MW00749408

101 YEARS OF
ALL BLACK TRIVIA

101 YEARS OF ALL BLACK TRIVIA

Fascinating facts and foibles

Graham Hutchins

Harper*Sports*

An imprint of HarperCollins*Publishers*

National Library of New Zealand Cataloguing-in-Publication Data

Hutchins, Graham.
101 years of All Black trivia : fascinating facts and foibles /
Graham Hutchins.
ISBN 1-86950-592-1
1. All Blacks (Rugby team)—Miscellanea. 2. All Blacks (Rugby
team)—History. 2. Rugby Union football players—New Zealand
—Miscellanea. 3. Rugby Union football players—New Zealand
—History. I. Title.
796.3330993—dc 22

Harper*Sports*
An imprint of HarperCollins*Publishers*

First published 2006
HarperCollins*Publishers (NewZealand) Limited*
P.O. Box 1, Auckland

Copyright © Graham Hutchins 2006

Graham Hutchins asserts the moral right to be identified
as the author of this work.

All rights reserved. No part of this publication may be reproduced,
stored in a retrieval system or transmitted in any form or by any means,
electronic, mechanical, photocopying, recording or otherwise,
without the prior written permission of the publishers.

ISBN 1-86950-592-1

Cover design by Darren Holt, HarperCollins Design Studio
Typesetting by Janine Brougham
Printed by Griffin Press, Australia, on 79 gsm Bulky Paperback

Contents

Acknowledgements

I wish to acknowledge the help and support of Bob Howitt of HarperCollins in compiling this collection. His knowledge and experience were invaluable in seeking out and hunting down a good deal of the more distinctive material, much of which is seeing the light of day for the first time. Another Bob — Luxford — of the New Zealand Rugby Museum, is also acknowledged with gratitude. The Rugby Museum website was an excellent source of information and enlightenment.

About the author

Graham Hutchins first came to prominence while writing a regular humorous column for *Rugby News* in the 1980s. *101 Years of All Black Trivia* is his 25th book and while he has written books about unrelated topics, it is always rugby he has returned to, either in humorous, light-hearted fashion or in more formal offerings. *Rugby Rabbits*, *Tall Half-backs*, *New Zealand Rugby Yarns* and *Tales from the 22* fall into the first category, while *Black Magic*, *Magic Matches — Great Days of New Zealand Rugby*, *A Score to Settle* and *The Road to Cardiff* were more sober reflections of the national pastime.

Still a King Country man at heart, Hutchins was swept up in the 'Northern drift', which deposited him over the border at Hamilton, where he now lives with his family.

Our 1064
All Blacks trivialised

Harry Louis 'Bunny' **ABBOTT**, a 1905 and 1906 All Black, actually played against the All Blacks for British Columbia when the Canadians were found to be short of players. Abbott, showing no favouritism, scored a try for British Columbia.

George Thomas Augustus **ADKINS**, an All Black in 1935 and 1936, who was born and died in Timaru, served with the RNZAF in the Pacific and was later president of the South Canterbury Rugby Union.

Ioane Fitu 'John' **AFOA**, an All Black on the 2005 Grand Slam tour, used his entire match fee and bonus payment after Auckland won the NPC final in 2003, to buy a classic 1971 Fairmont with mag wheels.

George Gothard **AITKEN**, a 1921 All Black, first played provincial rugby for Buller as a 16-year-old, attended Oxford as a Rhodes Scholar and went on to represent Scotland, Oxford University and the UK Barbarians.

Pita Faiva-ki-moana **ALATINI**, an All Black from 1999 to 2001, played NPC rugby for four provincial unions — Counties-Manukau, Southland, Otago and Wellington — and Super 12 rugby for four teams — the Crusaders, Chiefs, Highlanders and Hurricanes. He is the son of a 1969 Tongan rep.

Beethoven **ALGAR**, an All Black in 1920 and 1921, was a carpenter from a musical family and was named after the German composer Ludwig van Beethoven.

James **ALLAN**, a New Zealand rep in 1884, was one of four brothers who played for Otago. Weighing 90 kg, he was known as the 'Taieri Giant'.

Frederick Richard 'Fred' **ALLEN**, an All Black in 1946, 1947 and 1949, once caught a 25.5 lb snapper, which was good enough to take out a trophy presented by the Kawau Island Boating Club. An outstandingly successful coach, of Auckland and the All Blacks, he acquired the nickname of 'Needle'.

Lewis **ALLEN**, a New Zealand rep in 1896, 1897 and 1901, was nicknamed 'Snip'.

Mark Richard **ALLEN**, an All Black from 1993 to 1997, was nicknamed 'Bull' and his stamping ground — Rugby Park, New Plymouth — became known as the 'Bullring'.

Nicholas Houghton 'Nicky' **ALLEN**, an All Black in 1980, once convinced a traffic officer of his sobriety in respect of driving a car, by walking a straight line — on his hands.

Geoffrey Thomas **ALLEY**, an All Black in 1926 and 1928, was the brother of Rewi Alley. In 1964 he became New Zealand's first National Librarian; he also wrote a book on the 1930 British Isles tour of New Zealand.

Albert **ANDERSON**, an All Black from 1983 to 1988, went on the Cavaliers' tour of South Africa in 1986. He captained the All Blacks in four fixtures on the 1988 Australian tour.

Brent Leslie **ANDERSON**, an All Black lock in 1986 and 1987, went close to making the 1987 World Cup squad, missing out to another lock named Anderson — Albert, of Canterbury.

Eric James **ANDERSON**, a 1960 All Black, is the only prop to play for New Zealand while representing Bay of Plenty. He also coached Bay of Plenty to win the inaugural NPC in 1976.

Sosene Raymond **ANESI**, an All Black in 2005, has also represented New Zealand and Samoa at sevens rugby.

James Albert 'Jim' **ARCHER**, a 1925 All Black, was a well-known professional middle-distance runner and also represented Southland at rifle shooting.

William Robert 'Robin' **ARCHER**, an All Black from 1955 to 1957, is involved in the thoroughbred racing industry and bred Songline, the dam of the great Sunline.

Walter Garland 'Wally' **ARGUS**, an All Black in 1946 and 1947, withdrew from the 1949 All Black tour of South Africa because of business reasons.

Alexander McNaughton 'Barney' **ARMIT**, a New Zealand rep in 1897, died two years later at the age of 25 as a result of injuries sustained in a rep match between Otago and Taranaki in Dunedin, when he attempted to hurdle Alf Bayly and fell and broke his neck.

Adam 'Loftus' **ARMSTRONG**, a 1903 New Zealand rep, was a black-smith, before becoming a farmer.

Derek Austin **ARNOLD**, a 1963 to 1964 All Black, who acquired the nickname of 'Bluey', represented Christchurch West High School at 11 different sports — rugby, soccer, hockey, cricket, golf, tennis, wrestling, gymnastics, swimming, softball and athletics (high hurdles).

Keith Dawson **ARNOLD**, a 1947 All Black, was a shock omission from the 1949 tour of South Africa. A devastating flanker, he acquired the nickname of 'Killer' because he killed the reputations of so many opposing halfbacks.

Desmond 'Lloyd' **ASHBY**, a 1958 All

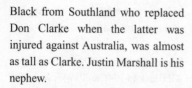

Black from Southland who replaced Don Clarke when the latter was injured against Australia, was almost as tall as Clarke. Justin Marshall is his nephew.

Albert Arapeha 'Opai' **ASHER**, a 1903 All Black, is believed to have played in a sub-union game between Tauranga and Auckland at the age of 13. He was the oldest of six sons of an Arawa chieftainess. His nickname — 'Opai' — came from the 1898 Great Northern Hurdles winner.

Barry Graeme **ASHWORTH**, a 1978 All Black, missed selection for Auckland in 1979 because of boundary qualification problems.

John Colin **ASHWORTH**, an All Black prop from 1977 to 1985, was an advertising artist for the *Christchurch Press* before becoming a farmer.

Benjamin Alo Charles 'Ben' **ATIGA**, a 2003 All Black, a nephew of former All Black Joe Stanley, suffered a fearful facial injury when a heavy weight crashed onto his face while he was working out at a gym.

Henry James 'Harry' **ATKINSON**, a 1913 All Black, was — at 88 kg — the heaviest player in the 1913 All Blacks.

Henry Esau **AVERY**, a 1910 All Black, had an illustrious military career, receiving the CMG, CBE and the American Legion of Merit. He was also the founder of Avery Motors, one of Wellington's biggest motor companies.

Graeme Thomas Miro **BACHOP**, an All Black from 1987 to 1995, attained national honours before he had played for his province, Canterbury. The following year he played only one game for Canterbury but was still selected as an All Black.

Stephen John **BACHOP**, an All Black from 1992 to 1994, is the uncle of Aaron and Nathan Mauger. His wife Sue (née Garden) was a New Zealand women's rugby rep.

Cecil Edward Oliver 'Ces' **BADELEY**, an All Black from 1920 to 1924, toured Britain with the Invincibles but played in only two matches out of 32. An Aucklander, he represented the South Island in 1922 as a replacement, opposing his brother Vic, a replacement for the North Island.

Victor Ivan Roskill 'Vic' **BADELEY**, a 1922 All Black, suffered a serious head injury in the 1924 trials that ended his playing days. A benefit match was staged to raise funds for the Badeley family. Vic lived to 72.

Keith Parker **BAGLEY**, an All Black in 1953 and 1954, played provincial rugby for Poverty Bay, Waikato, Manawatu and East Coast.

David Lindsay 'Scotty' **BAIRD**, a 1920 All Black, died as a result of injuries suffered in a coal-mining accident.

James Alexander Steenson 'Jim' **BAIRD**, a 1913 All Black, played a total of three first-class fixtures — two for Otago plus a test appearance (as a late replacement, there being no time to get an outside player to Dunedin) against Australia. He died aged 23, while serving with the New Zealand forces in France.

William **BALCH**, a New Zealand rep in 1894, became a school inspector. He wrote *Sentence Structure and Hints on Composition*, an English textbook in New Zealand primary schools. He was also an authority on daffodils.

Nelson **BALL**, an All Black from 1931 to 1936, was the father of Murray Ball, the cartoonist responsible for the 'Footrot Flats' series.

Robert John 'Bob' **BARBER**, a 1974 All Black, was able to play at flanker, No. 8 or prop. On the 1974 Australian tour he turned out at lock against Queensland Country and prop versus Fiji.

Connan Keith 'Con' **BARRELL**, a 1996 to 1997 All Black prop, played the role of hooker in his first season of first-class rugby. He became the first player to achieve 50 appearances for two different unions — Northland and Canterbury.

James 'Buster' **BARRETT**, an All Black in 1913 and 1914, was the Auckland Marist Club's first All Black. He played for the Catholic Club in 1912 and was one of the few All Blacks not to have his obituary printed in the *New Zealand Rugby Almanack*.

Edward Fitzgerald 'Ned' **BARRY**, an All Black in 1932 and 1934, joined the police force in 1932.

Kevin Edward **BARRY**, an All Black from 1962 to 1964, played 23 matches for New Zealand, none of which were tests. He broke into rep rugby for Thames Valley at 18 from the tiny Mercury Bay Club. One son, Liam, became an All Black; another, Mike, played for Northland and North Harbour.

Liam John **BARRY**, an All Black in 1993 and 1995, was the first third-generation All Black. His father, Kevin Barry, and grandfather, Edward Fitzgerald Barry, also played for New Zealand. All three were loose forwards.

Steven **BATES**, an All Black in 2004, played for the Warriors Under-19 league team.

Grant Bernard **BATTY**, an All Black from 1972 to 1977, scored 70 tries for the Kuranui College First XV in the Wairarapa in 1969. He had to be resuscitated after losing consciousness while swimming in Joe Karam's swimming pool in the 1980s. After moving to Australia's Sunshine Coast, he coached successfully at club level and became assistant coach of the Queensland Reds.

Walter **BATTY**, an All Black in 1928, 1930 and 1931, was not related to Grant Batty. He was born in Tonga and served with the 6th Field Regiment in the Second World War, winning the DCM in Libya.

Alfred **BAYLY**, a New Zealand rep in 1893, 1894 and 1897, represented his province Taranaki from six different club teams: Hawera, Waitara, Manganui, Stratford, Clifton and Tukapa. He also represented West Coast (North Island) at 16 and Egmont.

Walter **BAYLY**, a New Zealand representative in 1894, was a brother of Alfred Bayly. Four other brothers played for Taranaki — Charles, Frank, Henry and George.

George Edward **BEATTY**, a 1950 All Black, also represented his province, Taranaki, at cricket. He switched to league in 1950, playing for Leigh and Bellvue Rangers.

James Raymond 'Wampy' **BELL**, a 1923 All Black, later became a selector of South Island Railways. He played front row for New Zealand Maori, wing forward for Southland and five-eighth for the South Island.

Raymond Henry **BELL**, an All Black in 1951 and 1952, suffered a serious knee injury playing in a test match against Australia at Wellington, which ended his rugby career.

Reginald Clive **BELL**, a 1922 All Black, drowned while fishing in the Taieri River, aged 67.

Ernest Arthur 'Moke' **BELLISS**, an All Black from 1920 to 1923, was the grandfather of Peter Belliss, the celebrated lawn bowler. Peter Belliss himself played for Wanganui.

Robert 'Bob' **BENNET**, a 1905 All Black, was a tailor in Dunedin, making his solitary international appearance against Australia at Tahuna Park while the Originals were in the UK.

Trevor **BERGHAN**, an All Black in 1938, went on to become a dentist in Auckland.

Martin Joseph 'Marty' **BERRY**, an All Black in 1986 and 1993, made his only test appearance in the last minute of the third test against Australia in 1986, when he went on as a replacement.

Norman Rangi **BERRYMAN**, a 1998 All Black, first played first-class rugby for North Auckland as an 18-year-old weighing 105 kg. He scored seven tries in an NPC game against Wairarapa-Bush.

John Jeffries **BEST**, an All Black in 1935 and 1936, played representative rugby for Marlborough, Waikato and Bay of Plenty.

Vincent David 'Vince' **BEVAN**, an All Black from 1947 to 1954, played for the 22nd Battalion side that won the Freyberg Cup during the Second World War.

William Murray 'Bill' **BIRTWISTLE**, an All Black in 1965 and 1967, had a nephew, Mark Birtwistle, who represented Western Samoa in the 1990s.

John Edwin **BLACK**, an All Black in 1976 and 1980, was a member of the New Zealand Juniors team that beat a full-strength All Black side in 1973.

Neville Wyatt **BLACK**, a 1949 All Black, later played league for Wigan, Keighley and Ngongotaha.

Robert Stanley 'Bobby' **BLACK**, a 1914 All Black, lost his life during the Battle of the Somme, at the age of 23, while a corporal with the Otago Mounted Rifles.

Todd Julian **BLACKADDER**, an All Black from 1995 to 2000, first played provincial rugby for Nelson Bays. He carries a scar on his face from a car accident.

Ben Austin **BLAIR**, an All Black in 2001 and 2002, is an avid follower of rugby statistics and trivia. He created some of his own by scoring 37 points in his international debut against Ireland A at Belfast. Both his father and grandfather represented Buller.

John Alexander **BLAIR**, an 1897 New Zealand representative, was the first All Black from the Kaierau Club, Wanganui.

Alan Walter 'Kiwi' **BLAKE**, a 1949 All Black, missed the second test against the touring Australians because of a family bereavement. He was of African ancestry and captained Wairarapa to its 3-nil Ranfurly Shield win over Canterbury at Christchurch.

John Muldoon 'Jackie' **BLAKE**, an All Black in 1925 and 1926, once scored five tries for Hawke's Bay in a Ranfurly Shield defence.

Samuel **BLIGH** was Buller's first All Black, in 1910. His real name was Percival, but he played as Samuel because his mother disapproved of rugby. He eventually switched to league and played for Blackball from 1915 to 1921.

FOR RATHER OBVIOUS REASONS.... I DUB THEE - PINETREE !!!

©DARYL CRIMP

Andrew Francis **BLOWERS**, an All Black in 1996 and 1999, initially toured South Africa with Western Samoa, but because he played no test matches, he became eligible to play for New Zealand.

Kenneth Charles **BLOXHAM**, a 1980 All Black from Otago, died of cancer at the age of 46. He played most of his rugby out of the small Tokomairiro club in South Otago.

John William **BOE**, a 1981 All Black (replacing an injured Doug Rollerson on the All Blacks' 1981 tour to Romania and France), became a successful coach of Samoa.

Eric George **BOGGS**, an All Black in 1946 and 1949, played his club rugby in 1942 for an Auckland side known as Countess of Ranfurly's Own.

Jack 'Garth' Parker **BOND**, a 1949 All Black, played 19 games for the 'Kiwis'.

Roger John **BOON**, a 1960 All Black, is credited with giving Colin Meads his nickname, 'Pinetree'.

Ernest Edward 'General' **BOOTH**, an All Black from 1905 to 1907, later played for New South Wales in 1908 and 1909. He was controversially appointed as a professional coach of

Southland in the 1920s, and, as a journalist, he accompanied the 1908–1909 Australian side on its tour of the UK as a press correspondent.

Kevin Grant **BOROEVICH**, an All Black in 1983, 1984 and 1986, the nephew of All Black Percy Erceg, first played representative rugby, as a prop with King Country, at the age of 17.

Frano Michael **BOTICA**, an All Black from 1986 to 1989, played a World Cup qualifying match for Croatia against Latvia in 1997.

Ian James **BOTTING**, a 1949 All Black, played two test matches for England in 1950 while studying at Oxford University. He became a chaplain in Christchurch and was later knocked off his bike and killed.

Noel James Gordon **BOWDEN**, a 1952 All Black, established a long jump record of 22 feet and 6 inches while at Auckland Grammar School in 1944. The record stood for many years.

Richard 'Guy' **BOWERS**, an All Black in 1953 and 1954, was a tobacco grower. He was christened Richard, but became known as Guy because his birthday was on the 5th of November.

Albert William 'Snow' **BOWMAN**, an All Black in 1938, played provincial rugby for Hawke's Bay, Wellington and Nelson.

Nicholas Martin **BRADANOVICH**, a 1928 All Black, was a Pukekohe dentist and president of the Franklin Racing Club.

Henry Yule **BRADDON**, a New Zealand rep in 1884, was the son of Sir Edward Braddon, the premier of Tasmania. He was born in Calcutta and became Sir Henry following a distinguished business career in Australia.

Daniel John **BRAID**, an All Black in 2002 and 2003, is the son of ex-All Black Gary Braid. He attended Kings College with Angus MacDonald, also the son of an ex-All Black lock — Hamish MacDonald.

Gary John **BRAID**, an All Black in 1983 and 1984, played soccer at school. In 2002–2003 he coached the Auckland University senior rugby team, a side that included his talented son Daniel.

Leonard 'John' **BRAKE**, a 1976 All Black, made his New Zealand debut at Montevideo against Uruguay.

Selwyn George 'Mick' **BREMNER**, an All Black in 1952, 1956 and 1960, represented New Zealand at four-yearly intervals and became known as the 'leap year All Black'.

Michael Robert 'Mike' **BREWER**, an All Black from 1986 to 1995, was called into the All Blacks in 1993 while temporarily based in the UK as a rep for Canterbury Clothing.

Kevin Charles 'Monkey' **BRISCOE**, an All Black from 1959 to 1964, was listed as being 5 foot 3 inches in 1959 and 5 foot 7 inches in 1963.

Robin Matthew **BROOKE**, an All Black from 1992 to 1999, acquired his nickname of 'Foodbill' when he toured with the 1993 All Blacks without playing in any of the team's games.

Zinzan Valentine **BROOKE**, an All Black from 1987 to 1997, could shear 300 sheep in a day at 14. His early aspiration was to be the Golden Shears champion. He made his senior club debut, for Warkworth, at 15.

Mark **BROOKE-COWDEN**, an All Black in 1986 and 1987, was a great-grandson of Wiri Nehra of the 1888 Native team.

Frank Jenner **BROOKER**, a New Zealand rep in 1897, was 1.92 m in height — an exceptional height for the times.

Sam Roger **BROOMHALL**, an All Black in 2002, was an opening batsman for the Canterbury Under 20 cricket reps while playing for Ellesmere College.

Charles 'Charlie' **BROWN**, an All Black in 1913 and 1920, was a Pakeha who appeared as a 'guest' for New Zealand Maori in a charity match against Australia in 1913.

Handley Welbourne **BROWN**, an All Black from 1924 to 1926, was the father of Ross Handley Brown. Both first played for the All Blacks at the age of 19.

Henry Mackay **BROWN**, an All Black in 1935 and 1936, played six first-class games for King Country, Auckland and Poverty Bay over nine seasons. He was the brother of All Black Handley Brown, who played all his provincial rugby for Taranaki.

Olo Max **BROWN**, an All Black from 1990 to 1998, is a chartered accountant. He was an avid chess player while on tour with the All Blacks.

Ross Handley **BROWN**, an All Black from 1955 to 1962, won a Ranfurly Shield match for Taranaki in 1964 by kicking three dropped goals against North Auckland.

Tony Eion **BROWN**, an All Black first five-eighth from 1999 to 2001, scored three tries in a test match against Samoa in 2001. He came from Kaitangata.

Cyril James **BROWNLIE**, an All

Black from 1924 to 1928, was the first player to be sent off in a test match, against England at Twickenham.

Jack Laurence 'Laurie' **BROWNLIE**, a 1921 All Black, was the youngest of the three Brownlie brothers, (the others being Maurice and Cyril) to play for New Zealand. He was also the first to be selected for New Zealand.

Maurice John **BROWNLIE**, one of the most famous All Black forwards, who represented his country between 1922 and 1928, was also an accomplished boxer, making it to the final of the New Zealand amateur heavyweight championship in 1921 where he lost to Brian McCleary, who also became an All Black.

John Alexander 'Alex' **BRUCE**, an All Black in 1913 and 1914, once scored a double century in Wellington club cricket, playing for the now defunct St James Club. He represented Wellington at rugby and cricket in teams that held the Ranfurly Shield and Plunket Shield.

Oliver Douglas 'Doug' **BRUCE**, an All Black in 1974 and from 1976 to 1978 and who was Alex Wyllie's sidekick during Canterbury's great Ranfurly Shield reign in the 1980s, is a schoolteacher at Geraldine who paints in watercolours.

Ronald Frederick **BRYERS**, a 1949

All Black, became headmaster of Mount Maunganui School. His daughter, Rhonda Bryers, became a well-known entertainer.

John Alexander Sheperd **BUCHAN**, a 1987 All Black, became the central figure in a Ranfurly Shield match between Auckland and Canterbury when he was ordered off and, because Canterbury purportedly didn't have a front-row replacement, Golden Oldie scrums became the norm.

Alfred **BUDD**, a 1910 All Black, toured Australia with the All Blacks and decided to stay on after the tour. He died in Melbourne in 1962.

Thomas Alfred 'Alf' **BUDD**, an All Black in 1946 and 1949, was born in Bluff, played his provincial rugby for Southland and later became works manager of the Northland Harbour Board.

George Arthur Hardy **BULLOCK-DOUGLAS**, an All Black in 1932 and 1934, scored five tries for the North Island in the inter-island match of 1932.

Frank Eneri **BUNCE**, an All Black from 1992 to 1997, was 30 years of age when he first played for New Zealand. He is a direct descendant of George Rex, a son of the union of Yorkshire draper Hannah Lightfoot and King George III.

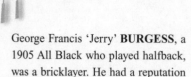

George Francis 'Jerry' **BURGESS**, a 1905 All Black who played halfback, was a bricklayer. He had a reputation as 'a persistent squealer'.

Gregory Alexander John **BURGESS**, a 1980 All Black prop, played for the University club in Dunedin as a wing threequarter and the Union Club in Dunedin as a No. 8, before settling at prop. He won a national power-lifting title in 1985 and a silver medal in the shot put at the 1984 and 1985 nationals.

Robert Edward 'Bob' **BURGESS**, an All Black from 1971 to 1973, swallowed his tongue while playing against the British Lions at Athletic Park in 1971. The problem was identified by the Lions' fullback J.P.R. Williams, who was a medical student. Williams promptly prised open Burgess' mouth and alleviated the situation. Burgess was taken unconscious from the field and spent two days in hospital.

Michael Martin **BURGOYNE**, a 1979 All Black, played in several Ranfurly Shield defences for North Auckland that year. He made his rep debut at the relatively advanced age of 26.

Peter Standish **BURKE**, an All Black in 1951, 1955 and 1957, won the Taranaki mixed tennis doubles title with his sister Judy.

John Francis 'Jake' **BURNS**, a 1970 All Black, was listed as a concrete worker at the time of his New Zealand selection.

Patrick James 'Paddy' **BURNS**, an All Black in 1908, 1910 and 1913, played five tests for New Zealand — once as a halfback, once as a wing, and the other three as a centre.

James Thomas **BURROWS**, a 1928 All Black, was a brigadier in the Second World War, winning the DSO, bar and Order of Valour. In 1954 he was commander of K force in Korea. He received a CBE in 1959.

Hugh Cameron **BURRY**, a 1960 All Black, later settled in England, where he coached the Guy's Hospital side.

John Robert **BURT**, a New Zealand rep in 1901, played one match for his country, against Wellington as a replacement for Walter Augustus Drake when the latter failed to arrive in time. Drake, in his turn, also played one match for New Zealand — in 1901 — when he turned up in time to play against New South Wales.

Ronald George **BUSH**, an All Black in 1931, scored 14 points in his only game for New Zealand — as a fullback against Australia. He later played for Auckland and the North Island as a loose forward. He was the uncle of photographer Peter Bush and co-founder of the New Zealand Barbarians.

William Kingita Te Pohe 'Billy' **BUSH**, an All Black from 1974 to 1979, worked as a commercial diver.

Henry **BUTLAND**, a New Zealand rep in 1893 and 1894, played for his country before playing representative rugby for West Coast. He was a gold-miner who worked for a time in the Klondike and was also the father of Sir Jack Butland, one of New Zealand's wealthiest industrialists.

Victor Claude **BUTLER**, a 1928 All Black, became, in 1953, the first headmaster of Mount Roskill Grammar School.

John Burns **BUXTO**... in 1955 and 1956, p... rugby for Manawa... Otago and Auckland. He published his autobiography *Blood and Guts* in 1999, having enjoyed a significant career in the meat industry.

Phillippe Sidney de Quetteville 'Sid' **CABOT**, a 1921 All Black, was born at Rough Ridge, Central Otago. He studied at Columbia, Princeton and Harvard Universities and completed a doctorate with a special interest in pediatrics.

Michael Joseph 'Mick' **CAIN**, an All Black in 1913 and 1914, played 104 first-class games after making a late start to the game at age 21.

Umberto Primo **CALCINAI**, a 1922 All Black, was nicknamed 'Bert'. He descended from an Italian family that settled in Wellington in the late 19th century.

John Arthur **CALLESEN**, an All Black from 1974 to 1976, had a spinal fusion operation to correct vertebrae problems caused by farm work and poorly designed scrum machines.

Joseph John **CALNAN**, an 1897 New Zealand rep, had his playing career interrupted by a two-year suspension for alleged drunkenness and bad language. At the time of his work retirement in 1932, he was custodian of Wellington's Te Aro baths.

Dennis Hugh **CAMERON**, a 1960 All Black, played for Mid-Canterbury and Counties, then in 1964 switched to league. He was subsequently re-instated and became an administrator with Waikato and Bay of Plenty.

Donald **CAMERON**, a 1908 All Black, scored four tries for his province Taranaki against Manawatu in 1906. He played in five unsuccessful Ranfurly Shield challenges against Auckland in 1906, 1908, 1909, 1910 and 1912 .

Lachlan Murray 'Lachie' **CAMERON**, an All Black in 1979, 1980 and 1981, was a keen rower before moving to the Manawatu to study for an Agricultural Science degree at Massey University.

Sydney Russell **CARLETON**, a 1928 and 1929 All Black, toured Australia with the 1929 team, where he played centre in the first test, fullback in the second and second five-eighth in the third.

Kenneth Roy **CARRINGTON**, an All Black in 1971 and 1972, played representative rugby in his first year out of school.

Alphonsus John 'Phonse' **CARROLL**, a Manawatu All Black in the 1920s, played rep rugby with four of his brothers: Frank, William, Mick and Vince. He was a conscientious objector during the First World War.

William Nicol 'Bill' **CARSON**, a 1938 All Black, was also an outstanding batsman in cricket, sharing a world-record second-wicket partnership of 445 for Auckland against Otago. He was severely wounded in Italy in 1944, contracted jaundice on a hospital ship returning to New Zealand and died aged 28. His farm 'Snake Gully' was for 40 years the venue of Sunday cricket matches.

Daniel William **CARTER**, an All Black from 2003 to 2005, scored 10 tries in his first 21 tests. At age 22, he was the youngest recipient of the Kel Tremain Player of the Year Award in 2004 and won it again in 2005. His partner Honor Dillon plays hockey for New Zealand.

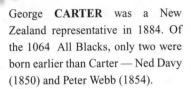

George **CARTER** was a New Zealand representative in 1884. Of the 1064 All Blacks, only two were born earlier than Carter — Ned Davy (1850) and Peter Webb (1854).

Mark Peter **CARTER**, an All Black in 1991 and 1997–1998, played league for the Auckland Warriors in 1996. He worked for his father making corks for wine bottles.

Scott Calvert **CARTWRIGHT**, a 1976 All Black, scored seven tries in his seven matches for New Zealand, including a hat trick against Uruguay at Montevideo.

Stephen Timothy **CASEY**, an All Black from 1905 to 1908, who was born in and died in Dunedin, never scored a point in his 38 matches for New Zealand.

Adrian Richard **CASHMORE**, an All Black in 1996 and 1997, gained selection for the 1996 All Black tour to South Africa, but had to return home because of injury before the first match.

Evelyn Haswell 'Has' **CATLEY**, a famous All Black hooker in 1946, 1947 and 1949, made his test debut when he was 30.

Thomas Harcourt Clarke 'Pat' **CAUGHEY**, an All Black from 1932 to 1937, scored three tries against Scotland on the 1935–1936 tour of Britain. He was knighted in 1972 for services to the Auckland Hospital Board, of which he was chairman for 15 years.

Ralph Walter **CAULTON** of Wellington, an All Black from 1959 to 1964, scored two tries in each of his first two tests for New Zealand. He was one of the better pianists amongst the post-war All Blacks.

Nau Paora 'Brownie' **CHERRING-TON**, an All Black in 1950 and 1951, used to smoke a pipe, but not while playing.

Desmond Lawrence **CHRISTIAN**, a 1949 All Black, was chosen for the 1949 South African tour as a prop, but played in the final test as a No. 8. His nickname was 'Stuffy'.

Michael **CLAMP**, an All Black in 1984 and 1985, represents Quicksilver Surfing Equipment in Biarritz, France. Because of injury he played in only one tour match in Argentina in 1985 — against Mar del Plata — but scored three tries.

Donald William **CLARK**, the Otago forward who played for the All Blacks in 1964, suffered a serious farm accident at Cromwell that ended his playing days in 1967. His cousin Kerry represented New Zealand at bowls at the Commonwealth Games and became president of Bowls New Zealand.

Francis Leslie 'Frank' **CLARK**, a 1928 All Black, was an electrician. In 1927 he played in the first Canterbury team to win the Ranfurly Shield (off Manawhenua).

Lindsay Allan **CLARK** is famous for being the individual who replaced Keith Murdoch after the Otago prop was sensationally expelled from the 1972–1973 All Black tour of the UK and France for attacking a security guard. Clark did not play for his country again following that tour.

William Henry 'Bill' **CLARK**, an All Black from 1953 to 1956, used to play in white headgear, the better, some pundits reasoned, for selectors to notice his whereabouts. His father was captain of Golden Bay-Motueka. In 1975 his and Ron Jarden's business phone numbers, 660-450 and 660-455, were separated by a difference of five — equal to a converted try in the 1950s. Such a numerical coincidence seemed appropriate, for Clark and Jarden cooked up a lot of five-pointers.

Adrian Hipkins **CLARKE**, an All Black from 1958 to 1960, was an unsuccessful parliamentary candidate.

Donald Barry **CLARKE**, an All Black from 1956 to 1964, who achieved legendary status as a goal-kicker, represented the North Island at cricket in 1952–1953.

Eroni **CLARKE**, an All Black in 1992 and 1993, was still playing NPC rugby for Counties-Manukau in 2005 at the age of 36.

Ian James **CLARKE**, an All Black from 1953 to 1964, was a famously durable prop. In 1955, however, the selectors named him as a No. 8 — and captain — for the three-match series against Australia. Nicknamed 'Wishbone', he used to entertain team-mates with his rendition of the Inkspots' famous number 'The Best Things in Life are Free'.

Philip Hipkins **CLARKE**, a 1967 All Black, was the RNZAF and Combined Services sprint champion.

Ray Lancelot **CLARKE**, a 1932 All Black from Taranaki, was a cheesemaker.

Donald Gordon **COBDEN** of Canterbury, a 1937 All Black, was seriously injured in his only test match against the 1937 Springboks and left the field after 25 minutes of play. He was an RAF pilot during the Second World War, losing his life during the Battle of Britain, when he was shot down on his 26th birthday.

Eric Arthur Percy **COCKCROFT**, an

All Black in 1913 and 1914, was the author of *The Modern Method of New Zealand Football* (W.H. Foden, 1924). He also represented New Zealand at bowls in 1953 and was headmaster of Ashburton High School for 20 years (1929–1949).

Samuel George **COCKCROFT**, a New Zealand representative in 1893 and 1894, was at the time of his death in 1955, the oldest surviving All Black. Two years after playing for New Zealand he captained Queensland in 1896 on a tour of New Zealand.

Maurice Stanley 'Snow' **COCKER-ILL**, a 1951 All Black, disappeared from first-class rugby at the age of 22, after he suffered a bad knee injury in the Taranaki-Waikato game of 1951.

Brett William **CODLIN**, a 1980 All Black, played provincial rugby for Canterbury and Counties, after initially representing Poverty Bay Colts.

Phillip Hone **COFFIN**, a 1996 All Black from King Country, was one of the few All Blacks to make his debut when over the age of 30.

George Lindsay 'Lin' **COLLING**, an All Black in 1972 and 1973, made the New Zealand side from Otago but ended up captaining Auckland

for three seasons. His niece Belinda captained New Zealand at netball. He was working as a shepherd in the Lake Wakatipu region when first selected for New Zealand and may well be the last shepherd to become an All Black.

Arthur Harold **COLLINS**, an All Black in 1932 and 1934, scored for New Zealand in four different ways: one try, 35 conversions, 11 penalty goals and one dropped goal.

Jerry **COLLINS**, an All Black from 2001 to 2005, was one of the youngest players to captain a senior club team when he led Porirua's Northern United at 18 years of age.

John Law **COLLINS**, a 1964 and 1965 All Black from Poverty Bay, spent some time on active service in Malaya.

William Reuben 'Bill' **COLLINS**, a 1935 All Black, suffered from heart strain during the 1935–1936 All Black tour to Britain. At 100 kg he was the heaviest tourist. Collins lived to be 83.

John Thomas Henry 'Jack' **COLMAN**, a 1907 and 1908 All Black, who was nicknamed 'Ginger', appeared for New Zealand as both a back and a forward. In Australia in 1907 he played first as a wing forward, then at fullback.

Stuart Bruce **CONN**, an All Black in 1976 and 1980, played club rugby in Auckland for three different teams: Northcote, Takapuna and Grammar.

Leo Stephen **CONNOLLY**, a 1947 All Black, was, at 5 foot 10 inches (1.8 m), the shortest forward on the New Zealand tour to Australia in 1947.

Desmond Michael **CONNOR**, an All Black halfback from 1961 to 1964, toured New Zealand as a Wallaby and then applied for a teaching position through the *Education Gazette* and was appointed as Physical Education master at Takapuna Grammar. He arrived in New Zealand in 1959 and two years later became an All Black.

William John McKeown 'Bill' **CONRAD**, a 1949 All Black, died of a heart attack while on duty as registrar of the Auckland Supreme Court.

Richard James 'Dick' **CONWAY**, an All Black in 1959, 1960 and 1965, was a migratory player, turning out for his Bay of Plenty club side and then travelling to Otago in the 1957, 1958 and 1959 seasons to play rep rugby there. A softball catcher who played for Rotorua, he broke a finger in a game; the finger was subsequently set badly and he decided to have it amputated rather than miss the 1960 tour of South Africa.

Albert Edward 'Bert' **COOKE** was an All Black from 1924 to 1930. A mercurial player, he scored 38 tries in 44 matches for New Zealand. He played league for a Post and Telegraph team in Auckland after leaving school.

Alfred Ernest **COOKE**, an 1894 New Zealand rep, died after being accidentally shot on a hunting expedition at Lake Ellesmere in 1900, aged 30.

Reuben James 'Ru' **COOKE**, a 1903 All Black, was ordered off in the first match of the 1903 tour of Australia and, although later cleared of any wrongdoing, gave the game away after the tour.

Mark Stephen Bill **COOKSLEY**, an All Black from 1992 to 2001, was the first All Black to receive a yellow card in 1995. Cooksley was sin-binned against a French Selection by Irish referee Gordon Black, who seemed unaware that the yellow and red card system had yet to be cleared for use in international rugby. 'Rugby colours — the rub of the green by Black, produces yellow', could have been a useful by-line to apply to the incident. Cooksley, at 2.05 m, was the tallest man to play for New Zealand.

Gregory John Luke **COOPER**, an All Black in 1986 and 1992, suffered from cancer while still at school. He played in the first test against Ireland in 1992 before having the unusual experience of losing his place to his brother Matt.

Matthew James Andrew **COOPER**, an All Black from 1987 to 1996, scored 23 points, against Ireland, this being an All Black record for a player on debut, until beaten in 1995 by Andrew Mehrtens who scored 28 points in his first test against Canada.

John **CORBETT**, a 1905 All Black, became a Buller selector and worked in Reefton and Westport as a baker.

Thomas George **CORKILL**, a 1925 All Black, although primarily a halfback, also played representative rugby at fullback, wing and five-eighth.

Mervyn Miles Nelson **CORNER**, an All Black from 1930 to 1936, was awarded the Military Cross in the Second World War. He was general manager of the Auckland Savings Bank from 1968 to 1973, was president of the Auckland Trotting Club and served on the NZ Racing Authority and Totalisator Agency Board. He was awarded the OBE.

Raymond Reginald 'Mick' **COSSEY**, a 1958 All Black, played provincial rugby for Auckland, Poverty Bay and Counties. As a schoolteacher at Patutahi, Gisborne, in the 1950s he taught Ian Kirkpatrick. He was killed in a railway crossing accident in 1986 at the age of 51.

Anthony Ian 'Beau' **COTTRELL**, an All Black from 1929 to 1932, appeared in New Zealand's last 2-3-2 scrum against Australia in 1931.

Wayne David **COTTRELL**, an All Black from 1967 to 1971, was nicknamed 'Baker'. He was a baker.

Manuera Benjamin Riwai 'Ben' **COUCH**, an All Black in 1947 and 1949, later became Postmaster General and Minister of Maori Affairs and Police in Robert Muldoon's National government.

Thomas Desmond **COUGHLAN**, a 1958 All Black, played very well in his only match — the first test against the 1958 Australians. Despite this he never played for New Zealand again. His uncle, Tom Lynch, was an All Black in 1913 and 1914 and his first cousin, who was also named Tom Lynch, was an All Black in 1951.

Quinton James 'Jimmy' **COWAN**, a 2004–2005 All Black, is regarded as a Justin Marshall lookalike. He was sent home from the 2005 Junior All Blacks tour of Australia for misbehaviour.

John Neville **CREIGHTON**, a 1962 All Black, was a hooker but still managed to score four tries in his six games for New Zealand.

Ronald Te Huia **CRIBB**, an All Black in 2000 and 2001, gave away a crucial penalty try against Australia in 2001.

Scott **CRICHTON,** an All Black prop between 1983 and 1985, was considered to be too heavy for his high school First XV at Wanganui Boys College. He played soccer and later became a 'bikie', roaring around Wanganui on a Triumph. At one point his weight hit 170 kg.

Stewart Edward George **CRON**, a 1976 All Black, is the brother of Mike, the scrummaging guru with Graham Henry's 2005 All Blacks.

Thomas **CROSS**, who represented New Zealand in 1901, 1904 and 1905, was nicknamed, somewhat creatively, 'Angry'. He was ordered off in a club game in 1907 and after being suspended for the season, accepted an offer to join the All Golds league team on its tour of the UK. He never returned to rugby.

Graeme Murray **CROSSMAN**, an All Black in 1974, 1975 and 1976, later became export manager of a kiwi fruit marketing company.

Kieran James **CROWLEY**, an All Black from 1983 to 1991, was working on the farm at Kaponga when Terry Wright was injured during the 1999 World Cup. Crowley was rushed to the UK and played in the losing semi-final against Australia.

Patrick Joseph Bourke **CROWLEY**, an All Black in 1949 and 1950, was regarded in his day, at 1.88 m and nearly 90 kg, as a huge man for a flanker.

Simon David **CULHANE**, an All Black in 1995 and 1996, played in five of his six test matches when Andrew Mehrtens was injured.

Christian Mathias **CULLEN**, an All Black from 1996 to 2002, was known as the 'Paekakeriki Express'. After suffering two heavy tackles in his first test against Samoa he later announced that, 'Those first tackles settled me down a bit'.

William **CUMMINGS**, an All Black in 1913 and 1921, played two tests against the 1913 Australians before the First World War broke out and later, after the war, played a further test against New South Wales. His two playing stints were eight years apart.

Rawi Tama **CUNDY**, an All Black in 1929, was the first player to achieve 100 points in a first-class season. He did this as Wairarapa's goal-kicker in 1927.

Gary Richard **CUNNINGHAM**, an

All Black in 1979 and 1980, played test match rugby as a wing, a centre, as well as a second five-eighth. He became assistant coach to Brad Johnstone with Fiji at the 1999 World Cup.

William 'Bill' **CUNNINGHAM**, a New Zealand rep from 1901 to 1908, was described as a 'rotund, cheerful and durable player'. Once, after unsuccessfully chasing a flying winger, he was asked by his teammates why he had bothered. 'He might have dropped dead,' replied the plodding Cunningham.

Leslie Frank **CUPPLES**, an All Black from 1922 to 1925, won the Military Medal in the First World War. He undertook his rugby training before breakfast.

William Douglas Roy 'Bill' **CURREY**, a 1968 All Black, scored eight tries in seven matches for New Zealand. In 1977 he completed the demanding three-day Dhuzi canoe marathon from Pietermaritzburg to Durban in South Africa.

Clive James **CURRIE**, an All Black in 1978, suffered a broken jaw and concussion in the 1978 test against Wales. His replacement, Brian McKechnie, developed legendary status by kicking three penalty goals, including the controversial match-winner in the dying moments of the game. Currie represented New Zealand schools and Wellington as a cricketer.

John Elliott **CUTHILL**, a 1913 All Black, was born at Inverleith and was invited to captain the 1914 All Black tourists to Australia. He declined and pulled out of the team to devote time to his university studies. He later served as secretary of the Southland racing and trotting clubs.

William Charles 'Bill' **DALLEY**, an All Black from 1924 to 1929, was 1.65 m in height. He later became chairman of the Canterbury Rugby Union and represented Canterbury at lawn bowls.

Andrew Grant 'Andy' **DALTON**, an All Black from 1977 to 1985, and again in 1987 (although he was unable to play because of injury), was the son of All Black Raymond Alfred Dalton. Both father and son played in the front row. Andy Dalton was the president of the NZRFU in 1999 and 2000.

Douglas **DALTON**, an All Black from 1935 to 1938, later gave sterling service to the St John Ambulance Association.

Raymond Alfred **DALTON**, an All Black in 1947 and 1949, served in the Second World War as a flight-lieutenant in the RNZAF.

George 'Nelson' **DALZELL**, a 1953 and 1954 All Black, suffered serious wounds serving in the Pacific during the Second World War, but recovered to become an All Black at the age of 32. He is the brother-in-law of All Black Allan Elsom and his son-in-law is All Black Graeme Higginson. Dalzell was capable of heaving full 44-gallon drums on to the tray of a truck.

Archibald Edgar **D'ARCY**, a New Zealand rep in 1893 and 1894, later became joint manager of the New Zealand Insurance Company in Sydney. In 1889 he became the first player to kick a penalty goal (dropped) in an inter-union game in New Zealand, when playing for Wairarapa against Wellington.

Murray Geoffrey **DAVIE**, an All Black prop in 1983, scored a try in his only test — as a replacement against England. He also played water polo for New Zealand.

William Anthony 'Tony' **DAVIES**, an All Black in 1960 and 1962, was primarily a fullback, although his three test matches saw him playing twice as a second five-eighth and once as a first five-eighth. He played for Blackheath (1971–1972) and London Irish (1972–1974) while furthering his medical studies in the UK.

Chresten Scott **DAVIS**, a 1996 All Black, gained selection for Manawatu as a flanker after playing only two club games — and those at lock.

Keith **DAVIS**, an All Black from 1952 to 1958, was a 5 foot 6 inch halfback. His brother Morris, who played for Waikato and New Zealand Maori, was a hulking tight-forward. Keith Davis won the Tom French Cup in 1952, 1953 and 1954.

Lyndon John **DAVIS**, an All Black in 1976 and 1977, played his first game for New Zealand at the age of 32. He became a tomato grower and was nicknamed 'Scaley'.

William Leslie 'Bill' **DAVIS**, an All Black from 1963 to 1970, was also a New Zealand softball rep in 1973 and 1976.

Edwin 'Ned' **DAVY**, a New Zealand rep in 1884, was described as a 'capital collarer'. He was also a major in the Salvation Army. At 33 he was the oldest player in the first All Black touring team.

Ian 'Bruce' **DEANS**, an All Black in 1987, 1988 and 1989, played 23 matches at halfback for New Zealand and scored 14 tries. He was the grandnephew of Bob Deans.

Robert George 'Bob' **DEANS**, an All Black in 1905, 1906 and 1908, died shortly after playing in the third test against the 1908 Anglo-Welsh side, from complications of an appendectomy at the age of 24. The son of Canterbury pioneers, he was a millionaire when he toured Britain in 1905.

Robert Maxwell 'Robbie' **DEANS**, an All Black in 1983, 1984 and 1985, married Jock Hobbs' sister.

Graham Wallace **DELAMORE**, a 1949 All Black, was deputy principal of Takapuna Grammar School when he retired from teaching. Nicknamed 'Red', he played Hawke Cup cricket for Hutt Valley and won many centre titles in bowls.

Stephen John **DEVINE**, an All Black in 2002 and 2003, played for the Australian Under-21 side in 1997 and the Australian Sevens in 1998. The son of an electrician, he was born at Boggabri. 'Simplydevine' is his email address. He and Des Connor, halfbacks both, are the only Australians to play for New Zealand.

Henry 'Norkey' **DEWAR**, a 1913 All Black, was killed at Chunuk Bair in the Gallipoli campaign, dying close to his 32nd birthday. He captained the Wellington Mounted Rifles team when they played in Egypt.

Ernest Sinclair 'Tuppy' **DIACK**, a 1959 All Black, retired from first-class play at the age of 32 after scoring 53 tries.

John **DICK**, an All Black in 1937 and 1938, scored six tries in a 1937 All Black trial match. He missed the 1938 Australian tour when he contracted measles after selection, but when he recovered New Zealand supporters financed his late arrival in Australia, where he played in three games, including the final test.

Malcolm John **DICK**, an All Black from 1963 to 1970, was nicknamed 'Farmer'. He managed the 1987 All Blacks to Japan and was made a life member of the Auckland Rugby Union.

George Ritchie **DICKINSON**, a 1922 All Black, disappeared from first-class rugby at the age of 21. He was one of only seven men who have represented New Zealand at rugby and cricket, playing for the New Zealand cricket team from 1924 to 1932.

David McKee **DICKSON**, an All Black in 1925, was a back-row forward who kicked goals. He became a surgeon in Christchurch and his medical studies caused him to be unavailable for the 1924 All Blacks. He also took up refereeing and adjudicated the 1937 match between the Springboks and Manawatu.

Maurice James 'Morrie' **DIXON**, an All Black from 1953 to 1957, had a reputation as a tap dancer.

WHY DIDN'T I TACKLE HIM? I WASN'T SURE WHICH LEGS TO GO FOR !!!

© DARYL CRIMP

Ronald Leslie **DOBSON**, a 1949 All Black, was Bob Scott's business partner in their painting and paper-hanging operation.

Ernest Henry **DODD**, a New Zealand representative in 1901 and 1905, was the youngest player in the New Zealand side that played Wellington and New South Wales in 1901. He was one of the 13 All Blacks killed in the First World War, dying at the age of 38.

Andrew John **DONALD**, an All Black in 1981, 1983 and 1984, preceded David Kirk as halfback in the Wanganui Collegiate First XV.

James George 'Jim' **DONALD**, a Wairarapa All Black from 1920 to 1925, played for several Wairarapa club

sides, including Featherston Liberal. A wing forward for Wairarapa, he appeared at second five-eighth in a Ranfurly Shield challenge which his side lost 77-14 against Hawke's Bay.

Quentin **DONALD**, an All Black from 1923 to 1925, was selected for the North Island at the age of 19. He and Maurice Brownlie were sent off in the infamous Hawke's Bay-Wairarapa 'Battle of Solway' Ranfurly Shield game in 1927.

Mark William **DONALDSON**, an All Black from 1977 to 1981, had his jaw broken by a fellow All Black in an off-field fracas in Australia in 1980 and had to be replaced. Later that year on the tour of Wales he was reprimanded for crash-tackling coach Eric Watson at a practice session at Newport.

John Patrick **DOUGAN**, an All Black in 1972 and 1973, played first-class cricket for Hutt Valley and Hawke's Bay. He scored the first four-point try for New Zealand against Australia in 1972.

James Burt **DOUGLAS**, a 1913 All Black, born at Shag Point, was expelled from the game in 1915 by the Otago Rugby Football Union after accepting bribes. He was readmitted after the war, in 1922.

Craig William **DOWD**, an All Black from 1993 to 1997, played in 37 tests in partnership with Sean Fitzpatrick and Olo Brown. He now helps coach London Wasps.

Graham William **DOWD**, a 1992 All Black, was selected as a hooker but made his test debut as a replacement prop.

Albert Joseph 'Doolan' **DOWNING**, an All Black in 1913 and 1914, became the first New Zealand rugby representative to die in the First World War when he was killed at Gallipoli, aged 29.

John Alan **DRAKE**, an Auckland All Black in 1985, 1986 and 1987, initially played club rugby in Dunedin. He made his first-class debut playing for New Zealand Universities. He is currently a Sky TV rugby comments person.

Walter Augustus **DRAKE**, a 1901 New Zealand representative, arrived too late to play for New Zealand against Wellington in 1901, although he made it in time for the later match against New South Wales. A Canterbury representative, he had three brothers — Frank, Victor and Reg — who also represented that province. Walter served as a New Zealand selector in 1923.

Robert Hamilton 'Bob' **DUFF**, an All Black from 1951 to 1952 and 1955 to 1956, was the youngest Justice of the Peace in New Zealand when appointed to the role, and served as deputy mayor of Lyttelton. He was a member of the NZ Racing Authority for 10 years from 1984.

Rhys John Llewellyn **DUGGAN**, a 1999 All Black, was one of three New Zealand halfbacks selected for the 1999 World Cup, the others being Justin Marshall and Byron Kelleher.

John Thomas **DUMBELL**, a New Zealand rep in 1884, was described as having 'a capital pot at goal'. He was born in Liverpool, came to New Zealand at the age of 13 and was considered by some pundits to be less than 50 kg in weight, although he played in the forwards.

James 'Jimmy' **DUNCAN**, a New Zealand rep in 1897, 1901 and 1903, captained the All Blacks in the first official test match in 1903. The five-eighths pattern of back configuration was considered to have been his brainchild. He was a saddler by trade, and had a remarkably compressed rugby career, going from All Black in 1903 to All Black coach in 1904–1905 and ending up as a test referee in 1908.

Michael Gordon 'Mick' **DUNCAN**, a 1971 All Black, although primarily a centre or wing for Hawke's Bay, made his test debut as a replacement second five-eighth against the British Lions.

William Dow **DUNCAN**, an All Black in 1920 and 1921, worked as a telephone linesman and cable joiner.

Edward 'Eddie' **DUNN**, an All Black from 1978 to 1981, played in an All Black trial in 1975, although he was not a member of his provincial side, Auckland. He first represented North Auckland at the age of 18 while at Dargaville High School.

Ian Thomas Wayne **DUNN**, an All Black in 1983 and 1984, was the brother of Eddie Dunn. Both were first five-eighths. A third brother, Richard, played halfback for Auckland and New Zealand Maori.

John Markham 'Jack' **DUNN**, a 1946 All Black, was involved in a boundary dispute between the Auckland RFU and the South Auckland sub-union. He was educated at Ararimu School.

Andrew Thomas 'Andy' **EARL**, an All Black from 1986 to 1992, played test rugby at three positions: lock, flanker and No. 8. He was famous for never combing his hair and acquired the nickname 'Worzel'. In 1992 he went straight from battling snow blizzards on his North Canterbury farm to playing for New Zealand in Australia's heat. While playing in England his photo featured in the Rugby Football Club programme, modelling clothing sponsored by Rugby Cement. In 2005 he cycled around New Zealand raising funds and awareness for couples afflicted by infertility. He is the first player to have played against every New Zealand rugby union.

Barry 'Peter' **EASTGATE**, a Canterbury All Black in 1952, 1953 and 1954, played his early club rugby on the West Coast for Hokitika Kiwi. Following the 1953–1954 tour to Britain, Eastgate was admitted to a Christchurch sanatorium with tuberculosis, and retired from rugby at 27 years of age. He later became a prosperous businessman, dealing in scrap metal.

Jason **EATON**, an All Black on the 2005 Grand Slam tour, is the grandson of Bevan Jones, who played regularly for Manawatu and New Zealand Maori in the 1950s. A shock selection, Eaton was only in the Taranaki Development Squad in 2004.

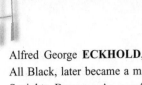

Alfred George **ECKHOLD**, a 1907 All Black, later became a maltster at Speights Brewery. As a referee, he controlled the unofficial test between New Zealand and New South Wales in 1923 and adjudicated four Ranfurly Shield games. He was also an Otago cricket rep and a notable rifle shooter.

Ian Matheson **ELIASON**, an All Black in 1972 and 1973, was not a noted try scorer, but managed two on the All Blacks' internal tour in 1972. He was nicknamed 'Legs' and ended up playing in 222 games for Taranaki, which equalled Fergie McCormick's Canterbury tally. He is also credited with throwing himself out of a lineout in a Taranaki-King Country match to achieve a penalty against Colin Meads. Apparently he was put up to it by coach J.J. Stewart.

Kenneth George 'Red' **ELLIOTT**, a 1946 All Black (who died in 2006 aged 83), became the Senior Lay Canon at Christchurch Cathedral. In 1944 he had the unique experience of playing against Wellington (for NZ Combined Services) and for Wellington (against Canterbury). A keen squash player, he organised volunteers to build squash courts in an old reservoir condemned after the Napier earthquake.

Marc Christopher Gwynne **ELLIS**, an All Black in 1992, 1993 and 1995, later became a well-known TV personality. He made it on to the New Zealand rich list after establishing the Charlie's fruit juice company.

Thomas Rangiwahia **ELLISON**, a New Zealand rep in 1893, was the first Maori to become a lawyer. He also conceived the All Black jersey and the silver fern, and wrote *The Art of Rugby Football*, published in 1902.

Allan Edwin George **ELSOM**, an All Black from 1952 to 1955, was one of the few All Black centres to kick a dropped goal in a test match.

Ronald Rutherford **ELVIDGE**, an All Black in 1946, 1949 and 1950, later became an obstetrician and gynecologist. As a member of the 1949 All Blacks — and a qualified doctor — he assisted passengers injured in a train crash in Rhodesia that involved the All Black touring party.

William Lister 'Bill' **ELVY**, an All Black in 1925 and 1926, was the Canterbury amateur welterweight boxing champion and worked as an engine driver with New Zealand Rail.

Charles 'Percy' **ERCEG**, an All Black in 1951 and 1952, also represented New Zealand Maori and later coached the same side.

Cyril Edward **EVANS**, a 1921 All Black, played only two games in the 1921 season: for Canterbury in their

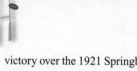

victory over the 1921 Springboks, and for New Zealand against New South Wales. He was nicknamed 'Scrum'. He represented Canterbury at cricket in the 1920s.

David Alexander **EVANS**, a 1910 All Black, represented New Zealand at league in 1911 and 1912. He was instrumental in persuading Hawke's Bay clubs Clive, Ahuriri and Kia Toa to switch to league in 1911.

Nick **EVANS**, a 2004 and 2005 All Black, played Australian Rules when he was young.

Kevin **EVELEIGH**, an All Black in 1974, 1976 and 1977, also played for Rhodesia in 1979 and Zimbabwe in 1980. His eldest son, Jason, has represented South Africa at mountain biking. Kevin, or 'Hayburner' as he is known, runs a stud farm for showjumping horses near Johannesburg and imports breeding stock from Holland.

Alfred Henry Netherwood **FANNING**, a 1913 All Black, was a founding member of the Christchurch Marist Club. One of his brothers was Bernard John Fanning. Another brother, Leo, was a journalist who wrote a rugby book in 1910 called *Players and Stayers*.

Bernard John **FANNING**, an All Black in 1903 and 1904, was regarded as the best lock forward of his time.

Colin Paul **FARRELL**, a 1977 All Black, was the first All Black produced by the Suburbs Club in Auckland.

Christopher Louis 'Kit' **FAWCETT**, a 1976 All Black, was selected for his country while playing for Auckland University. However, he never represented Auckland, although he played for Otago and Waikato. He is remembered for his infamous quote at the beginning of the 1976 All Black tour to South Africa that the All Blacks would score more 'off the field than on'.

William Rognvald **FEA**, a 1921 All Black, was also New Zealand squash champion in 1936 and 1937.

Gregory Edward **FEEK**, an All Black from 1999 to 2001, represented Taranaki and Canterbury in the NPC but first played Super 12 rugby for the Chiefs.

Brian Edward Louis **FINLAY**, a 1959 All Black flanker, played provincial rugby at fullback, wing threequarter, centre and five-eighth before moving into the forwards.

Jack **FINLAY**, a 1946 All Black, first played provincial rugby as a five-eighth, but later played as a loose forward. In three All Black trial matches in 1937 he played as prop or hooker. His only test match for New Zealand was as a No. 8.

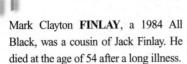

Mark Clayton **FINLAY**, a 1984 All Black, was a cousin of Jack Finlay. He died at the age of 54 after a long illness.

Innes 'Bunny' **FINLAYSON**, an All Black from 1925 to 1930, made his first-class debut for North Auckland in the latter's inaugural provincial match against South Island Country in 1920. His brothers were known as 'Bain' and 'Tote'. When he was ordered off against Transvaal in 1928 he required police protection to get to the sanctuary of the changing sheds.

Thomas **FISHER**, a 1914 All Black, played club rugby in Buller for a team called Hill United in 1919. He was a coalminer who became a publican and a prominent racehorse owner.

Charles James **FITZGERALD**, a 1922 All Black, was killed in a car accident in 1961. He was Marlborough's first All Black.

James Train 'Jim' **FITZGERALD**, an All Black from 1952 to 1954, scored an early try on the occasion of his test debut against Australia in 1952, but was subsequently dropped when New Zealand came out on the wrong side of a 14-9 scoreline. Earlier he had played in the same Hutt Valley High First XV as Ron Jarden, Colin Loader and John Reid, the cricketer.

Brian Bernard James **FITZ-PATRICK**, an All Black second five-eighth in 1951, 1953 and 1954, is the father of Sean Fitzpatrick. He first played rep rugby for Poverty Bay at the age of 18.

Sean Brian Thomas **FITZPATRICK**, an All Black from 1986 to 1997, weighed 69.9 kg at the age of 12 and was placed in the 3D team in his first year at Sacred Heart College. This was a weight-restricted side for the worst players at the school. He later went on to play 92 tests for New Zealand, the most by an All Black.

Troy Vandem **FLAVELL**, an All Black in 2000 and 2001, scored three tries on debut as a lock against Tonga.

John Kingsley **FLEMING**, an All Black in 1978, 1979 and 1980, played provincial rugby for Auckland and Wellington, before taking the field for Waikato. However, he was unlucky enough to break an ankle after only five minutes' play for Waikato against Horowhenua. His nickname was 'Bones'.

Charles John Compton **FLETCHER**, an All Black in 1920 and 1921, toured Australia with the All Blacks in 1920 but was unable to play because of an injury suffered before departure. He was the only All Black to make more than one appearance who was never in a winning side, and the only one to play more than one game for teams who failed to score a point. His matches resulted in scores of 0-17 against New South Wales and 0-0 versus South Africa.

Corey Robert **FLYNN**, an All Black in 2003 and 2004, has an uncle, Robbie, who has played test rugby for the USA, a father, Shaun, who represented Southland and a nephew, Aaron, who played for Canterbury and the Crusaders.

Richard 'Dick' **FOGARTY**, a 1921 All Black, played two games against the 1921 Springboks — one as a loose forward, the other as a hooker. He served in the First World War with the New Zealand Rifle Brigade and won the Military Medal. He lived to be 88.

Brian Robert **FORD**, an All Black in 1977, 1978 and 1979, was described as being a crushing and cartage contractor in Kaikoura.

William August **FORD**, an All Black in 1921, 1922 and 1923, was nick-named 'Jockey', probably because he stood 1.65 m and weighed only 65 kg. As a winger he scored a fast, jockey-like try that enabled Canterbury to beat the 1921 Springboks.

Stuart Thomas **FORSTER**, an All Black in 1993, 1994 and 1995, was nicknamed 'The Bear', and 'Bear Park', his mythical stamping ground,

was located in the street outside Carisbrook.

Grant James **FOX**, an All Black from 1984 to 1993, scored 1067 points for New Zealand, although he didn't become the All Blacks' regular goal-kicker until 1987. When in hospital in Toulouse suffering from a punctured lung, on the 1986 tour of France, he was given a carafe of wine with his first meal.

Arthur Reginald Howe 'Bolla' **FRANCIS**, an All Black from 1905 to 1910, transferred to league, eventually captaining New Zealand and playing professionally for Wigan and Hull. He won a Rugby League Cup Final Medal while playing for Hull.

William Charles 'Bill' **FRANCIS**, an All Black in 1913 and 1914, was just 19 when he first played for New Zealand. He was the youngest forward to play test rugby for the All Blacks, a record that still stands.

Bernard Gabriel 'Bernie' **FRASER**, an All Black from 1979 to 1984, was born in Lautoka, Fiji. He wrote a book *Ebony and Ivory* with Stu Wilson, and his daughter Brooke is a well-known New Zealand recording artist.

Harry Frederick **FRAZER**, an All Black in 1946, 1947 and 1949, was once awarded a penalty try in a test after being tackled without the ball against Australia in 1947.

William Stuart Scott 'Stu' **FREE-BAIRN**, an All Black wing three-quarter in 1953 and 1954, made the All Black tour to Britain and France after scoring three tries in an All Black trial. He is a Feilding chemist.

David 'Frank' Errol **FREITAS**, a 1928 West Coast All Black, was a commercial fisherman who lost his life in the *Wahine* disaster in 1968 at the age of 67.

Richard Trevor **FROMONT**, an All Black in 1993 and 1995, didn't play rugby until he was 18 years of age.

Harry **FROST**, an 1896 New Zealand representative, was the first New Zealand player to become a life member of the NZRFU. He was also a life member of the Auckland Rugby Union.

Frank Cunningham **FRYER**, an All Black wing threequarter in 1907 and 1908, was the first New Zealander to score five tries in a provincial match playing for Canterbury. He also scored five tries for New Zealand against Queensland in 1907.

William Bennett **FULLER**, a 1910 All Black, refereed the 1930 match between the British Lions and Wellington.

Blair Donald Marie **FURLONG**, a 1970 All Black first five-eighth, played an All Black trial in 1970 at fullback. He was one of three Maori to tour South Africa for the first time in 1970, the others being Buff Milner and Sid Going. Bryan Williams, of Samoan descent, also made the cut. As a cricketing off-spinner Furlong took a hat trick for New Zealand Under 23s against Canterbury.

David Richmond 'Davy' **GAGE**, a New Zealand rep in 1893 and 1896, later worked as a native interpreter. He had been a member of the New Zealand Native team in 1888 and became the subject of a TV mini-series *Savage Play*, shown on TV in the 1990s.

John Anthony **GALLAGHER**, an All Black from 1986 to 1989, converted to rugby league in 1990, the same year All Blacks Mathew Ridge, Frano Botica, John Schuster and Paul Simonsson also crossed the line. Gallagher is now head of physical education at Colfe's School, an independent school for boys in South London. His nickname, 'Kipper', bears a vague relationship with that of All Black Jamie Salmon's ('Trout'), but is believed to be based on the fact that Gallagher — as a Pom — came from the land of kippers.

David **GALLAHER**, an All Black from 1903 to 1906, gave his name to the Gallaher Shield, the Auckland

ACTUALLY - I THINK I GOT THE NICKNAME BECAUSE I LIKE THE ODD NAP.... EVERYONE THOUGHT I WAS A BIT OF A KIPPER!

© DARYL CRIMP

club championship trophy. While serving as a company sergeant major in the First World War he died of wounds inflicted at Passchendaele at the age of 43. His grave at Poperinge in Belgium has since become a shrine.

Phillip Charles **GARD**, an All Black in 1971 and 1972, died of cancer at the age of 43. He has been the only true-blue North Otago player to achieve All Black status.

Ashley John **GARDINER**, a 1974 All Black, had played for Taranaki for nine seasons before gaining All Black honours.

John Henry **GARDNER**, a New Zealand rep in 1893, was selected for the 1893 Australian tour before he had played first-class rugby. He was the publican of the Sporting Arms Hotel at Saltwater Creek.

Warren David **GATLAND**, an All Black from 1988 to 1991, went on four All Black tours without playing a test match. He subsequently coached Ireland and London Wasps before taking up the mantle of Waikato coach.

Rico **GEAR**, an All Black in 2004 and 2005, transferred to the Nelson Bays union in 2004. He had already played for Poverty Bay, Auckland, Bay of Plenty and North Harbour. His preferred sport from six till his mid-teens was swimming.

John Herbert 'Bert' **GEDDES**, a 1929 All Black, played six matches for New Zealand and scored seven tries. He was the son of the 1922 NZRFU president Arthur Geddes, who was also a New Zealand selector who happened to be on the panel that selected his son in 1929.

William McKail 'Mac' **GEDDES**, a 1913 All Black, was a major in the First World War and won the Military Cross. He gained the rank of lieutenant-colonel in the Territorial Artillery and was the Auckland Fortress Commander in 1940 and 1941.

Bruce McLeod **GEMMELL**, a 1974 All Black, earlier captained the 1973 Junior All Blacks who defeated the All Blacks. His son Fraser captained Oxford University against Cambridge.

Samuel William **GEMMELL**, a 1923 All Black who played one game against New South Wales, played his last first-class match when he was 45.

Victor Leslie 'Les' **GEORGE**, a 1938 All Black, was a New Zealand selector from 1964 to 1970.

Jonathan Brian 'Jono' **GIBBES**, an All Black in 2004 and 2005, was chosen for the 2004 tour to Europe but was unable to play because of injury. He captained New Zealand Maori to their historic victory over the British and Irish Lions in 2005.

Daryl Peter Earl **GIBSON**, an All Black from 1999 to 2002, graduated from Canterbury University with two degrees, specialising in education. Eight of his 19 test matches were played as a substitute.

Graham Duncan McMillan 'Mike' **GILBERT**, an All Black in 1935 and 1936, landed a vital 'pot' in the 13-12 win over Wales. He was born in Scotland and came to New Zealand as a small boy. On the boat trip from Britain he helped a sailor make rope quoits, and later back in Britain played 27 out of 30 games on the All Blacks 1935–1936 tour of the UK. He switched to league in 1937 and such was the sense of defection, he was not reinstated to rugby until 1995, when he was 84.

Charles Theodore **GILLESPIE**, a 1913 All Black, began his First World War service as a farrier-sergeant. He survived the Gallipoli campaign, although he was wounded at Passchendaele. He was awarded the Military Cross and lived to be 80.

William David 'Dave' **GILLESPIE**, an All Black in 1957, 1958 and 1960, played in seven successive All Black trials. Of his 23 games for New Zealand, only one of those was a test match.

George Arthur **GILLETT**, an All Black from 1905 to 1908, is reputed to have earlier played Australian Rules for Western Australia while living in Kalgoorlie.

Colin Cuthbert **GILLIES**, a 1936 All Black, first played senior provincial rugby for North Otago while attending Waitaki Boys High School. He also played cricket for North Otago while at the same school.

Colin MacDonald **GILRAY**, a 1905 All Black, later rose to the position of Deputy Chancellor of the University of Melbourne, after having been a Rhodes Scholar in 1907 at Oxford University, from which lofty status he represented Scotland.

Frederick James **GIVEN**, a 1903 New Zealand representative, toured Australia with the first New Zealand touring team. He later became a plumbing inspector.

Francis Turnbull 'Frank' **GLASGOW**, an All Black in 1905, 1906 and 1908, played provincial rugby for Wellington, Taranaki, Hawke's Bay and Southland. He served on the NZRFU executive from 1937 until his sudden death aged 58 in 1939.

William Spiers 'Billy' **GLENN**, an All Black in 1904, 1905 and 1906, was the first ex-All Black to become a member of Parliament, serving three political terms until 1928. During the First World War he was awarded the Military Cross while serving with the Royal Field Artillery.

Ernest **GLENNIE** was an 1897 New Zealand representative. His place of birth and place of death are unknown but what is known is that he was born and died on New Year's Day, 1871 and 1908, respectively.

John Wood 'Jack' **GODDARD**, an All Black in 1949, scored 13 points in a final All Black trial, which was a lot back then.

Maurice Patrick 'Morrie' **GODDARD**, an All Black in 1946, 1947 and 1949, played twice for England in war-time service internationals during the Second World War.

Kenneth Tautohe **GOING**, a 1974 All Black, had his appendix removed two weeks before he was named in the national side.

Sidney Milton **GOING**, an All Black from 1967 to 1977, was later awarded the MBE for his contribution to rugby. At one stage he spent three years as a Mormon missionary in Alberta, Canada. His bestselling biography was called *Super Sid*.

Jasin Alex **GOLDSMITH**, a 1988 All Black, was only 18 when he first played for New Zealand. As a 17-year-old he played 12 games for Waikato while attending Forest View High School, but after breaking his leg during the 1990 fixture between Auckland and Canterbury, he slowly drifted out of top rugby.

Alan **GOOD**, a New Zealand rep in 1893, was a lauded Maori linguist.

Hugh Maurice **GOOD**, a New Zealand representative in 1894, was a national champion in the high jump and shot put in 1898.

Steve Bryan **GORDON**, an All Black from 1989 to 1993, was an outstanding clay bird shooter who represented Waikato at provincial level. He also slept with the Ranfurly Shield after playing for Waikato in its famous victory at Eden Park in 1993.

William 'Rob' **GORDON**, an All Black in 1990 and brother of Steve, speaks fluent French, having lived in France for 15 years. A representative of Airbus Industries, he travels the world checking out the infrastructure at airports.

David 'John' **GRAHAM**, an All Black from 1958 to 1964, later became headmaster of Auckland Grammar School. He was named New Zealander of the Year by *North and South* magazine in 1999.

James Buchan **GRAHAM**, an All Black back-row forward in 1913 and 1914, was a goal-kicking forward who top scored with 66 points on the 1913 tour to America. He was disqualified from rugby in 1915 for allegedly accepting a bribe.

Maurice Gordon **GRAHAM** turned out as a guest player for the All Blacks against Queensland in Sydney in 1960. He and Eddie Stapleton made up the numbers for the day's double-header. He later became secretary of the Sydney Rugby Union.

Wayne Geoffrey **GRAHAM**, an All Black in 1978 and 1979, played in the first test against Argentina in 1979 when he replaced the luckless Ross Fraser, who broke his leg after being selected.

Kenneth William **GRANGER**, a 1976 All Black, became a car salesman. He suffered seriously from asthma as a child and never played a rugby game without puffing on his inhaler.

Lachlan Ashwell 'Lachie' **GRANT**, an All Black in 1947, 1949 and 1951, played three games for South Canterbury as a 17-year-old. He captained South Canterbury and kicked a penalty goal to help them lift the Ranfurly Shield from Wairarapa in 1950.

George Donaldson 'Doddy' **GRAY**,

an All Black in 1908 and 1913, played six consecutive games for the South Island. He was christened George but went by his second name, Donaldson, and his nickname 'Doddy'.

Kenneth Francis 'Ken' **GRAY**, an All Black from 1963 to 1969, had a renowned snarl. At the time of his premature death at 53, he had been selected as the Labour Party candidate for Western Hutt for the 1993 general election.

Roderick 'Rod' **GRAY**, an 1893 New Zealand rep, was described as 'a dashing type of forward that any side can do with'. He was reckoned to be the best miler in the Wairarapa in his day.

William Ngataiawhio 'Bill' **GRAY**, an All Black in 1955, 1956 and 1957, was the New Zealand Maori junior tennis champion in 1950. He received a telegram of sympathy from Prime Minister Walter Nash after breaking his leg playing for New Zealand Maori in Australia in 1958.

Craig Ivan **GREEN**, an All Black from 1983 to 1987, was best known as a wing threequarter. However, he played his first two tests as a second five-eighth, one as a replacement. He married an Italian woman, Antonella, who was a professional volleyball player. Their first baby, Marcus, was a cot death victim.

Kevin Michael **GREENE**, an All Black in 1976 and 1977, was the brother of Larry and Leo and son of Pat, who all played for Waikato.

Bertram Arthur 'Bert' **GRENSIDE**, an All Black in 1928 and 1929, scored 30 tries during Hawke's Bay's Ranfurly Shield tenure in the 1920s, a record for 60 years until Terry Wright eclipsed it in the late 1980s.

Jack Lester **GRIFFITHS**, an All Black from 1934 to 1938, rose to the rank of major in the Second World War, won the MC and was mentioned in dispatches. He served as aide-de-camp to General Freyberg.

Keith Eric **GUDSELL**, a 1949 All Black, later played for Australia against the 1951 All Blacks while studying veterinary science.

Richard Alan 'Richie' **GUY**, an All Black in 1971 and 1972, was chairman of the NZRFU in the mid-1990s when rugby converted from amateurism to professionalism. He won the barrel-carrying contest at the Waipu Highland Games on an annual basis.

Andrew Maxwell 'Andy' **HADEN**, an All Black in 1972, 1973 and from 1976 to 1985, at one stage registered his occupation as 'rugby player'. He is the business manager for such high-profile personalities as Rachel Hunter, Kylie Bax and A.J. Hackett.

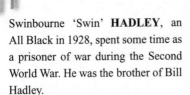

Swinbourne 'Swin' **HADLEY**, an All Black in 1928, spent some time as a prisoner of war during the Second World War. He was the brother of Bill Hadley.

William Edward 'Bill' **HADLEY**, an All Black in 1934, 1935 and 1936, suffered a broken jaw in the opening match of the All Blacks' 1935–1936 tour to Britain. He was the brother of Swin Hadley.

James Scott 'Jimmy' **HAIG**, a 1946 All Black, was born in Prestonpans, Scotland. He switched to league in 1947, became a Kiwi and played in 21 tests.

Laurence Stokes 'Laurie' **HAIG**, an All Black from 1950 to 1954, was a coalminer during his playing days. A brother of Jimmy Haig, he too was born at Prestonpans, Scotland. He came to New Zealand at the age of two and grew up at Kaitangata. He and Tony Brown share the distinction of being All Black first-fives to emerge from Kaitangata.

Duncan Alister **HALES**, an All Black in 1972 and 1973, later studied at the Palmer College of Chiropractic in the USA.

Donald Cameron **HAMILTON**, who played one test against the Anglo-Welsh in 1908, played in an exhibition league match in 1909 during the seemingly petty suspension of the Pirates and Brittania clubs in Southland. As a result of playing league, the players were declared professional and Hamilton's rugby career ended at that point.

Mark Garry **HAMMETT**, an All Black from 1998 to 2003, played 29 tests for New Zealand, all but three as a substitute.

Ian Arthur **HAMMOND**, an All Black in 1951 and 1952, was Marlborough's first test player. Hammond went on to become a life member of the union.

Robert Alexander **HANDCOCK**, a New Zealand representative in 1897, was a 12-stone (76.2 kg) front row forward in the days when the 2-3-2 scrum was in vogue.

William Robert 'Bill' **HARDCASTLE**, a New Zealand representative in 1897, toured Australia with the New Zealand team, liked what he saw and returned to live in Sydney. Before too long — in 1899 — he represented Australia at rugby from the Glebe Club and in 1908 he switched to league, in which code he also represented his adopted country.

Samuel **HARDING**, a 2002 All Black, played his only test match against Fiji. His father and two uncles played for Western Australia and his great-uncle, Rowe Harding, was a Welsh international in the 1920s and toured South Africa with the 1924 British Isles team.

Eric Tristram **HARPER**, an All Black in 1905 and 1906, died in Palestine in 1918. He is credited, with James Dennistoun, of discovering a pass to the West Coast at the head of the Rangitata River. A keen mountaineer, he died aged 40 while attempting to quieten horses during an artillery bombardment as a member of the Canterbury Mounted Rifles.

George 'Geo' **HARPER**, who represented New Zealand in 1893, made his first-class debut while still at Nelson College. Prior to the 1893 tour of Australia he played for a Combined XV against the New Zealand team, causing confusion by wearing a black jersey, which no doubt helped him score a runaway try!

Jack Hardy **HARRIS**, a 1925 All Black, scored only four points for the All Blacks — the result of a dropped goal. That goal enabled New Zealand to beat New South Wales 4-nil. He appeared at fullback in the final trial to select the 1924–1925 tourists to the UK, but the selectors opted to take only one fullback — George Nepia.

Perry Colin **HARRIS**, a 1976 All Black, won a test cap as a replacement

prop in South Africa, when Brad Johnstone and Bill Bush were injured and Kerry Tanner was ill.

William Albert 'Pat' **HARRIS**, who represented New Zealand in 1897, was suspended along with Joe Calnan for two years, for alleged drunkenness and bad language following New Zealand's match against Auckland after their Australian tour. He never played first-class rugby again.

Augustine Henry 'Gus' **HART**, an All Black in 1924 and 1925, although scoring 23 tries in 17 appearances for the Invincibles, could not command a regular position in the test team.

George Fletcher **HART**, an All Black from 1930 to 1936, toured to Australia in 1932, but because of injury played in one game only — against Darling Downs. A captain in the 20th Armoured Regiment, he died of wounds after being hit by a shell at Cassino in 1944, aged 53.

Brett Andrew **HARVEY**, a 1986 All Black, stood 1.94 m tall but weighed only 92 kg.

Ian Hamilton **HARVEY**, an All Black lock from 1924 to 1926 and in 1928, made his first-class debut for Wairarapa at fullback but played for New Zealand at lock.

Lester Robert **HARVEY**, an All Black

in 1949 and 1950, was described as a 'strong rucking forward'. He was the Matakanui Club's first All Black. He and Charlie Willocks played so many times together for Otago and New Zealand, they were known as 'Bacon and Eggs'.

Patrick 'Peter' **HARVEY**, a 1904 All Black, was selected for the 1905–1906 All Blacks but was unable to tour because of his highly specialised job. As a lip-reading teacher at the Sumner School for the deaf, and the only one in New Zealand, his services could not be spared. No less than New Zealand Premier Richard Seddon, made this decision.

Edward William 'Nut' **HASELL**, an All Black in 1913 and 1920, was nicknamed 'Nut' because his surname was pronounced 'Hazel'. He toured South Africa with the 1919 New Zealand Army side.

William Edward 'Scobie' **HAY-MACKENZIE**, a 1901 New Zealand representative, was the only back from the North Island team of 1905 to miss selection in the 1905–1906 All Black Originals. In 1894 he was dropped from an Otago-Southland match after partying until three o'clock in the morning on match day.

Carl Joseph **HAYMAN**, an All Black from 2001 to 2005, became the 1000th All Black in 2001.

Harold Owen **HAYWARD**, a 1908 All Black, was nicknamed 'Circus'. He transferred to league and made two tours of Australia, in 1912 and 1913, the second as Kiwi captain.

Edward John 'Jack' **HAZLETT**, an All Black in 1966 and 1967, was the nephew of Bill Hazlett, an All Black in 1926, 1928 and 1930. He went on to run a successful slink skins business in Southland.

William Edgar 'Bill' **HAZLETT** was a prominent sheep dog trialist as well as an All Black. A successful horse trainer based at Riverton, he was New Zealand's most successful owner from 1965 to 1969.

Thomas Roderick 'Rod' **HEEPS**, a 1962 All Black, kicked one conversion for New Zealand, won three national 100-yard sprint titles and scored eight tries for the All Blacks against Northern New South Wales at Quirindi.

Wiremu Rika **HEKE**, a 1929 All Black, played under the name Wiremu Rika. He didn't play rep rugby until he was 30 and toured with the 1926 New Zealand Maori team to Europe, Ceylon, Australia and Canada.

George Henry Noble **HELMORE**, a New Zealand representative in 1884, played as a wing, centre and forward for the 1884 New Zealand tourists

to Australia. He died in 1922 while holidaying in England.

Bruce Stephen **HEMARA**, a 1985 All Black, was chosen for the one-off test against the 1986 French tourists but had to withdraw through injury. He was replaced by Sean Fitzpatrick, who went on to play 92 tests. Hemara ended up coaching in Spain.

Ronald Courtney **HEMI**, an All Black from 1953 to 1957 and in 1959 and 1960, was only 20 when he played in all five of the All Blacks' tests while on tour in Britain and France in 1953–1954. As a cricketer he represented Auckland at the age of 17, opening the batting with Verdun Scott in three Plunket Shield matches.

Paul William **HENDERSON**, an All Black from 1989 to 1995, was nicknamed 'Ginge', although he had brown hair. He captained the All Blacks just once — at Bloemfontein during the 1995 World Cup, when his team beat Japan 145-17.

Peter **HENDERSON**, an All Black in 1949 and 1950, was the leading try scorer, with seven tries, on the 1949 All Black tour to South Africa. He won the national 100 yards sprint in 1949 and ran for New Zealand in the 1950 Empire Games in Auckland, qualifying for the 100 yards final.

James Malcolm 'Jamie' **HENDRIE** appeared as a guest player for the 1970 All Blacks when they played two games against Western Australian combinations while on their way to South Africa. Hendrie was summoned because the matches were staged on a Sunday and All Black halfback Sid Going was unavailable on religious grounds.

MacFarlane Alexander 'Mac' **HERE-WINI**, an All Black from 1962 to 1967, landed a penalty goal against France at Paris in 1964 for an All Black team that included Don Clarke. The latter had lost form to such an extent that he finally said to his captain, 'Give the ball to Mac.'

Maurice **HERROLD**, an 1893 New Zealand rep, was born in Calcutta, India. He died in Buenos Aires, Argentina.

David Norman **HEWETT**, an All Black from 2001 to 2003, lived in Hungary for three years as a teenager, where his father worked on an agricultural development project,

having been posted there by Pyne Gould Guinness.

Jason Alexander **HEWETT**, a 1991 All Black, played one match for New Zealand against Italy at the 1991 World Cup, and scored one try, which was worth four points at the time. He later spent six years in Japan as head coach and player for Mitsubishi Motors. He is a cousin of All Black prop Dave Hewett.

Norman Jason **HEWITT**, an All Black hooker from 1993 to 1998, achieved post-playing fame in 2005 in a TV series on ballroom dancing.

Allan Roy **HEWSON**, an All Black from 1979 to 1984, played for Wellington as a wing, centre and fullback in 1978. He played a season for the Wellington cricket team as a wicketkeeper-batsman.

Percy Hubert **HICKEY**, an All Black in 1922, conceded a penalty try for alleged shepherding against New South Wales.

Graeme **HIGGINSON**, an All Black from 1980 to 1983, was almost sent from the field when the All Blacks played Llanelli in 1980, but the two captains were able to convince referee Alan Hosie that he should stay.

David William **HILL**, a 2001 All Black, didn't play rugby until his seventh form year at college. Of Italian descent, he is a cousin of cricketer Daniel Vettori.

Stanley Frank 'Tiny' **HILL**, an All Black from 1955 to 1959, had two sons, Stan and John, who played basketball for New Zealand. He served nine months in Vietnam in the late 1960s as battalion sergeant major of the New Zealand battery at Nui Dat.

Geoffrey Robert **HINES**, a 1980 All Black, was selected for New Zealand at the age of 19. Earlier he won a New Zealand secondary schools hurdles title.

Frederick George **HOBBS**, an All Black in 1947, played in army matches in Egypt before gaining selection for the All Blacks. He worked as an accountant and manager with the *Christchurch Press* and organised the annual charity match between the police and Christchurch newspapers.

Michael James Bowie 'Jock' **HOBBS**, an All Black from 1983 to 1986, is the brother-in-law of Canterbury All Blacks Robbie and Bruce Deans. For many years he held the New Zealand franchise for Japanese boot and sports gear manufacturer Mizuno.

Carl Henry **HOEFT**, an All Black from 1998 to 2003, played 31 matches for New Zealand, 30 of them tests.

The single non-test match was against New Zealand A in 1999.

John **HOGAN**, a 1907 New Zealand representative, was also a member of the Wanganui water polo team that won the national title in 1905.

Martin Rowan 'Marty' **HOLAH**, an All Black from 2001 to 2005, was the 999th All Black to play for his country.

Arthur William 'Tubby' **HOLDEN**, a 1928 All Black halfback, partnered his club mate Nick Bradanovich at first-five in his two matches for New Zealand against New South Wales.

Edward Catchpole **HOLDER**, an All Black from Buller in 1932 and 1934, was a service car driver. He switched to league in 1935 and played for the Streatham and Mitcham club, and then Wigan, in the UK.

Bevan **HOLMES**, an All Black in 1970, 1972 and 1973, played twice for the All Blacks in one day when he performed as a replacement in the second of the two matches staged against Western Australian combinations at Perth. He went on four All Black tours without ever gaining test selection.

Llewellyn Simpkin 'Lew' **HOOK**, an All Black in 1928 and 1929, was a tobacconist.

John Alan 'Jack' **HOOPER**, an All Black in 1937 and 1938, played for the 1941 New Zealand Infantry Battalion side that beat a Fijian Battalion team in Fiji 32-9.

Aaron Remana **HOPA**, a 1997 All Black, died in a diving accident off the Coromandel Peninsula at the age of 27.

Alister Ernest **HOPKINSON**, an All Black from 1967 to 1970, was a stock agent and auctioneer. It was said there wasn't a person in North Canterbury he didn't know and not one who didn't like him.

Andrew Keith **HORE**, an All Black in 2002 and 2004, has a mother who played hockey for New Zealand. In 2005 he was convicted for shooting a seal.

John **HORE**, an All Black from 1928 to 1936, first played for New Zealand as a hooker in the old 2-3-2 scrum; but in 1932, when New Zealand first packed a 3-4-1 scrum, Hore, despite being less than 13 stone (82.5 kg), played as a prop. He was later a selector of the successful 1945–1946 Kiwis Army team and worked for 42 years at Dukes Butchery in George Street, Dunedin.

Ronald Hugh **HORSLEY**, an All Black lock in 1960, 1963 and 1964, had his appendix removed during the 1963–1964 tour of Britain and France. He was affectionately known as 'Honest Ron'.

John **HOTOP**, a Canterbury All Black in 1952 and 1955, initially played provincial rugby for Bush. As a trainee farm adviser he also played for Manawatu, Canterbury and Otago, and was selected for Southland, but injury prevented him playing.

Shane Paul **HOWARTH**, an All Black in 1993 and 1994, scored 34 points against the South of Scotland in 1993 and all of New Zealand's 34 points at Auckland and Sydney in 1994. He was the central figure in the 'Grannygate' inquiry that led to his suspension from Graham Henry's Welsh team, after a newspaper disclosed he had no Welsh grand-parentage.

James **HOWDEN** of Southland played one match for the All Blacks — against West Coast-Buller at Greymouth in 1928. The game was a 'work-out' between the second and third encounters against the New South Wales tourists.

Douglas Charles 'Doug' **HOWLETT**, an All Black between 2000 and 2005, has scored 39 tries in 48 test matches. As head boy at Auckland Grammar, he first represented Auckland as a 17-year-old while still playing First XV rugby. Later he became New

Zealand's youngest Super 12 player at 18 years, 230 days.

Arthur Maitland **HUGHES**, an All Black in 1947, 1949 and 1950, played for the All Blacks against Auckland in 1947 following the All Blacks tour to Australia. Both regular All Black hookers were injured and the little-known Hughes was called in. At the time he had not represented Auckland either. He was the managing director of Hughes and Cossar, wine and spirit merchants in Auckland, for many years, and also served as president of the New Zealand Racing Conference.

Daniel John **HUGHES**, who represented New Zealand in 1894, had his reminiscences published in *Taranaki Tales*. He was one of Taranaki's best wrestlers.

Edward 'Ned' **HUGHES**, an All Black in 1907, 1908 and 1921, was the oldest test player, being 40 years and 123 days old when he took the field in the second test against South Africa in 1921.

Laurence Clifford **HULLENA**, an All Black in 1990 and 1991, went on two All Black tours but never played in a test match.

George William **HUMPHREYS**, a New Zealand representative in 1894, was born in Wolverhampton.

Arthur Larwill 'Skinny' **HUMPHRIES**, a New Zealand rep in 1897, 1901 and 1903, once kicked a penalty goal for New Zealand in Queensland that was worth only two points. He later became manager of the New Zealand team involved in the 1908 series against the Anglo-Welsh.

Bruce Anthony **HUNTER**, an All Black in 1970 and 1971, is the first All Black to play two full matches for New Zealand on the one day — against Western Australia and an ARU President's XV in Perth (en route to South Africa) in 1970. He scored three tries in the first game and two in the second. He was also the holder of three New Zealand 800 metre titles.

James **HUNTER**, an All Black in 1905, 1906 and 1908, played 36 matches for the All Blacks and scored 49 tries. His first children, twin sons, died at birth, a daughter died of polio and a son (named Robert Deans Hunter after his 1905 team-mate) was killed fighting in Greece in 1941.

Ian Archibald **HURST**, an All Black from 1972 to 1974, was one of the few farmers to represent New Zealand in the 1970s who played as a midfield back. His son Ben represented Canterbury and the Crusaders as a halfback.

Alama **IEREMIA**, an All Black from 1994 to 2000, was in the All Black team that played England at the odd venue of Manchester. His sister April played netball for New Zealand and became a television newsreader.

Karl Donald **IFWERSON**, a 1921 All Black, scored 24 points for Auckland against a Wellington XV in 1922 — an extraordinary tally for the times. It was a record that stood for 33 years.

Craig Ross **INNES**, an All Black from 1989 to 1991, made his first-class debut in an All Blacks trial (1988), being unable to gain a spot for Auckland until later in the year. He scored a try for New Zealand the first time he touched the ball in a test — against Wales at Cardiff in 1989.

Gordon Donald **INNES**, a 1932 All Black, is believed to be the only ex-All Black to play league for England (against France in 1935).

Ian Bruce **IRVINE** played one test for the All Blacks as a hooker against the 1952 Wallabies. He is the brother of Bob Irvine, one of New Zealand's leading rugby commentators in the 1960s and 1970s.

John Gilbert 'Sal' **IRVINE**, a 1914 All Black, was a fireman.

William Richard 'Bull' **IRVINE**, an All Black from 1923 to 1926 and in 1930, played his Wairarapa club rugby

for Featherston Liberal. One of his sons, Ian, was an All Black in 1952 and the other, Bob, became a famous rugby commentator.

Mark William **IRWIN**, an All Black prop from 1955 to 1960, first played in All Black trials as an 18-year-old. He was a member of the New Zealand rowing eight in 1956.

Frederick Elder Birbeck **IVIMEY**, a 1910 All Black, became a captain in the regular force army. He served in the Boer War in South Africa prior to becoming an All Black.

Christopher Raymond **JACK**, an All Black from 2001 to 2005, scored a try 11 minutes into his debut test against Argentina in 2001, after coming on as a replacement.

Everard Stanley **JACKSON**, an All Black from 1936 to 1938, lost a leg in 1943 while serving in the Maori Battalion in the Western Desert campaign. His father, Fred Jackson, played for Leicester against the 1905 All Blacks before touring with the 1908 Anglo-Welsh tourists to New Zealand. He later settled in New Zealand, subsequently representing his new country at league.

Hohepa 'Harry' **JACOB**, Horo-whenua's first All Black, captained Manawhenua when it won the Ranfurly Shield from Wairarapa in

1927. He subsequently named his son Ran Furly Jacob.

John Phillip le Grande 'Phil' **JACOB** played for New Zealand in 1901. He was described as an itinerant character with bruising hips. He represented Wanganui, Taranaki, Wellington and Southland, and also played in New South Wales.

John Lyndon 'Lyn' **JAFFRAY**, an All Black from 1972 to 1979, scored five tries in his first five games on tour in South Africa with the 1976 All Blacks.

Mervyn William Rutherford **JAFFRAY**, a 1976 All Black, was forced to retire from the game in 1978 with a neck injury.

Ronald Alexander **JARDEN**, an All Black from 1951 to 1956, was selected for the All Blacks' 1951 tour of Australia while already on tour there with the Universities team. When he scored 38 points for the All Blacks against Central West, Jarden beat Billy Wallace's New Zealand record of 28 points in a game, which had stood since 1905. Wellington's *Evening Post* devoted its entire front page to Jarden after his shock death at 48. He was chairman of the New Zealand Broadcasting Corp, a trustee of the National Art Gallery and National Museum, and as a yachtsman he represented New Zealand at the Admirals Cup at Cowes.

Andrew Charles Reeves 'Andy' **JEFF-ERD** was East Coast's second All

I S'POSE THE POOR LITTLE BLIGHTER CAN BE THANKFUL YOU WEREN'T PLAYING IN THE LE QUESNE NEILSEN CUP!

© DARYL CRIMP

Black, in 1980 and 1981. He and the great George Nepia are the only two All Blacks chosen from East Coast.

Arthur Grahn **JENNINGS**, a 1967 All Black, represented Bay of Plenty, where he played club rugby for five clubs — Te Puke Rovers, Tauranga Cadet Old Boys, Ngongotaha, Kahukura and Eastern Suburbs.

Francis Mahon 'Doss' **JERVIS**, a New Zealand representative in 1893, kicked two goals from a mark for New Zealand.

Evan Morgan 'Ted' **JESSEP**, an All Black in 1931 and 1932, became New Zealand's first test hooker in a three-man front row. Sydney-born, he was also the first All Black to play both for and against his country in test matches, being a member of the first Australian team to win the Bledisloe Cup (1934).

Peter Arthur **JOHNS**, a 1968 All Black, was best known at provincial level as a centre, yet on the 1968 All Black tour to Australia he played as a second five-eighth and fullback. He was a Waiouru-based soldier when selected for the All Blacks.

Launcelot Matthew 'Lance' **JOHNSON**, an All Black in 1925, 1928 and 1930, played his last match for the All Blacks against North Otago. During an ostrich hunt at Burgersdorp on the 1928 tour of South Africa, he felled a bird at a range of more than 1000 metres.

David 'Davy' **JOHNSTON**, a 1925 All Black, gained his cap when he replaced James 'Wampy' Bell in the 1925 tourists to New South Wales. He died at the age of 35.

William 'Massa' **JOHNSTON**, an All Black in 1905 and 1907, was left in Britain at the end of the 1905 tour because of a throat infection. He had the distinction of being the first player to be ordered off in a Ranfurly Shield match, playing for Otago against Wellington. After retirement he became Commissionaire of the Royal Sydney Agricultural Showgrounds.

Bradley Ronald 'Brad' **JOHNSTONE**, an All Black from 1976 to 1980, was the son of Ron Johnstone, a member of the 'Kiwi' army team. He coached Fiji at the 1995 World Cup and, subsequently, Italy.

Campbell Robert **JOHNSTONE**, a 2005 All Black, is a keen stamp collector.

Peter **JOHNSTONE**, an All Black in 1949, 1950 and 1951, played soccer at school and represented Otago schoolboys before converting to rugby. The Taieri Club's ground in Dunedin is named after him.

Ian Donald **JONES**, an All Black from 1989 to 1999, was nicknamed 'Kamo' after the town in which he grew up. From the same street (Fisher Terrace) came Olympic equestrian eventer Blyth Tait, New Zealand table tennis player Angela Brackenbridge, New Zealand hockey rep Brian Maunsell and New Zealand Combined Services rugby player Richard Ackers.

Michael Niko **JONES**, an All Black from 1987 to 1998, refused to play on Sundays because of his religious beliefs. He has a masters degree in geography and a bachelors degree in town planning. He made his test debut at the age of 21 in 1986 — for Western Samoa against Wales in Apia.

Murray Gordon **JONES**, an All Black in 1973, tragically lost his life on Waitemata Harbour, Auckland, at the age of 32 while trying to save his son after a yachting mishap.

Peter Frederick Hilton **JONES**, an All Black from 1953 to 1960, was the highest try scorer (with 10) amongst the forwards on the All Black tour to Britain and France in 1953–1954. He achieved everlasting fame by telling the gathered crowd at Eden Park, after the series-clinching win over South Africa in 1956, that, 'I don't know how you feel, but I'm absolutely buggered'. The statement went out live over national radio.

Howard Thornton **JOSEPH**, a 1971 All Black, retired from top-level rugby after tearing knee ligaments in the same year he made the All Blacks. He worked as a journalist on the *Christchurch Star* while still playing first-class rugby.

James Whitinui 'Jamie' **JOSEPH**, an All Black from 1992 to 1995, was one of the 15 new All Blacks named in 1992. He played for Japan at the 1999 World Cup.

Jerome **KAINO**, a 2004 All Black, went to the same school as Joe Rokococo — St Kentigern College.

Gregory Norman **KANE**, a 1974 All Black, first played provincial rugby for Waikato at the age of 18. He later played for Wellington and Bay of Plenty. He also represented Waikato at the 1972 NZAAA championships as a javelin thrower.

Joseph Francis 'Joe' **KARAM**, an All Black from 1972 to 1975, who first played for his province Wellington as a 17-year-old, has campaigned strenuously in recent years for the release of convicted mass murderer David Bain.

Thomas **KATENE**, a 1955 All Black, made the national side while playing for Wellington, but also played eight seasons of provincial rugby for King Country.

Kieran James **KEANE**, a 1979 All Black from Canterbury, ended up coaching Hawke's Bay.

James Clarke 'Jim' **KEARNEY**, an All Black in 1947 and 1949, played representative rugby in Ashburton County for Canterbury Yeomanry Cavalry in 1943.

Byron Terrance **KELLEHER**, an All Black from 1999 to 2005, is a 91 kg halfback. He was named after poet Lord Byron by his poetry-loving father. Kelleher made headlines in 2005 when it was revealed that his new partner was a porn star.

John Wallace 'Jack' **KELLY**, an All Black in 1949, 1953 and 1954, became headmaster at Takapuna Grammar School. He had been the South Island junior shot put and discus champion in 1944.

Gerald Francis **KEMBER**, an All Black in 1967 and 1970, went on two major All Black tours during which he scored 185 points, but never played for New Zealand in a home game. He graduated from Victoria University as a lawyer.

Dean Julian **KENNY**, a 1986 All Black, was one of two All Black halfbacks playing for Otago at the time. The other was David Kirk, who was often shunted to the wing to accommodate him.

Alexander 'Sandy' **KERR**, a New Zealand rep in 1896, was a leather tanner by trade. He and Sydney Orchard became the first Linwood club players to represent their country.

Rodney Clive **KETELS**, an All Black in 1979, 1980 and 1981, was selected to tour with the All Blacks in 1978 but had to withdraw because of a leg injury. He later became a player manager, one of his charges being dynamic winger Joeli Vidiri.

Henry Arthur Douglas 'Mickey' **KIERNAN**, a 1903 All Black, usually wore white rugby boots.

Francis David 'Frank' **KILBY**, an All Black in 1928, 1932 and 1934, played provincial rugby for Southland, Wellington, Wanganui and Taranaki. He served 19 years on the NZRFU from 1955 and was a popular manager of Wilson Whineray's All Blacks on the 1963–1964 tour of the UK and France.

Brian Alexander **KILLEEN**, a 1936 All Black, was a proficient boxer during his school days and won provincial medals for being the most scientific boxer in 1925 and 1926.

Regan Matthew **KING**, a 2002 All Black, once played in the New Zealand Under-18 touch rugby team and worked at the Cambridge race track as a track worker.

Ronald Russell **KING**, an All Black lock from 1934 to 1938, made his provincial debut for West Coast as a wing. He was for many years licensee of King's Hotel in Greymouth, where the Queen stayed in 1953.

Charles Napoleon 'Nap' **KINGSTONE**, a 1921 All Black, played only 13 first-class games because of injuries received in a motor accident in 1922.

David Edward **KIRK**, an All Black halfback from 1983 to 1987, scored 17 tries in 34 matches for New Zealand. He studied at Oxford University as a Rhodes Scholar, served on Prime Minister Jim Bolger's staff and was CEO of one of Australia's largest media production companies, PMP, until his appointment in 2005 to head the Fairfax publishing empire.

Alexander **KIRKPATRICK**, an All Black in 1925 and 1926, was a foundation member of the Hastings Club, Hawke's Bay, in 1918. He later served on the NZRFU from 1952 to 1956 and was elevated to president in 1956.

Ian Andrew **KIRKPATRICK**, an All Black from 1967 to 1977, was the first player to captain both the North and South Island teams. He was a talented polo player, as were two of his brothers, David and Colin, who both represented New Zealand at polo.

Earle Weston **KIRTON**, an All Black from 1963 to 1970, was born in Taumarunui. He used to ride trackwork at Trentham when he was 16 and weighed only 7 stone (44.5 kg). While studying in London for a postgraduate course in dentistry he represented Harlequins, Middlesex and the Barbarians.

John James **KIRWAN**, an All Black winger from 1984 to 1994, played halfback for his school, De La Salle College. He grew 12 inches (30.5 cm) in a year while at De La Salle, which eventually led to a condition called Sherman's Disease, which placed stress on the sciatic nerve and manifested itself in hamstring problems. He was a butcher's apprentice when first chosen for the All Blacks.

Alfred Louis **KIVELL**, a 1929 All Black, made his New Zealand debut at the age of 32.

Arthur 'Bubs' **KNIGHT**, an All Black in 1926, 1928 and 1934, was an uncompromising forward, despite his nickname. He was the brother of Laurie Knight (the first) and lived to 84.

Gary Albert **KNIGHT**, an All Black from 1977 to 1981 with the nickname of 'Axle', won a Commonwealth bronze medal as a wrestler. He dislocated both hips in a fall from a tractor at the age of 14 and six pins had to be inserted to repair the damage. He later suffered bruised ribs when a spectator attacked him with a fence paling after the All Blacks' game against Nadroga at Lautoka ended in a riot.

Lawrence Alfred George 'Lawrie' **KNIGHT**, a 1925 All Black, was ordered from the field following a difference of opinion with the referee during the Auckland-British Lions match in 1930. He was the father of 1974–1977 All Black Lawrie Knight.

Lawrence Gibb 'Lawrie' **KNIGHT**, an All Black in 1974, 1976, and 1977, was a doctor of medicine, who lived and practised as a doctor in Johannesburg for almost 20 years.

Michael Orton **KNIGHT**, a 1968 All Black, played representative rugby for Hawke's Bay, Counties and Wellington, and then went offshore to play for Singapore. He had been the New Zealand national junior sprint champion in 1964. His father Wally represented England Combined Services.

Tohoa Tauroa 'Paul' **KOTEKA**, an All Black prop in 1981 and 1982, was also known as 'Bam-bam'. He went on to represent Western Australia.

Anthony John 'Tony' **KREFT**, a 1968 All Black prop replacement player, played four games for New Zealand and scored two tries.

Joshua Adrian 'Josh' **KRONFELD**, an All Black from 1995 to 2000, had two granduncles, David and Frank Solomon, who played for New Zealand. He is an enthusiastic surfer, owns a home in Raglan, and is a talented singer and harmonica player who often performs gigs in nightclubs and bars.

Robert **KURURANGI**, a 1978 All Black wing, was denied a place in Ranfurly Shield folklore when the referee ruled him offside as he was racing for the goal-line in Counties' 1982 challenge against Canterbury.

Christopher Robert **LAIDLAW**, an All Black from 1963 to 1970, had his appendix removed during the course of the All Blacks' tour to South Africa in 1970. He was awarded a Rhodes Scholarship and studied at Oxford University, where he completed a Bachelor of Letters. After serving with the New Zealand Embassy in France he became New Zealand's ambassador in southern Africa. He was Race Relations Conciliator before serving a brief stint in Parliament.

Kevin Francis **LAIDLAW**, a 1960 All Black, who was born in Nightcaps, Southland, won two New Zealand gun dog championships. He also owned a racehorse called Bell

Flight that won two steeplechases in Australia before crashing in the Australian Grand National when 100 metres in front.

Patrick Richard **LAM**, a 1992 All Black, also played for Western Samoa in the 1991 and 1995 World Cup campaigns.

Kent King **LAMBERT**, an All Black from 1972 to 1977, missed the second and third tests against the 1977 British Lions while recovering from an appendectomy. The first All Black front rower since 1905 to place kick a goal in Great Britain, he is the proprietor of the Commercial Hotel at Waipawa, having previously run hotels in Taranaki.

James Taylor **LAMBIE**, who represented New Zealand in 1893 and 1894, died from injuries inflicted by his horse while on the way home from watching the match between Taranaki and the 1904 British team.

Arthur 'Artie' **LAMBOURN**, who represented the All Blacks from 1934 to 1938, was a photoengraver.

Blair Peter **LARSEN**, an All Black from 1992 to 1996, was selected as All Black flanker in 1994, although he normally played lock forward.

Sione **LAUAKI**, an All Black in 2005, earlier played for the Pacific Islanders in 2004 against New Zealand, Australia and South Africa. He scored tries against all three. He was born at Ha'a Pai.

Casey Daniel Eti **LAULALA**, a 2004 All Black, likes the movie *How to Lose a Guy in Ten Days*. He was born at Moto'otua.

Arthur Douglas **LAW**, a 1925 All Black, played for the temporarily amalgamated Manawatu and Horowhenua unions (Manawhenua), and made the All Blacks from there. He was Palmerston North Boys High School's first All Black.

Gordon Pirie **LAWSON**, a 1925 All Black, was an auctioneer who played provincial rugby for South Canterbury, as did his three brothers, Douglas, Allan and William.

Jules Mathew **LE LIEVRE**, an All Black from 1962 to 1964, went on to become a broiler chicken farmer.

John Gage **LECKY**, a New Zealand rep in 1884, was a tinsmith by trade. He owed his All Black selection to the fact that the 1884 team was chosen on a quota system, with four players each from Otago, Canterbury, Wellington and Auckland getting the nod. When an Auckland player withdrew from the original selection, his replacement had to be an Aucklander. Come in, Lecky!

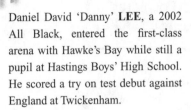

Daniel David 'Danny' **LEE**, a 2002 All Black, entered the first-class arena with Hawke's Bay while still a pupil at Hastings Boys' High School. He scored a try on test debut against England at Twickenham.

John **LEESON**, an All Black prop in 1934, weighed only 13 stone (about 82.5 kg). Remarkably, he played 31 seasons as a member of the Kereone senior team and represented Harlequins against Thames Valley at the age of 45.

Robert Noel 'Bob' **LENDRUM**, a 1973 All Black fullback, began his first-class career for Counties as a second-five.

Andrew Roy 'Andy' **LESLIE**, an All Black from 1974 to 1976, captained the All Blacks in all 34 matches he played for them. His two sons, John and Martin, both represented Scotland. Andy also played softball for New Zealand.

Howard Joseph **LEVIEN**, a 1957 All Black, was born in Taumarunui. Following a motorbike accident he had a leg amputated below the knee and never played rugby again. Later he became a New Zealand disabled golf champion.

Eric Tiki 'Tiny' **LEYS**, a 1929 All Black, played cricket for Wellington Town, won the Auckland B grade tennis title and was an Auckland representative lawn bowler.

Herbert Theodore 'Herbie' **LILBURNE**, an All Black from 1928 to 1932 and in 1934, remains the youngest ever All Black captain in a test, being 21 years and 112 days of age.

David Frederick **LINDSAY**, an All Black in 1928, was selected for the South African tour as a threequarter, but played all but one of his 14 matches as a fullback. He slept in during the 1928 South African tour and missed the bus taking the team to practice in Cape Town. Scorning breakfast, he made it to Newlands by borrowing a child's bicycle.

William George 'Bill' **LINDSAY**, a 1914 All Black, was nicknamed 'Dad'. Lindsay first played for his province, Southland, at the age of 32, and became an All Black two years later. He played club rugby in Dunedin with Pirates until he was 42.

Terence Raymond 'Terry' **LINEEN**, an All Black from 1957 to 1960, played his club rugby for Auckland Marist, who numbered amongst their ranks fellow All Blacks Keith Davis, Steve Nesbit and Paul Little. His son, Sean Lineen, made 70 appearances for Scotland and toured New Zealand in 1990.

WHATEVER YOU DO... DON'T CRITICIZE THE ALL BLACKS!

HAIRDRESSER

© DARYL CRIMP

Thomas Norman **LISTER**, an All Black from 1968 to 1971, was not the only sportsman in his family. His brother John was a prominent professional golfer who won a PGA tournament in the United States.

Paul Francis **LITTLE**, an All Black from 1961 to 1964, was a hairdresser.

Walter Kenneth **LITTLE**, an All Black from 1989 to 1998, played for New Zealand at centre, second five-eighth and first five-eighth. He and Frank Bunce were the subjects of a book about their careers, called *Midfield Liaison*.

Colin James **LOADER**, an All Black in 1953 and 1954, was one of the selectorial victims of the tour to Britain and France, for after playing four of the five tests, he was not called upon by the New Zealand selectors again.

Brian James **LOCHORE**, an All Black from 1963 to 1971, technically played for two provincial unions — Wairarapa (1959–1970) and Wairarapa-Bush (1971), after Wairarapa and Bush had amalgamated. He was knighted in 1998 before serving three years as chairman of the Hillary Commission. As a youngster, he won the Wairarapa junior tennis title on four successive occasions.

Terence McClatchey 'Terry' **LOCK-INGTON**, a 1936 All Black, was one of the few All Blacks who played neither a home test nor an overseas tour game. His one All Black appearance was against South Canterbury, staged between two home tests against the touring Wallabies.

Richard Wyllie **LOE**, an All Black from 1986 to 1992 and in 1994 and 1995, first played for the All Blacks during the 1986 tour to France. Loe was not a member of the official touring party, but happened to be playing for the Lyon club in France when called upon to reinforce the injury-ravaged forwards.

Arthur Robert 'Mick' **LOMAS**, an All Black in 1925 and 1926, appeared for Auckland in 1920 while playing for Thames RSA, at a time when the Thames sub-union was part of the Auckland union. A fisherman when he played for the All Blacks, Lomas later became one of Thames' leading citizens and headed the town's fire service.

Jonah Tali **LOMU**, an All Black from 1994 to 2002, was such an aggressive individual when he started at Wesley College that principal Chris Grinter set up a punching bag in the gymnasium, with instructions that whenever Lomu was angry he was to 'take it out on the punching bag'. Lomu lived his first seven years on the tiny Tongan island of Ha'apai

where he became known as 'The Water Rat'.

Andrew Thomas 'Paddy' **LONG**, an All Black in 1903, is one of the more obscure All Blacks. Details regarding his birth and death are not known. He had the honour, though, of playing in the first official test match. In 1904 he was suspended by the Auckland Rugby Union for offering a bribe to a City club player. The suspension lasted until 1911.

John Kelman **LOVEDAY**, a Manawatu All Black in 1978, was a chiropractor. He captained Palmer Chiropractic College, based at Davenport, Iowa, to victory in the 1972 American national inter-collegiate rugby championship.

David Steven 'Dave' **LOVERIDGE**, a Taranaki All Black from 1978 to 1983, and in 1985, farms pigs on his property in Rugby Road, Inglewood. He represented Auckland Under 23s and Taranaki at cricket, and is nicknamed 'Trapper'.

George **LOVERIDGE**, a Taranaki All Black in 1913 and 1914, was a telegraphist with the Post Office. He is not related to Dave Loveridge.

Keith Ross **LOWEN**, a 2002 All Black, was the first Chiefs player to score a hat trick of tries in Super 12 rugby. His nickname is 'Sumo'.

Frederick William **LUCAS**, an All Black from 1923 to 1930, was well-known for his immaculate appearance. Not surprisingly, he established his own menswear store in Auckland. He represented Piha at national surf lifesaving.

William Albert 'Bert' **LUNN**, an All Black in 1949, was one of the few players to take part in both unsuccessful tests against the 1949 Australians. His son Steve became a first-class referee and an NZRFU board member.

Thomas William **LYNCH** (ii), an All Black in 1913 and 1914, was popularly known as Tiger. His father, Thomas William Lynch (i), had represented Otago and the South Island in the 1880s. A speedy threequarter, 'Tiger' scored 37 tries in 23 outings for the All Blacks, most of them on tours of America and Australia. He twice scored four tries in a match.

Thomas William **LYNCH** (iii), an All Black in 1951, was the son of Thomas William Lynch (ii). He represented Otago in cricket at Brabin Cup and Colts level and also played professional league for Halifax in the UK from 1952 to 1956. He was a cousin of 1958 All Black Tom Coughlan.

George **MABER**, who represented New Zealand in 1894, had 'any amount of dash and was a good collarer'. The first All Black from the Petone Club, he died at the tender age of 25.

Charles Luke **McALISTER**, a 2005 All Black, scored 99 points for the 2002 New Zealand Secondary Schools team.

Francis Stevens 'Frank' **McATAM-NEY**, an All Black prop in 1956 and 1957, was a converted lock forward. His son Steve played for Mid-Canterbury in the 1980s as a lock. The latter was not converted into a prop.

Bernard Joseph 'Bernie' **McCAHILL**, an All Black from 1987 to 1991, had eight brothers and sisters, one sister, Terri-Anne, representing New Zealand at soccer. His father Barney enjoyed considerable success as a racehorse owner, winning the Wellington and Auckland Cups with Castletown. After his career wound down McCahill coached London Harlequins with Zinzan Brooke.

Patrick **McCARTHY** was ordained as a Catholic priest in 1920 and played his only game for the All Blacks in 1923. He spent most of his life in Australia.

Terence Michael **McCASHIN**, an All Black hooker in 1968, played provincial rugby for four teams:

Horowhenua, Wellington, King Country and Marlborough. As a brewer, he established the 'Macs' range of beers.

Richard Hugh 'Richie' **McCAW**, an All Black since 2001, became New Zealand's 60th test captain when he led his country against Wales in 2004. He grew up on the family farm at Hakataramea in North Otago and can play the bagpipes.

William Alexander 'Bill' **McCAW**, an All Black in 1951, 1953 and 1954, was also a South Island softball rep. He is not related to Richie McCaw.

Brian Verdon **McCLEARY**, an All Black in 1924 and 1925, was New Zealand and Australasian amateur heavyweight boxing champion in 1920 and 1921. He beat another future All Black, Maurice John Brownlie, in winning the national title.

William Graham 'Monty' **McCLYMONT**, a 1928 All Black, wrote the official war history, *To Greece*. He retired as first assistant at Otago Boys' High School in 1961.

Michael John **McCOOL** played one test for the All Blacks in 1979. During his time with Wairarapa-Bush, McCool often locked the scrum with a teenaged Andy Earl.

Archibald George 'Archie' **McCORMICK**, a 1925 All Black, was also New Zealand amateur heavyweight boxing champion in 1922 and 1923. He was the father of Fergie McCormick.

James **McCORMICK**, a 1947 All Black hooker, played for Wairarapa, Wellington and Hawke's Bay. During the 1947 tour to Australia he became, like the leading hooker 'Has' Catley, injured, thus allowing Arthur Hughes to make his All Black debut before he had played for Auckland.

William Fergus 'Fergie' **McCORMICK** played for the All Blacks in 1965, and from 1967 to 1971. His first wife, Helen, was a national hockey rep. Fergie at one time worked as a slaughterman.

John Francis **McCULLOUGH**, a 1959 All Black, was one of the few farmers to play first five-eighth for New Zealand.

Alexander **McDONALD**, an All Black from 1905 to 1908 and again in 1913, was captain of the All Blacks on their pioneering tour to North America in 1913. He became a New Zealand selector, co-manager of the 1938 All Blacks in Australia and assistant manager of the 1949 All Blacks in South Africa.

Angus James **MacDONALD**, an

All Black on the 2005 Grand Slam tour, is the son of All Black Hamish MacDonald and the nephew of Doug Bruce, who starred at first-five when the All Blacks completed their only other grand slam in the UK, 27 years earlier. Multi-talented, Angus was invited to join the Auckland Cricket Academy in the same year he was signed up by the Auckland Rugby Academy. He sacrificed cricket.

Hamish Hugh **MacDONALD**, an All Black lock from 1972 to 1976, scored a try against Scotland in six inches of water in the 'flood' test at Eden Park. Both his father, H.J. Macdonald and son, Angus, played representative rugby, one for Northland, the other for Auckland.

Leon Raymond **MacDONALD**, an All Black from 2000 to 2003, and in 2005, kicked 16 consecutive conversions at the 2003 World Cup.

Joseph Michael 'Joe' **McDONNELL**, a 2002 All Black, scored a try in his first test against Italy, an unusual feat for a prop forward.

Peter **McDONNELL**, who represented New Zealand in 1896, was the first player to score four tries in a New Zealand provincial match — for Wanganui against Manawatu.

Steven Clark **McDOWELL**, an All Black prop from 1985 to 1992, also represented New Zealand at judo.

John Thompson **McELDOWNEY**, an All Black in 1976 and 1977, propped the Taranaki scrum with his brother Bryce for several years. He was listed at one stage as a bitumen worker.

Ian Neven 'Nev' **MacEWAN**, an All Black from 1956 to 1962, was unable to play in the fourth test against the 1959 British Lions because of an attack of measles. He served a term as president of the New Zealand Rugby Museum.

Paul William **McGAHAN**, an All Black in 1990 and 1991, represented both Counties and North Harbour.

Brian **McGRATTAN**, an All Black from 1983 to 1986, was a prop forward who scored four tries in 16 games. Following a club match he required approximately 60 stitches to a head wound inflicted by an opponent.

Alwin John 'Dougie' **McGREGOR**, a 1913 All Black, also played rugby league for New Zealand in 1919 and 1920.

Ashley Alton **McGREGOR**, a 1978 All Black on the tour to Britain, played in only three of the 18 tour matches. Unfortunately, one of those games was the traumatic 12-nil loss to Munster.

Duncan **McGREGOR**, an All Black from 1903 to 1906, scored four tries in the 1905 test against England. He switched to league and toured with the 1907 All Golds. Remaining in England, he joined the Merthyr Tydfil club and on his return to New Zealand, became a league referee and national selector.

Neil Perriam **McGREGOR**, an All Black in 1924, 1925 and 1928, toured South Africa with the 1928 All Blacks, but because of injuries played in only four matches. His final first-class game was an All Black trial in 1930.

Robert Wylie 'Dick' **McGREGOR**, a New Zealand rep in 1901, 1903 and 1904, scored a controversial try in New Zealand's first official test match against Australia in 1903. He was one of six brothers who played rugby in the Thames district. Before he moved to Australia a benefit match was arranged on his behalf as he had been in poor health for most of his later life.

Maurice James 'Morrie' **McHUGH**, an All Black in 1946 and 1949, was the New Zealand amateur heavyweight boxing champion in 1938. He later became a cartage contractor, a rubber worker and an insurance agent.

Charles Nicholson **MacINTOSH**, who represented New Zealand in 1893, was born in Timaru. A former mayor of Timaru, he edited a newspaper in

Buenos Aires and died, aged 49, in Rio de Janeiro, Brazil.

Donald Neil **McINTOSH**, an All Black in 1956 and 1957, was later the only non-member of a referee's association to ref a rep match (Wairarapa v. East Coast, 1968).

Donald William **McKAY**, an All Black in 1961, 1962 and 1963, was a surprise omission from the All Black touring team to Britain and France in 1963–1964. He was a sprint and swimming champion while at Takapuna Grammar School.

James Douglas **MACKAY**, a 1928 All Black, was later awarded the MBE. He served for 15 years as a warden at Lincoln College after being a RNZAF education officer during the Second World War.

Brian John **McKECHNIE**, an All Black from 1977 to 1979, also played cricket for New Zealand. He was the batsman on the receiving end of the infamous underarm delivery dished up by the Australians in 1981.

Gerald Forbes **McKELLAR**, a 1910 All Black, volunteered to serve in the Boer War while still a schoolboy.

Richard John 'Jock' **McKENZIE**, an All Black in 1913 and 1914, later became publican of the Hamilton Hotel. Wounds suffered in the First World War ended his rugby career, but he was reported to have subsequently represented Waikato at hockey.

Robert Henry Craig 'Crow' **MACKENZIE**, a 1928 All Black, later wrote the biography *Walter Nash: Pioneer and Prophet*. He also wrote a history of Hutt Hospital and represented Wellington at cricket.

Robert Hugh 'Rab' **McKENZIE**, a New Zealand representative in 1893, scored Auckland's only try against the 1888 British touring team as an 18-year-old. He ended up as chairman of the New Zealand Co-operative Dairy Company.

Roderick McCulloch **McKENZIE**, an All Black from 1934 to 1938, was a side-row and lock forward who kicked a goal from a mark for New Zealand. He retired as a mailroom supervisor with the New Zealand Post Office.

William 'Mac' **McKENZIE**, who represented New Zealand from 1893 to 1897, was known as 'Offside Mac', as a result of his fringing play. In 1893 he was ordered off against New South Wales, but disguised his shame by affecting an exaggerated limp to give the impression he had been forced from the field by injury. Rheumatism cut short his rugby playing days.

William Henry Clifton 'Billy'

MACKRELL, a New Zealand representative in 1905 and 1906, switched to league and played in the first ever New Zealand league test — against Wales on a UK tour. He died of a paralytic seizure at the age of 35.

John Victor **MACKY**, a 1913 All Black, qualified as a public accountant, in the process winning the Shaw Prize in 1908 for the highest marks in New Zealand.

Jon Stanley **McLACHLAN**, a 1974 All Black, scored four tries against South Australia during the course of the All Black tour to Australia in 1974. It was his debut match. When he was called into the second test team he became the College Rifles Club's first test All Black.

Hugh Campbell **McLAREN**, a 1952 All Black, played in every forward position during his provincial rugby career. His only game for the All Blacks was at No. 8. He was invalided out of the second test selection of 1952 with a nose injury.

Andrew 'Leslie' **McLEAN**, an All Black in 1921 and 1923, first played for Auckland in 1916 against the 17th Reinforcements at the age of 17, at a time when, for patriotic reasons, selection was restricted to players under 20.

Charles 'Chas' **McLEAN**, a 1920 All Black, was born at Cape Foulwind. As a loose forward he scored seven tries in his five All Black appearances. He was awarded the Military Medal during the Gallipoli landings.

Hubert Foster 'Hugh' **McLEAN**, an All Black from 1930 to 1936, helped set up the Barbarians club in New Zealand in 1937, along with another ex-All Black, Ronald George Bush. His father, four uncles and two brothers also played provincial rugby. Another brother, Terence Power McLean, was a famous sporting journalist and writer.

John Kenneth 'Jack' **McLEAN**, an All Black in 1947 and 1949, played provincial rugby for Auckland, Canterbury, Waikato and King Country. He was an accomplished athlete and his best time for the 100 yards was 10 seconds flat.

Robert John 'Robbie' **McLEAN**, a 1987 All Black prop, made the All Blacks in his first year of first-class rugby. He was one of several players from Wairarapa-Bush to play for New Zealand in the 1980s.

Bruce Edward **McLEOD**, an All Black hooker from 1964 to 1970, scored a try in his first test against Australia in 1964. His life after rugby was blighted by severe alcohol problems and he died in 1996 at the age of 56.

Scott James **McLEOD**, an All Black in 1996, 1997 and 1998, played in New Zealand's first night test match at home — against Western Samoa in 1996.

David Thomas McLaggan **McMEE-KING**, a 1923 All Black, played 'spasmodically' for Otago after which he gave stalwart service to Dunedin's Kaikorai club as an administrator and coach.

Archibald Forbes 'Archie' **McMINN**, a 1903 and 1905 All Black, later became a Dannevirke fishmonger. His father, Alexander McMinn, a journalist, founded the *Manawatu Evening Standard* newspaper.

Francis Alexander 'Paddy' **McMINN**, a 1904 All Black, was the brother of Archibald McMinn. He was also the brother of Gordon, Garnet and Leslie, who all played for Manawatu.

Raymond 'Frank' **McMULLEN**, an All Black from 1957 to 1960, scored a try in each of his first two tests for New Zealand — against Australia in 1957. He later became a test match referee and had control of the 1973 England test at Eden Park.

John Alexander 'Jack' **McNAB** toured Australia with the All Blacks in 1925 but played only one match before being struck down with appendicitis. He came from Hawke's Bay.

John Ronald 'Jack' **McNAB**, an All Black in 1949 and 1950, couldn't play rugby at school because the Owaka District High School didn't have enough boys. He first represented Otago from the Catlins club. As an administrator he served 40 years on the Owaka club committee, becoming president of the Otago RFU in 1980.

Alan Murray **McNAUGHTON**, an All Black in 1971 and 1972, was reputedly selected for the 1971 All Blacks specifically to 'look after' British Lions kingpin Barry John.

James 'Jim' **McNEECE**, an All Black in 1913 and 1914, also represented Southland at cricket. He died at Messines, Belgium, during the First World War, at the age of 29.

Alasdair Lindsay Robert 'Sandy' **McNICOL** was an All Black in 1973. His father, Stew, played rep rugby for Wellington, King Country, Wanganui and New Zealand Universities, and New Zealand Services in the United Kingdom in 1944. 'Sandy' McNicol played for French club Tarbes from 1973 to 1976.

Bruce Eric **McPHAIL**, a 1959 All Black, once scored seven tries for Canterbury against Combined

Services. He was the national veteran sprint champion in 1979–1980.

Donald Gregory **MacPHERSON**, an All Black in 1905, became assistant medical officer at Weston Hospital in London. He represented Scotland against England in 1910 while playing for London Hospital.

Gordon **MacPHERSON**, an Otago All Black in 1986, originally played for Poverty Bay. He became a one-test All Black, along with Brett Harvey, when he played in the 1986 test for the Baby Blacks against France.

Ian Robert **MacRAE**, an All Black from 1963 to 1970, was a big second five-eighths at 6 foot 2 inches (1.88 m) and 13 stone 7 lb (85.7 kg). Danny Hearn, the England centre, ended up in a wheelchair following a mistimed tackle on him in 1967. MacRae was the first chairman of the ill-fated NPC second-division team Central Vikings.

John Alexander 'Jack' **McRAE**, a 1946 All Black hooker, made his New Zealand debut as a replacement prop for the injured Harry Frazer, although he was only 13 stone 6 lb (85.4 kg) in weight. He was the Southland rugby selector in 1959.

Nisbet **McROBIE**, a New Zealand rep in 1896, later unsuccessfully contested the Ohinemuri seat for the Reform Party in the 1911 General Election. He was the president of the Remuera Bowling Club in 1924–1925. He was also manager of the *New Zealand Times*, owner of the *Waihi Daily Times* and manager of Business Printing Works in Auckland.

Ruben George **McWILLIAMS**, an All Black in 1928, 1929 and 1930, was educated at Eureka School in the Waikato. He later became assistant coach of the Ponsonby Club.

James Richard **MAGUIRE**, a 1910 All Black, was a member of the Waitemata rowing crew that won the national fours title in 1909.

Atholstan **MAHONEY**, an All Black from 1929 to 1936, was killed in a car accident near Pahiatua. The Bush union's only All Black, he was nicknamed 'Tonk' and was a great personal friend of commentator Winston McCarthy.

Laurence William 'Laurie' **MAINS**, an All Black fullback in 1971 and 1976, who played his early rugby as a first five-eighth, is an avid fisherman and once caught a 17.3 kg salmon in the Waitaki River.

John **MAJOR**, an All Black in 1963, 1964 and 1967, acted as back-up hooker to two long-serving All Black hookers — Dennis Young and Bruce McLeod. His only test match came in 1967 against Australia, when McLeod was suspended.

Isitola **MAKA**, a 1998 All Black, weighed 122 kg. Born in Longoteme, Tonga, he was one of 14 children.

Thomas 'Simon' **MALING**, an All Black from 2001 to 2004, played for the Harlequins in London at the end of 2004.

John Eaton 'Jack' **MANCHESTER**, an All Black from 1932 to 1936, was nicknamed 'Lugger' because of his prominent ears.

Simon James **MANNIX**, an All Black in 1990, 1991 and 1994, became an All Black in his first year of provincial rugby.

Paul Francis **MARKHAM**, a 1921 All Black, was also known as Father Paul Kane, having been ordained as a Roman Catholic priest. He was a member of the Society of Mary.

Justin Warren **MARSHALL**, an All Black from 1995 to 2005, captained New Zealand in four tests in 1997. When he first played rugby he was a freezing worker in Mataura. Once, after scoring a try, in an attempt to arouse the crowd, he effected an impromptu skipping technique which, when allied with flapping arms, led to the development of a dance step that lasted two matches.

Matemini Christopher 'Chris' **MASOE**, an All Black on the 2005 Grand Slam tour, won a gold medal as a member of the 2002 New Zealand sevens team at the Kuala Lumpur Commonwealth Games. His nickname is 'Mussy'.

David Frank 'Tim' **MASON**, a 1947 All Black, scored a try for New Zealand in his first test while acting as a replacement, an unusual feat. He was a brother of celebrated playwright Bruce Mason and settled in South Africa, where he twice played for Western Province. Mason died in Johannesburg at the age of 67.

Frederick 'Harold' **MASTERS**, a 1922 All Black, was regarded as 'a huge player for his time', at 15 stone 6 lb (about 98 kg). Masters had the unusual record of being a national selector in two different countries, being All Black selector in 1936 and 1937, and later in 1946 and 1947 after moving to Australia, becoming selector for New South Wales and Australia. Masters won the Military Medal at Messines during the Second World War.

Robin 'Read' **MASTERS**, an All Black in 1923, 1924 and 1925, later became one of the editors of the *Rugby Almanack of New Zealand* in 1935 and was associated with it

ER... IS THERE AN ALL BLACK IN THE CROWD ?!

© DARY CRIMP

until his death in 1967. He was an All Black selector in 1949 and NZRFU president in 1955.

Hawea Karepa **MATAIRA**, a 1934 All Black, later played rugby league and departed on the New Zealand league team's 1939 tour of England, only to be forced to return home with the team after two matches because of the outbreak of the Second World War. He was charged with manslaughter after a fight with fellow New Zealand Maori player B.E. Rogers in 1936, Rogers dying of a fractured skull. Mataira was subsequently acquitted after Rogers was found to be the aggressor.

Jeffrey David **MATHESON**, an All Black in 1972, made the All Blacks from Otago but ended his provincial playing days captaining North Otago.

He was the technical adviser to the Sri Lankan Rugby Union from 1990 to 1994.

Robert George **MATHIESON**, a 1922 All Black, was born in the Chatham Islands. He represented Otago in 1918, at the age of 18.

John Tabaiwalu Fakovale 'Tabai' **MATSON**, an All Black in 1995 and 1996, gained selection in an impromptu fashion. He was following the All Blacks' 1995 tour of Italy and France as a sponsor's representative when he was invited to play as injuries took their toll.

Herman Alfred **MATTSON**, a 1925 All Black, was unable to play representative rugby for Auckland because of a knee injury in 1923 and a broken jaw in 1924. His rugby playing days ended when he suffered a broken collarbone in 1926. As a banker, he had a reputation for looking after people down on their luck. Refugees from Europe were always treated with kindness, though he had to stretch bank rules to allow this.

Aaron Joseph Douglas **MAUGER**, an All Black from 2001 to 2005, has played 32 test matches, 28 of which have produced victories.

Nathan Keith **MAUGER**, a 2001 All Black, broke a leg in 1999 after an accidental collision with his brother Aaron, while playing for New Zealand Colts. His mother was not only the sister of two All Blacks (the Bachop brothers) but also the mother of another two.

Donald Stanfield 'Don' **MAX**, an All Black in 1931, 1932 and 1934, broke his ankle while touring Australia in 1934 and did the same again the following season. In 1949 he was president of the NZRFU. His debut match for the All Blacks coincided with the last 2-3-2 scrum fielded by New Zealand in 1931.

Norman Michael Clifford **MAX-WELL**, an All Black lock from 1999 to 2004, scored a try in his first test against Samoa, and another one in his first World Cup match against Tonga.

Mark Andrew **MAYERHOFLER**, an All Black in 1998, was nicknamed 'Bubs'. He had the misfortune to play most of his tests during the infamous losing streak of the 1998 All Blacks.

Colin Earl **MEADS**, the legendary 'Pinetree' who was an All Black from 1957 to 1971, still holds the record for most appearances for New Zealand, 133. In 1999, he was named All Black of the Century and in 2001 he was created a distinguished Companion of the New Zealand Order of Merit (the equivalent of a knighthood). Daughter Rhonda represented New Zealand at netball.

Stanley Thomas **MEADS**, an All Black from 1961 to 1966, locked the New Zealand scrum with his brother Colin in 11 tests. He was born in Arapuni. During his time as King Country selector-coach, King Country beat Canterbury, 48-28, at Te Kuiti, in 1995.

Keven Filipo **MEALAMU**, an All Black from 2002 to 2005 is, at 1.81 m in height, New Zealand's shortest hooker since Dennis Young.

Kevin Francis **MEATES**, a 1952 All Black, in later years befriended Prime Minister Norman Kirk.

William Anthony 'Bill' **MEATES**, an All Black in 1949 and 1950, was the brother of Kevin Meates. He played 13 matches for the Kiwis army team.

Kees Junior **MEEUWS**, an All Black from 1998 to 2004, scored 10 test match tries — an astonishing and record-breaking figure for a prop — in 42 tests. His later adventures in France were produced in book form, with the help of author Heather Kidd, in *Le Rugbyman* in 2005.

Andrew Philip **MEHRTENS**, an All Black from 1995 to 2004, was the grandson of George, an All Black fullback who played for New Zealand in New Zealand in 1928 — he died aged 47 — and the son of Terry, who represented New Zealand Juniors against the Springboks in 1965. Andrew was born in Durban, his parents having lived there for five years. Possessed of a photographic memory, he is gifted at calculus.

George Martin **MEHRTENS**, a 1928 All Black, retired from the game at the early age of 21. He was the grandfather of Andrew Mehrtens.

Thomas Charles **METCALFE**, an All Black in 1931 and 1932, was the first All Black to play at No. 8.

Graham George **MEXTED**, an All Black in 1950 and 1951, won selection for Wellington while playing senior B rugby for Tawa. The father of Murray, he established Mexted Motors in Tawa. The family are descendents of George Mexted, one of Wellington's earliest settlers in 1840.

Murray Graham **MEXTED**, an All Black from 1979 to 1985, married New Zealand's Miss Universe, Lorraine Downes. A veteran TV rugby commentator with Sky, he set up the International Rugby Academy in Wellington.

Bradley Moni **MIKA**, a 2002 All Black, weighed 123 kg. Although gaining his All Black cap as a lock forward, he produced good form for Auckland in 2005 as a No. 8.

Dylan Gabriel **MIKA**, a 1999 All Black, is related to Bradley Mika and is an insulin-dependent diabetic.

James Joseph 'Jimmy' **MILL**, an All Black halfback from 1923 to 1926 and in 1930, played provincial rugby for four teams: Poverty Bay, Hawke's Bay, East Coast and Wairarapa. While playing for Nelson College First XV he also played for Nelson in a second-class match. He was a member of the Poverty Bay cricket side that won the Hawke Cup in the 1918–1919 season.

Paul Charles **MILLER**, an All Black in 2001, played two matches (against Ireland A and Scotland A) for New Zealand, but has yet to play a test.

Todd James **MILLER**, an All Black fullback in 1997, played no rugby in 1995 and 1996 as he was undertaking Mormon church missionary work. He is a nephew of Sid Going, another All Black Mormon missionary.

Harold Maurice **MILLIKEN**, a 1938 All Black, transferred to rugby league in 1939 and was reinstated to the 15-man code in 1950.

Hugh Parsons **MILLS**, an 1897 New Zealand representative, was described as an all-round forward. He had a 'penchant for launching dribbling rushes'.

John Gordon **MILLS**, a 1984 All Black, replaced the injured Andy Dalton in the Cavaliers in 1986. As a hooker he gained the unusual distinction of being part of the New Zealand team at the Hong Kong Sevens in 1984.

Edward Bowler **MILLTON**, a New Zealand rep in 1884, was described as 'one of the best dribblers'. From 1911 to 1921 he commanded the Eighth South Canterbury Rifles as a lieutenant-colonel.

William Varnham **MILLTON**, a New Zealand rep on tour to Australia in 1884, played his first tour game at fullback before seeing out the tour's duration in the forwards. He later saved the life of a passenger during the plight of the vessel *Melrose*, which foundered near Timaru. He was captain of New Zealand's first-ever touring side, to Australia in 1884. At the age of 29 he died of typhoid.

Henare Pawhara 'Buff' **MILNER**, a 1970 All Black, first played provincial rugby for East Coast while still a pupil at Tokomaru Bay High School. During the 1970 All Black tour to South Africa, Milner played at fullback, wing, centre and second five-eighth. He died of cancer in 1996 at the age of 50.

John Eric Paul **MITCHELL**, an All Black No. 8 in 1993, was elevated suddenly to higher honours after having played for Waikato for nine years, and never having gained selection for any national team. He became an often controversial All Black coach and presided over New Zealand's 2003 World Cup campaign.

Neville Alfred 'Brushy' **MITCHELL**, an All Black from 1935 to 1938, also played cricket for Southland. He later became a hotel manager, bookseller and a wholesale liquor merchant.

Terry William **MITCHELL**, an All Black in 1974 and 1976, first played representative rugby for Golden Bay-Motueka as a 17-year-old. He later became a tobacco company rep.

William James 'Billy' **MITCHELL**, an All Black in 1910, worked in a fruit shop. He was born in Melbourne.

Frank Edwin **MITCHINSON**, an All Black from 1907 to 1913, scored for New Zealand in four different ways — 22 tries, two conversions, two penalty goals and one dropped goal. His test match try-scoring record of 10 stood for 60 years until bested by Ian Kirkpatrick in 1973.

James Edward 'Jim' **MOFFITT**, a 1920 and 1921 All Black, was initially a tailor's cutter by trade. During his short All Black career he played in all games on the New Zealand tour to Australia in 1920, and in all three tests against the 1921 Springboks.

Brian Peter John **MOLLOY**, an All Black halfback in 1957, became a scientist with the DSIR's botany division in Christchurch.

Graham John Tarr **MOORE**, an All Black in 1949, became an eye specialist in Masterton and was appointed as honorary doctor for the Wairarapa and Wairarapa-Bush unions.

Raymond Claude **MORETON**, an All Black in 1962, 1964 and 1965, was one of several players considered unlucky to miss selection for the tour of Britain and France in 1963–1964. He became a South Island Universities selector in 1974.

Herman 'David' **MORGAN**, a 1923 All Black, played only eight first-class games, including one match for New Zealand against New South Wales. He was the New Zealand 440 yards hurdles champion in 1926.

Joseph Edmund 'Joe' **MORGAN**, an All Black in 1974 and 1976, scored a remarkable try against South Africa from set play, in which he crossed the line untouched — an unheard of feat. And Morgan was better known for his defence. He died in an accident at a Whangarei construction site at the age of 57.

Trevor James **MORRIS**, an All Black fullback in 1972 and 1973, was 30 years of age when first selected to play for his country. He was the first All Black to represent the Nelson-Bays union.

Terry Geoffrey **MORRISON**, a 1973 All Black, later played for London New Zealand, the Harlequins and Middlesex.

Thomas Clarence **MORRISON**, an All Black in 1938, was voted on to the NZRFU executive in 1946 at the age of 33 while still playing representative rugby for Wellington. He ran a menswear shop in partnership with Ivan Vodanovich, who also coached the All Blacks. He represented South Canterbury at athletics and swimming.

Brian Lewis **MORRISSEY**, a 1981 All Black, captained the New Zealand junior basketball team in 1968.

Peter John **MORRISSEY**, a 1962 All Black, was the Canterbury 440 yards athletic champion in 1961, with a time of 48.7 seconds.

Graham Neil Kenneth **MOURIE**, an All Black from 1976 to 1982, captained the New Zealand Juniors against Romania in 1975 and scored his side's only two tries. His first wife was an Argentinian.

John **MOWLEM**, a New Zealand rep in 1893, was the first player to play for both sides during the course of a New Zealand first-class fixture. This came about when he was asked to change sides during the course of a trial match in 1893. He later became a hunter in South Africa before returning to New Zealand, where he became involved with setting up big game fishing operations at Tauranga.

Junior Malili 'Mils' **MULIAINA**, an All Black in 2003, 2004 and 2005, can play equally well at fullback, wing or centre. He grew up in Southland before coming north to attend Kelston Boys' High School, Graham Henry's old school.

Brian Leo **MULLER**, an All Black from 1967 to 1971, was generally regarded as being the heaviest prop to play for New Zealand. In a reflection of his strength, it was reported that he was in the habit of trimming hedges with a lawnmower.

William John 'Bill' **MUMM**, an All Black prop in 1949, was also a national champion sawyer. Not surprisingly, he was a sawmiller. He became a Buller selector in the 1960s and 1970s.

Henry Gordon 'Abe' **MUNRO**, an All Black in 1924 and 1925, was at 11 stone 12 lb (75.4 kg), one of the lightest ever All Black forwards. He was president of the Otago Rugby Union in 1949 and 1950.

Keith **MURDOCH**, the infamous All Black prop of 1970 and 1972, played provincial rugby for Otago, Hawke's Bay and Auckland. Following his banishment from the 1972–1973 tour to Britain, he has spent most of his time in the outback of Australia.

Peter Henry **MURDOCH**, an All Black in 1964 and 1965, scored tries in each of his first two test matches. His father, 'Doc', a former Auckland rep, became well known as a masseur and baggage man for many touring teams to New Zealand.

Frederick Steele Miller **MURRAY**, a New Zealand rep in 1893 and 1897, could play equally well in any forward position. He also played cricket for Auckland.

Harold Vivian 'Toby' **MURRAY**, an All Black in 1913 and 1914, played much of his representative rugby as a wing threequarter, although he appeared for New Zealand as a wing-forward. He had won the Ladies Challenge cup for the under-16 mile while at school.

Peter Chapman **MURRAY**, an All Black in 1908, was born in Southern Grove. He became a member of the Waimarino County Council.

Richard George 'Dick' **MYERS**, an All Black in 1977 and 1978, was a shock selection for the All Blacks' tour to France in 1977, and just as big a shock selection when named for his only test match against Australia in 1978.

Harry Jonas 'Simon' **MYNOTT**, an All Black rep from 1905 to 1907 and in 1910, was a first five-eighth who made his test debut against Ireland as a wing threequarter. At provincial level he became known as one of the 'Taranaki twins', who formed a strong five-eighths combination. The other 'twin' was Jimmy Hunter.

Waka Joseph **NATHAN**, an All Black from 1962 to 1967, played in 14 tests and was never on the losing side. The French dubbed him the Black Panther. He made a habit of breaking his jaw on All Black tours of Britain, achieving the feat in 1963–1964 and again in 1967. A butcher at Mangere, he became president of the Auckland Rugby Union.

Keith Alister **NELSON**, an All Black in 1962, 1963 and 1964, is a dentist. He served for several years on the Auckland RFU management committee and is one of the few All Blacks to receive life membership of the Ponsonby Club.

George **NEPIA**, an All Black from 1924 to 1930, played twice for his province East Coast in 1947 at the age of 42. In 1950 he became the oldest player to turn out in a first-class fixture when he captained the Olympian Club against Poverty Bay. The latter team was captained by Nepia's son, George junior. This fixture was also distinctive in being the only occasion when a father and son combination have appeared on opposing sides in New Zealand first-class rugby.

Steven Roberto **NESBIT**, an All Black first-five in 1960, later lived in the United States. He returned to New Zealand as a member of a Californian Universities team. His occupation at one stage was listed as 'barman'.

Wayne Ronald **NEVILLE**, a 1981 All Black, played for three North Auckland clubs — Kaitaia Pirates, Awanui and Kaitaia. Following his sudden elevation to All Black status, he disappeared from the scene and didn't even play further provincial rugby for North Auckland. He was never an age grade rep and played in no trials or inter-island games.

Craig Alan **NEWBY**, a 2004 All Black, played 12 sevens tournaments for New Zealand.

Frederick **NEWTON**, an All Black in 1905 and 1906, was, at 15 stone (95.3 kg), the heaviest forward on the 1905 All Black tour to Britain. He was nicknamed 'Fatty'. He gained one of his three test caps while replacing Bill Cunningham, who had a cold.

Harold Garwood 'Doc' **NICHOLLS**, a 1923 All Black, was not a doctor.

Harry Edgar 'Ginger' **NICHOLLS**, an All Black halfback from 1921 to 1923, missed out on the All Black tour to Britain in 1924–1925, but accompanied the tour in his capacity of correspondent for the *Free Lance* magazine. His two brothers, Marcus Frederick and Harold Garwood, also played for New Zealand. Following Ginger Nicholls' performance against South Africa in the first test of the 1921 series against the Springboks,

he was awarded a gold medal by the NZRFU for being New Zealand's best back. He was then dropped for the second test.

Marcus Frederick 'Mark' **NICHOLLS**, an All Black first-five from 1921 to 1930, once scored in four different ways for Wellington against Taranaki: a try, conversion, penalty goal and a goal from a mark (taken by a team-mate). He was the author of a book based on the All Blacks' 1928 South Africa tour — *With the All Blacks in Springbokland*.

George William **NICHOLSON**, an All Black loose forward from 1903 to 1907, was referred to as 'Long Nick'. He was a boot-maker. When he died in 1968, only Billy Wallace and 'Bunny' Abbott of the 1905–1906 Originals survived him.

Ma'a Allan **NONU**, an All Black in 2003, 2004 and 2005, was born in Wellington. As a 'modern' All Black, he was not averse to wearing eyeliner on the odd occasion.

Rangitane Will 'Tane' **NORTON**, a Canterbury All Black hooker from 1971 to 1977, first played provincial rugby for Mid-Canterbury. He was one of the first six-foot hookers of the modern era. After almost 30 years as a tomato grower, in 2005 he became the owner of the Pacific Park Hotel

IT'S A DISGRACE ... ALL BLACKS WEARING EYE LINER !

WAIT 'TIL THEY START PUTTING THEIR HAIR IN ROLLERS !!

© DARYL CRIMP

in Christchurch with his son Richard, who is managing the operation.

Andrew James 'Jim' **O'BRIEN**, a 1922 All Black, made his first-class debut in the 1922 North-South match before playing for Auckland, and toured with the All Blacks to New South Wales, again before playing provincial rugby.

John Gerald 'Jack' **O'BRIEN**, an All Black in 1914 and 1920, broke his leg against New England while touring Australia. After he appeared in the 1919 Kings Cup Competition for the New Zealand Services team, the Prince of Wales, impressed with his soundness, made the following claim: 'If I dropped my kitbag from the dome of St Paul's, O'Brien would catch it.'

Joseph 'Jack' **O'BRIEN** played his only game for New Zealand in 1901, when a player called Tom Cross failed to arrive on time for the game against Wellington. Until 2002 no photo had ever been found of him, but a member of the public came forward with one after a news item on TV.

Michael William 'Mick' **O'CALLA-GHAN**, a Manawatu All Black in 1968, won four blues for Cambridge University. He became a lecturer in veterinary surgery and radiology at Massey University.

Thomas Raymond 'Ray' **O'CALLA-GHAN**, a 1949 Wellington All Black, also played representative cricket and hockey for West Coast.

Timothy Beehane **O'CONNOR**, a

New Zealand rep in 1884, was born in Kilenenan, Ireland. He won three national shot put titles and became the Australasian shot put champion. He also held the hammer throw title.

Robert John 'Bob' **O'DEA**, an All Black in 1953 and 1954, is one of only two Thames Valley representatives to have played for New Zealand. Kevin Barry is the other. O'Dea also played cricket for Thames Valley.

Desmond Hillary **O'DONNELL**, a Wellington All Black prop in 1949, played his last game for the Raetihi club in 1964 at the age of 43, after having served as coach and treasurer of the club from 1952 to 1958.

James **O'DONNELL**, a New Zealand rep in 1884, was arrested prior to touring Australia in 1884, on the basis of being indebted to trades people in the deep south of the South Island. It was strongly felt that O'Donnell had no intentions of returning from Australia. He didn't and went on to play for New South Wales.

Bernard Clement 'Barney' **O'DOWDA**, a New Zealand rep in 1901, was born in India. He played for Brighton and Sussex before emigrating to New Zealand in 1895. After setting up a brewery at Waitara with James Donald Watson, another former New Zealand rep, he became a Taranaki oil driller.

Jason David **O'HALLORAN**, an All Black in 2000, only just made it to All Black status. He did so by playing the last few minutes as a replacement against Italy at Genoa in 2000. Prior to that he had played against the Asian Barbarians in a match that, because of replacement breaches, was ruled out as a first-class fixture. Then a family bereavement caused O'Halloran to miss the first week of the European leg of the tour and he only just made it back in time to be included in the squad for the Italian match.

Geoffrey Haldane **OLD**, an All Black loose forward from 1980 to 1983, was a policeman. He played against the 1981 Springboks at a time when policemen, in general, were expected to turn their back on on-field activity and watch the crowd.

Michael Joseph 'Joe' **O'LEARY**, an All Black in 1910 and 1913, was the first player to captain New Zealand in a test from the fullback position. He also played in the 1909 'Australian Club Championship' for Ponsonby in a match against Newtown in Sydney. His brother Humphrey captained New Zealand Universities and later became Chief Justice, while Michael, himself, was a blacksmith.

Robert **OLIPHANT**, who represented New Zealand in 1893 and 1896, was awarded the Royal Humane Society's

Certificate of Merit after saving a boy from drowning. He was born in County Tyrone, Ireland.

Anton David **OLIVER**, an Otago All Black from 1996 to 2005, first played provincial rugby for Marlborough in 1993. His biography *Anton Oliver — Inside* was published in 2005.

Charles Joshua **OLIVER**, an All Black from 1928 to 1936, also played cricket for New Zealand. He was forced to withdraw from an All Black test selection in 1931 following a bout of blood poisoning — the result of having been bitten in a provincial match. Oliver co-wrote, with fellow All Black Eric Tindill, a book called *The Tour of the Third All Blacks*.

Desmond Oswald 'Des' **OLIVER**, an All Black in 1953 and 1954, was christened Oswald Desmond Oliver. At one stage he became the director of the renal unit at the Churchill Hospital in Oxford, England.

Donald Joseph **OLIVER**, a 1930 All Black, worked as a prison officer and hydatids inspector. He played for five separate provincial unions in six seasons — Otago (1929), Wellington (1930), Wairarapa (1931), Waikato (1933 and 1934) and Southland (1935).

Francis James 'Frank' **OLIVER**, an All Black from 1976 to 1981, was recruited from Australia where he had played a charity game, to lock against the Springboks in 1981 after Graeme Higgonson freakishly broke his ankle in training. His son Anton is a current All Black, who, like his father, has captained New Zealand at test level.

Sydney Arthur **ORCHARD** of Canterbury, who represented New Zealand in 1896 and 1897, also played cricket for Canterbury. As a bowler he twice took a hat trick.

Jack **ORMOND**, an All Black in 1923, was an MP for Eastern Maori under his Maori name Tiaki Omana.

Rex William **ORR**, a 1949 All Black, was born in Gore. He captained New Zealand Services between 1953 and 1955 while a flight lieutenant in the New Zealand Air Force.

Glen Matthew **OSBORNE**, an All Black from 1995 to 1999, first played provincial rugby for Wanganui as a first five-eighth. He used to be in the habit of collecting rocks wherever he went as an All Black and was probably lucky he had a group weight concession.

William Michael 'Bill' **OSBORNE**, an All Black from 1975 to 1978 and again in 1980 and 1982, played in all seven matches on the All Blacks' 1980 Welsh Centenary tour. In his first All Black trial in 1974 he made seven line-breaks. With fellow All Black Bruce Robertson, he wrote a coaching book in 1984.

James Michael 'Jimmie' **O'SULLIVAN**, an All Black in 1905 and 1907, played in all four internationals on the 1905–1906 Originals tour to Britain. He was possibly the only All Black to receive all his education at Matapu School.

Terence Patrick Anthony 'Terry' **O'SULLIVAN**, an All Black in 1960, 1961 and 1962, scored a try in the first test against France in 1961, as a result of French centre Guy Boniface feeling the effects of a sprained ankle and dropping the ball. Ironically, O'Sullivan was forced out of the second test with a sprained ankle.

Lui **PAEWAI**, an All Black in 1923 and 1924, was the youngest player, at 17 years and 45 days, to play for New Zealand.

James Russell 'Rusty' **PAGE**, an All Black from 1931 to 1935, had a distinguished military career, retiring from the New Zealand Army as a brigadier. He received the DSO in 1942 and the CBE in 1954.

Milford Laurenson 'Curly' **PAGE**, an All Black in 1928, also captained the 1937 New Zealand cricket team on their tour to England. He scored 3247 runs in 88 first-class cricket matches for New Zealand.

Bertram Pitt 'Bert' **PALMER**, an All Black in 1928, 1929 and 1932, died of a head injury after making a tackle in a club match between Otahuhu and Auckland University in 1932. The Bert Palmer Memorial Trophy for sportsmanship among Auckland junior boys' teams was instigated in his honour.

James Hislop 'Jim' **PARKER**, an All Black in 1924 and 1925, was a wing forward who was deemed to be the fastest man in the Invincibles team that toured Britain. He managed the 1949 All Blacks in South Africa and was elected a life member of the NZRFU in 1959. He also served as chairman of the New Zealand Apple and Pear Marketing Board and received the CBE.

Allan Archibald **PARKHILL**, an All Black forward in 1937 and 1938, was a butcher.

Ross Michael 'Mike' **PARKINSON**, an All Black in 1972 and 1973, was the son-in-law of Johnny Smith, the legendary 1940s' All Black. Both were mid-field backs.

Alexander Marshall **PATERSON**, an All Black in 1908 and 1910, later died while a spectator at Carisbrook, Dunedin.

Henry **PATON**, an All Black in 1907 and 1910, was a lock forward who played his early club rugby at threequarter. As a consequence he knew the way to the try-line and scored six tries for New Zealand in only eight matches. He later became a New Zealand provincial referee.

Thomas Gibson **PAULING**, a New Zealand rep in 1896 and 1897, retired as a senior sergeant in the Sydney CIB. He had also been a prominent referee in Australia, controlling three games played by the 1903 All Blacks, Australia v. Great Britain (1904), New South Wales v. Anglo Welsh (1908) and the first test between New Zealand and Australia in 1914.

Arran Rewi Brett **PENE**, an All Black in 1992, 1993 and 1994, took up a contract to play in Japan in 1995.

Cyril Stennart **PEPPER**, an All Black in 1935 and 1936, won the Military Cross at Sidi Rezegh in the Second World War. He died of his war wounds at the age of 31.

Arnold **PERRY**, a 1923 All Black, was a doctor. He was regarded as a likely captain of the 1924–1925 Invincibles before indifferent trial form ruined his chances.

Richard 'Grant' **PERRY**, a Mid-Canterbury All Black in 1980, was summoned as a replacement on the New Zealand tour to Australia and Fiji, when Hika Reid, the Bay of Plenty hooker, was injured. Perry himself was injured in his first game.

Louis Charles **PETERSEN**, a 1921 to 1923 All Black, was born in Akaroa. He switched to league and represented New Zealand at the new code from 1925 to 1927. On the 1926–1927 league tour of England, a player revolt erupted and Petersen was one of seven players banned from league for life as a result.

William John 'Bill' **PHILLIPS**, an All Black in 1937 and 1938, was one of only two backs to represent the All Blacks while playing for the King Country union. The other was another wing, Jack McLean. Phillips is well remembered for his feat of running down the South African speedster Dai Williams in the second test of 1937. He was immediately dropped for his troubles.

Shayne **PHILPOTT**, an All Black in 1988, 1990 and 1991, played in two test matches — against Italy and Scotland — as a replacement on both occasions. He was nicknamed 'Rita'.

Ernest Arthur 'Rex' **PICKERING**, an All Black from 1957 to 1960, was born in Te Kuiti and educated at Otorohanga Primary School and Nelson College.

Murray James **PIERCE**, an All Black from 1984 to 1990, played first-class rugby for Combined Services before making the Wellington side.

Steven Tahurata **POKERE**, an All Black from 1981 to 1985, played soccer at secondary school and was good enough to gain selection for the South Island Under 12 and Under 14 soccer teams. In 2005 he was sentenced to a prison term for fraud.

Harold Raymond 'Bunk' **POLLOCK**, an All Black in 1932 and 1936, was one of the skinniest All Blacks at 1.78 m tall but weighing less than 60 kg. He became the driver for Caltex 'boss' Jack Sullivan.

Harry Graeme **PORTEOUS**, a 1903 All Black, was born at Blueskin Bay. He played for the combined Otago-Southland team that drew with the 1905 Originals before they set sail on their tour.

Clifford Glen **PORTER**, an All Black from 1923 to 1930, was born in Edinburgh, Scotland. He became a partner in a paper bag factory in the Hutt Valley. His final first-class game was as captain of his own XV against Marlborough in 1933.

Waate Pene 'Pat' **POTAKA**, a 1923 All Black, played first-class rugby in every backline position.

Jon Paul **PRESTON**, an All Black from 1991 to 1997, was also a talented cricketer who represented Canterbury at age grades through to the second XI. He is prominent on Sky TV these days as a sideline comments person.

Alexander 'Nugget' **PRINGLE**, an All Black in 1923, was almost 2 metres tall. He was one of the few fortunate Wellington team members who missed out on playing in Wellington's 58-8 thrashing at the hands of Hawke's Bay in 1926.

Walter Peter **PRINGLE**, a New Zealand representative in 1893, was a forward who weighed only 12 stone 2 lb (77.2 kg). He played in the days when the Petone club was bolstered by its amalgamation with the Epuni club — in 1891.

Albert Charles 'Joe' **PROCTER**, a 1932 All Black, scored four tries against Newcastle during the All Blacks' 1932 Australia tour. The number four agreed with him, for he had earlier scored four tries for Otago against North Otago. In his final match for Otago, the southern side uplifted the Ranfurly Shield from Canterbury.

Charles Alfred **PURDUE**, a New Zealand rep in 1901 and 1905, played club rugby in Sydney for Marrickville, prior to playing for New Zealand.

Edward 'Pat' **PURDUE**, a New Zealand rep in 1905, played his one game for New Zealand alongside his brother Charles, against Australia in 1905.

George Bamberry **PURDUE**, an All Black in 1931 and 1932, was the son of Edward Purdue and the nephew of Charles Purdue. All three Purdues played for Southland.

Graham Herbert **PURVIS**, an All Black from 1989 to 1993, retired in 1993 but returned to the Waikato fold in 1997 at the age of 36 to play in all of Waikato's games that season.

Neil Alexander **PURVIS**, a 1976 Otago All Black wing threequarter, first played provincial rugby for Wairarapa-Bush as an 18-year-old five-eighth. He also played Brabin Cup cricket for Otago in 1973. He was an owner of the 2004 Wellington Cup winner, Cluden Creek.

Charles Edward **QUAID**, an All Black in 1938, is the only player with a surname starting with Q to have represented New Zealand.

Caleb Stanley **RALPH**, an All Black from 1998 to 2003, scored New Zealand's 100th World Cup try when he touched down against Canada in 2003. He was romantically linked at one stage to Zara Phillips, daughter of Princess Anne and Captain Mark Phillips.

Richard 'Mark' **RANBY**, a 2001

All Black, has a BA degree and is a talented musician.

Taine Cheyenne **RANDELL**, an All Black from 1995 to 2002, first played for Otago at 17 and New Zealand at 20, becoming, at 21 years and 275 days — during the 1996 tour of South Africa — one of the youngest players to captain the All Blacks. A product of Lindisfarne College, Hastings, he achieved degrees in law and commerce at Otago University.

Roger Quentin **RANDLE**, a 2001 All Black, has scored five tries in a first-class match twice and four tries twice.

Ronald Edward **RANGI**, an All Black from 1964 to 1966, was placed under suspension by the NZRFU for misbehaviour. He was later reinstated. At one stage he served in the RNZAF.

John George **RANKIN**, an All Black flanker in 1936 and 1937, had a son, Alistair, who played for the Australian state of Victoria against the 1971 Springboks.

William Joseph **REEDY**, a 1908 All Black, was a blacksmith who worked at the Petone railway workshops.

Alan Robin 'Ponty' **REID**, an All Black from 1951 to 1957, played club rugby in the Waikato for Raglan, Frankton and Kereone. He was perhaps the smallest man to play for the All Blacks.

Hikatarewa Rockcliffe 'Hika' **REID**, an All Black from 1980 to 1986, slept in his All Black jersey prior to his debut at Adelaide in 1980.

Keith Howard **REID**, a 1929 All Black, played for Wairarapa for 14 seasons and was the sole Wairarapa selector for 12 seasons.

Sana Torium 'Tori' **REID** was an All Black lock and flanker in 1935, 1936 and 1937. In his final season of rep rugby he toured Australia with New Zealand Maori at the age of 37.

Bruce Trevor **REIHANA**, a 2000 All Black, was called into the 1999 New Zealand World Cup squad when Carlos Spencer was injured, but he neither played nor was a reserve.

Walter Brown **RESIDE**, a 1929 All Black, played for Wairarapa for nine seasons. He also represented New Zealand Maori.

Patrick Keith **RHIND**, a 1946 All Black, played in the first post-war test series against Australia. He later became managing director of Rhind's Transport.

Johnstone 'Jock' **RICHARDSON**, an All Black from 1921 to 1925, was educated at Normal School, Dunedin and later became an Otago shot put champion. He lived to 95 and was the last survivor of the Invincibles tour.

Haydn 'Hud' **RICKIT**, a 1981 All Black, played for Queensland against the 1974 All Blacks.

Matthew John **RIDGE**, a 1989 All Black, later became a league star and a television personality. According to some reports, he still suffers from 'foot in mouth' disease.

Alexander James 'Jimmy' **RIDLAND**, an All Black in 1910, died from his wounds during the last week of the First World War.

Charles Calvin **RIECHELMANN** chalked up six test appearances in 1997 without once being in the starting line-up. The players he replaced to earn those caps were Michael and Ian Jones, Zinzan Brooke (twice), Robin Brooke and Josh Kronfeld. In the 1996 Super 12 final against the Bulls, Riechelmann, playing for the Blues, scored a try with an extravagant dive that caused an injury.

Leonard Stephen **RIGHTON**, an All Black in 1923 and 1925, was a clerk with Auckland Tramways. He also served as secretary of the Ponsonby club for many years.

Edward James 'Teddy' **ROBERTS**, an All Black from 1913 to 1921, was an accurate short-range goal kicker who kicked 35 conversions for New Zealand, but no penalty goals. His father Henry ('Harry') was a tourist in the first New Zealand touring team in 1884.

Frederick **ROBERTS**, an All Black from 1905 to 1910, was the only halfback selected for the 1905–1906 Originals to Britain. He played in 29 of the 32 matches in Britain. Suffering from tonsillitis, he remained behind when the All Blacks' boat sailed for home from San Francisco. Along with Duncan McGregor and Tom Cross, Roberts was the first player to turn out for both the North and South Islands.

Henry 'Harry' **ROBERTS**, who represented New Zealand in 1884, scored New Zealand's first ever try — against a Wellington XV. He was also the first New Zealand rep to have a son play for his country — Teddy Roberts, who played for the 1913 All Blacks. Harry Roberts was a pastor in the Pentecostal Church.

Richard William 'Dick' **ROBERTS**, an All Black in 1913 and 1914, made his debut against Australia in a game that was played in four 20-minute quarters instead of two halves, because of the heavy conditions. He was also a prominent racehorse owner.

William 'Cocky' **ROBERTS**, a

New Zealand rep in 1896 and 1897, was suspended for two years by the NZRFU for alleged misbehaviour.

Bruce John **ROBERTSON**, an All Black centre from 1972 to 1980, scored 33 tries and two dropped goals for New Zealand. While participating in the TV series *Superstars* in 1979, he clocked 11.1 seconds in the 100 metres race.

Duncan John **ROBERTSON**, an All Black from 1974 to 1977, scored a remarkable solo try in his first test against Australia in 1974, on a very wet field. His other test match try was scored on an even wetter field — Eden Park — in 1975 against Scotland.

George Scott **ROBERTSON**, a New Zealand rep in 1884, was described as 'a first-rate dribbler and unsurpassed at long chucking'. He played for the English club Blackheath in 1878–1879 and in 1907 was the founder and first coach of the Harihari rugby club on the West Coast.

Scott Maurice **ROBERTSON**, an All Black from 1998 to 2002, was nicknamed 'Razor'. He was related by marriage to Greg Davis, the Australian rugby captain of the 1960s and 1970s.

Alan Charles Compton **ROBIL-LIARD**, an All Black from 1924 to 1928, broke a bone in his foot playing for the 1924–1925 All Blacks against Somerset. He was a jeweller.

Bryce Graeme **ROBINS**, a 1985 All Black from Taranaki, also represented his province at league. His son, also named Bryce, has played rugby for Taranaki.

Alastair Garth **ROBINSON**, a 1983 All Black lock with ginger hair, got his chance when the three All Black test locks of 1983 were unavailable for the end-of-season tour of England and Scotland.

Charles Edward 'Eddie' **ROBINSON**, an All Black flanker in 1951 and 1952, spent the best part of a test match against Australia deputising for an injured winger. In this impromptu position he scored one try and set up another, but was never chosen for the All Blacks again. He had earlier been a provincial rower for Southland.

Keith John **ROBINSON**, an All Black in 2002 and 2004, once played in a Thames Valley primary school rep side that was captained by Australian hooker Jeremy Paul. He is a big pig-hunting fan.

John Topi 'Toby' **ROBINSON**, a 1928 All Black, had a brother, Tom, who toured Europe with the 1926–1927 New Zealand Maori team. They both played out of the Te Kotahitanga club in Banks Peninsula.

Mark Darren 'Sharkey' **ROBINSON**, a 1997, 1998 and 2001 All Black, was the son of Lindsay Robinson, who played for Horowhenua; the grandson of Ray Robinson, who played for Horowhenua; and the great-grandson of R.L. Robinson, who played for Horowhenua.

Mark Powell **ROBINSON**, an All Black centre in 2000 and 2002, was the second player named Mark Robinson to play for New Zealand at approximately the same time. The first was Mark Darren, the North Harbour halfback.

Josevata Taliga 'Joe' **ROKOCOKO**, an All Black in 2003, 2004 and 2005, was the first All Black to score two or more tries in four successive tests, including hat-tricks against France and Australia.

Douglas Leslie **ROLLERSON**, an All Black in 1976, 1980 and 1981, played for Middlesex in 1979. He was appointed to the position of Chief Executive of the North Harbour RFU in 1997.

Roy Alfred **ROPER**, an All Black in 1949 and 1950, scored five tries for the Fourth Division against the First Division during the Second World War. He was also Taranaki's sprint, long jump and triple jump champion.

John Charles 'Jock' **ROSS**, a 1981 All Black, was still playing for Mid-Canterbury at the age of 37. At 2.03 m, he was one of the tallest All Blacks.

Gregory David **ROWLANDS**, a 1976 All Black, was one of the first New Zealand goal-kickers to employ the 'round-the-corner' method. His father, E.H. Rowlands, played for King Country in 1945.

Harrison Cotton Banks 'Harry' **ROWLEY**, a 1949 All Black, died as a result of injuries suffered in a level crossing crash at the age of 32. He played provincial rugby for Bush, Wanganui, Thames Valley and North Auckland.

Eric James **RUSH**, an All Black wing from 1992 to 1996, began his provincial career as a flank forward and became an All Black winger and represented New Zealand at sevens from 1988 to 2004. He is a qualified lawyer.

Xavier Joseph **RUSH**, an All Black in 1998 and 2004, is the brother of the New Zealand women's rugby team's Annaleah Rush. They featured in the curtain-raiser and main fare in internationals against Australia at Eden Park in 1998.

Charles Archibald **RUSHBROOK**, a 1928 All Black, scored 17 tries from 10 appearances on the All Blacks' 1928 tour to South Africa and Australia.

Seven of the tries were scored against the Victorian state side.

Leicester Malcolm **RUTLEDGE**, an All Black from 1978 to 1980, was a shock omission from the New Zealand team that toured England and Scotland in 1979. During his school days he was considered too heavy for rugby and played league instead for the Hornby club. He was appointed assistant coach of Italy in 2002.

Edmond 'Eddie' **RYAN**, an All Black in 1910 and 1914, was one of seven brothers who played for the Petone senior club side.

James **RYAN**, an All Black in 1910 and 1914, captained the New Zealand Services side that won the King's Cup after the First World War. He also represented a Mother Country selection.

James Andrew Charles **RYAN**, a 2005 All Black, is 2.00 m tall. Although a regular Otago player, he made his provincial debut for Marlborough in 2002.

Patrick John **RYAN**, a 1976 All Black, first played provincial rugby for the Bush Union, before its amalgamation with Wairarapa. His father Bill also played for Bush.

Thomas **RYAN**, a New Zealand rep in 1884, kicked the first conversion and dropped goal for New Zealand — against a Wellington XV before the commencement of the 1884 New Zealand tour to Australia. He later studied art in Paris and one of his paintings ended up in the Auckland City collection. Ryan ran a launch service on Lake Taupo before moving to Great Barrier Island.

Bernard Sydney 'Joey' **SADLER**, an All Black in 1935 and 1936, 'possessed a very effective body wriggle'. He suffered an apparently minor knee injury in a club match in 1937, but the damaged nerve was so debilitating that he never played again. He retired at 22.

James Lionel Broome 'Jamie' **SALMON**, an All Black in 1980 and 1981, later played for England, thereby becoming the first player to be capped by both New Zealand and England. Ironically, Salmon played his first game for England in the first test of 1985 against New Zealand at Lancaster Park — in that very English city, Christchurch.

Herbert 'Paul' **SAPSFORD**, a 1976 All Black, is a dental surgeon. In London, he played for Harlequins, London New Zealand and Middlesex.

Laurence Theodore 'Larry' **SAVAGE**, a 1949 All Black, represented Canterbury, Wellington and Bush. He was a New Zealand Universities selector from 1965 to 1977.

Charles Kesteven 'Charlie' **SAXTON**, an All Black in 1938, wrote the book, *The ABC of Rugby*, published in 1960. He rose to the rank of major during the Second World War and later served on the NZRFU council, becoming president in 1974 and a life member in 1976.

Mark **SAYERS**, an All Black in 1972 and 1973, later moved to South Africa, where he played for Witwatersrand University in 1978. As an All Black tourist in 1972–1973 he was as highly regarded for his humorous outlook as he was for his mid-field play.

Kevin James **SCHULER**, an All Black from 1989 to 1995, played one of his four tests — against Australia — when Michael Jones was unavailable because the game was staged on a Sunday. Schuler was a product of Thames Valley, for whom his father Herb played in the 1950s. Kevin, in fact, is known as 'Herb'.

Nesetorio 'Jonny' **SCHUSTER**, an All Black in 1987, 1988 and 1989, was known as John. After switching to league, Schuster returned to rugby and in 1999, at the age of 35, played a few internationals for Samoa in an attempt to play World Cup rugby. However, injury prevented this.

Robert William Henry 'Bob' **SCOTT**, an All Black from 1946 to 1954, was a member of the Divisional Ammu-nition Company rugby team while serving in the Middle East during the Second World War. He played Auckland club rugby for the Motor Transport Pool team in 1942, the year they won the Gallaher Shield. He was also famous for his barefoot goal kicking displays, often landing goals from half way.

Stephen John **SCOTT**, an All Black in 1980, scored four tries in his debut match against Queensland Country, a record for an All Black halfback. He died at the age of 39.

Alistair Ian **SCOWN**, an All Black flanker in 1972 and 1973, began his rep career for Taranaki as a wing. Indeed, in 1975, after playing as a flanker for New Zealand, he returned to the wing for two games for Taranaki. He became a well-known racehorse stud breeder. He is the father of Sonia Scown, who represented New Zealand in the single sculls at the 2000 Sydney Olympics.

George **SCRIMSHAW**, a 1928 All Black, played his early club rugby for the Cust club in North Canterbury. He was a surprise selection ahead of Cliff Porter for the 1928 New Zealand tour to South Africa. He also played in Canterbury's first Ranfurly Shield win — over Manawhenua in 1927.

Gary Alan **SEEAR**, an All Black from 1976 to 1979, played most of his test rugby at No. 8, after first gaining New Zealand selection as a lock.

Charles Edward **SEELING**, an All Black from 1904 to 1908, rejoiced in two nicknames: 'Tiger' and 'Bronco'. He was described as being 'sturdily built, with grand loins, very fast, and long arms'. He turned to league and played for Wigan, where he became the licensee of the Roebuck Hotel. In 1956, not long before he planned to return to New Zealand, he died in a motor accident.

George Maurice Victor **SELLARS**, a 1913 All Black, was killed in the First World War, aged 31, while carrying a wounded comrade to safety. He played in the first official New Zealand Maori team in 1910.

Kevin **SENIO**, a 2005 All Black, is the first Bay of Plenty All Black halfback. He is married to Anna, a former Silver Fern.

Dallas James **SEYMOUR**, a 1992 All Black, was born in Tokoroa. His wife Julie was an outstanding net-baller who captained the Silver Ferns.

Graham **SHANNON**, a New Zealand rep in 1893, had two lucky breaks in making the cut. For the 1893 tour to Australia 'Mother' Elliott withdrew, and Elliott's original replacement, Charlie Caradus, suffered a late injury.

Shannon was the son of the founder of the Shannon district in Manawatu.

Mark William **SHAW**, an All Black from 1980 to 1986, first played rep rugby for Horowhenua. His nickname 'Cowboy' attested to his uncompromising approach. Before becoming an All Black he played socially for Belsize Park while touring Britain.

Jack Douglas **SHEARER**, an All Black in 1920, played senior club rugby for Poneke, mostly as a loose forward, until he was 35. A grand servant for Wellington, he appeared in 18 Ranfurly Shield matches. Like his brother Sydney, he was a plumber.

Sydney David **SHEARER**, an All Black in 1921 and 1922, made his international debut against New South Wales in Christchurch at the age of 30. He played club rugby until he was nearly 40.

Thomas Reginald **SHEEN,** an All Black in 1926 and 1928, damaged a knee cartilage against Orange Free State and gave the game away. He worked for Collins Brothers in Glasgow before becoming a director of D.W. Paterson, printing and paper merchants, in Melbourne.

Frank Nuki Ken **SHELFORD**, an All Black from 1981 to 1985, played

© DARYL CRIMP

in the Opotiki College First XV for three years, and the hockey First XI for one. He later represented Bay of Plenty at tennis.

Wayne Thomas 'Buck' **SHELFORD**, an All Black from 1985 to 1990, spent eight years in the Navy, serving on HMNZS *Otago* and visiting such exotic destinations as Darwin, Singapore, Manila, Pago Pago, San Diego and Alaska. An inspirational leader of the haka, he grew up unable to speak Maori but is now undergoing an intensive course in the Maori language.

Kurt **SHERLOCK**, a 1985 All Black second-five, transferred to rugby league a year later. As a league player he developed one or two extra strings: an ability to kick goals and an adapta-

bility that saw him play hooker for the Roosters, because of his ease of passing off either hand as a dummy half.

Stanley 'Keith' **SIDDELLS**, a 1921 All Black, was described as 'a big fellow with a high action'. He later became mayor of Pahiatua.

Harold James 'Harry' **SIMON**, an All Black halfback in 1937, worked as a sugar boiler. He and his Otago cohort at first-five, Dave Trevathan, played together in all three tests against the 1937 Springboks. Their perceived sluggishness was seen as one of the main reasons South Africa beat New Zealand and, as scapegoats, neither played for the All Blacks again.

Paul Lennard James **SIMONSSON**,

an All Black in 1987, played two matches for New Zealand and scored seven tries. After switching to league he returned to rugby and represented New South Wales in 1996 and Australia at the Fijian Sevens.

John George **SIMPSON**, an All Black in 1947, 1949 and 1950, later represented Wellington and Northern Districts at lawn bowls. He was known as the 'Iron Man' because of his renowned strength in the front row.

Victor Lenard James **SIMPSON**, a 1985 All Black, played for Gisborne Boys' High First XV for four years, and for Poverty Bay, before making his mark in Canterbury. Reports have it that when coach Alex Wyllie suggested that Simpson play on the wing, he declined. Craig Green subsequently moved to the wing and went on to enjoy a lengthy spell as an All Black.

Graham Scott **SIMS**, an All Black in 1972, is the brother-in-law of Ross Murray, the one-time New Zealand amateur golf champion. Sims was a team-mate of Andy Haden's at Wanganui Boys High.

Robert Gemmell Burnett 'Jimmy' **SINCLAIR**, a 1923 All Black, was a doctor; he died at the age of 35 after an appendix operation left him in poor health.

Sitiveni Waica **SIVIVATU**, a 2005 All Black, was the only second division NPC player to win a Super 12 contract in 2002, making the cut from the Counties-Manakau side. In 2004, while playing for Waikato, he scored five tries in a record-breaking victory over Auckland.

Jack Robert **SKEEN**, a 1952 All Black, played for New Zealand before playing in All Black trials.

Kevin Lawrence **SKINNER**, an All Black from 1949 to 1956, won the New Zealand heavyweight amateur boxing title in 1947.

George Rupuha **SKUDDER**, an All Black in 1969, 1972 and 1973, caused a sensation in 1969 by gaining All Black selection in the second test against Wales, and then caused another by scoring an early try, beating illustrious Welsh defender J.P.R. Williams in the process.

Gordon Leonard **SLATER**, a 1997 All Black, was one of two Taranaki props to rise to prominence in the 1990s, the other being Mark Allen. His brother Andy Slater was often spoken of in terms of possible All Black selection. Gordon played 174 matches for Taranaki, six fewer than his brother Andy.

Peter Henry **SLOANE**, an All Black in 1973, 1976 and 1979, was the third of three North Auckland hookers to play in only one test match, the others being Ian Irvine and Des Webb.

Alan Edward **SMITH**, an All Black in 1967, 1969 and 1970, also played cricket for Taranaki and Central Districts Colts as a pace bowler. His uncle, John Walter, played rugby for New Zealand in 1925.

Bruce Warwick **SMITH**, an All Black in 1983 and 1984, scored a try against France in 1984 after the ball had rebounded from the upright. He scored seven tries in his first five matches for Waikato and later played for Bay of Plenty.

Charles Herbert 'Herb' **SMITH**, a 1934 All Black, coached the RNZAF team at Taieri in 1940. He was captain of Otago in 1935 when that team won the Ranfurly Shield for the first time. In some publications his initials were recorded, incorrectly, as H.A.

Conrad Gerard **SMITH**, an All Black in 2004 and 2005, scored a try the first time he touched the ball in his debut test against Italy in 2004. He is a law graduate from Wellington's Victoria University. His father Trevor played for Taranaki in the 1970s.

George William **SMITH**, a New Zealand rep in 1897, 1901 and 1905, was also a jockey. Some claim he won the 1894 New Zealand Cup on Impulse, although this is disputed. The jockey

in question weighed 7 st 9 lb, while Smith the All Black weighed 11 st 9 lb.

Ian Stanley Talbot **SMITH**, an All Black from 1963 to 1966, was nicknamed 'Spooky'. He was also known as the 'Gimmerburn Ghost'.

John Burns 'J.B.' **SMITH**, an All Black in 1946, 1947 and 1949, was the first Maori player to receive the Tom French Cup (in 1949). Ineligible to tour in 1949 because of South Africa's apartheid policy, he captained the 'other' All Blacks in two tests against the Wallabies.

Peter **SMITH**, an All Black in 1947, scored four tries against Combined Northern during the All Blacks' 1947 tour of Australia. He died suddenly in his sleep at the age of 29.

Ross Mervyn **SMITH**, a 1955 All Black, was the first New Zealander to score over 100 tries in first-class games. He became a selector for both Hawke's Bay (1973–1975) and Nelson-Bays (1976).

Wayne Ross **SMITH**, an All Black from 1980 to 1985, kicked four dropped goals for New Zealand. He became an All Black coach.

William Ernest **SMITH**, a 1905 Nelson All Black, was the largest first five-eighth to play for New Zealand, at 1.88 m and 90 kg. He was taller and heavier than most forwards playing in the 1900s.

Bernard Francis **SMYTH**, a 1922 All Black, played a total of only five first-class games. He was born at a place called Boatmans, near Inangahua.

Wallace Frankham 'Frank' **SNOD-GRASS**, a Nelson All Black in 1923 and 1928, also played tennis for Nelson. After first playing for New Zealand in 1923 he had to wait another five years before regaining national colours. Even then, he was, in an unusual move, bracketed with Monty McClymont prior to an international. Minutes before kick-off he was omitted when it was decided that he would not suit the wet conditions.

Eric McDonald 'Fritz' **SNOW**, an All Black in 1928 and 1929, was one of two Nelson reps to play for the All Blacks in 1928. The other was Frank Snodgrass. When he made his All Black debut on the 1928 tour to South Africa, Snow was aged 30. Four other tourists were in their 30s — Maurice and Cyril Brownlie, Bert Grenside and Lance Johnson — at a time when such a demographic was unusual for an international team.

David **SOLOMON**, an All Black in 1935 and 1936, was born in Levuka, Fiji. His brother Frank, also an All Black, was born in Pago Pago, American Samoa.

Frank **SOLOMON**, an All Black in 1931 and 1932, was the last New Zealand rep to play in the wing forward position.

Greg Mardon **SOMERVILLE**, an All Black from 2000 to 2005, lists *Braveheart*, the Mel Gibson classic, as his favourite movie.

William Theodore Charles 'Charlie' **SONNTAG**, a 1929 All Black, gained selection for New Zealand on his 35th birthday. At the time of selection he was the oldest player to make his All Black debut. This remains the case.

Rodney **SO'OIALO**, an All Black from 2002 to 2005, was a member of the New Zealand sevens team that won the Rugby World Cup title at Mar del Plata in 2001.

Alistair John 'Ack' **SOPER**, a 1957 All Black, played for the English club side Blackheath in 1960–1961. In 1955 he captained the New Zealand Colts team that toured Australia and Ceylon (Sri Lanka), a combination that included Wilson Whineray and Colin Meads.

Robert **SOUTER**, a 1929 All Black, was born in Cambusnethan, Scotland. He was a front-rower but stood only 1.70 m tall and weighed 80 kg.

Charles Richard Barton 'Copper'

SPEIGHT, a New Zealand representative in 1893, was a forward who weighed only 78 kg. He became a member of the Hamilton Borough Council.

Michael Wayne **SPEIGHT**, a 1986 All Black, was the great-grandson of All Black Charles 'Copper' Speight.

Carlos James **SPENCER**, an All Black from 1995 to 2004, first played rep rugby for Horowhenua as a 16-year-old. As a first five-eighth he scored more than 100 first-class tries, an unusually high tally for an inside back.

George **SPENCER**, a 1907 All Black, was described as being 'slow but sound with a slashing kick'. He missed out on playing a test for the All Blacks, but in 1908, after switching to league, he toured Australia and played in one of the tests for the New Zealand league team.

John Clarence 'Jack' **SPENCER**, who played for New Zealand in 1903, 1905 and 1907, was the brother of George Spencer, a 1907 All Black. He was the first All Black replacement in a test match when he came on for Jack Colman against Australia in 1907.

John Edmunde **SPIERS**, an All Black from 1976 to 1981, was regarded as one of the best maulers in New Zealand rugby. He played 27 games for New Zealand during the course of five tours, but never played for the All Blacks in New Zealand.

Augustine Patrick 'Gus' **SPILLANE**, a 1913 South Canterbury All Black, had three brothers who also played for South Canterbury. One of them, Charles Spillane, donated the Spillane Cup for competition among North Island Marist clubs.

John **STALKER**, a 1903 All Black, was described as 'a nuggetty stamp of a player'. At the time of his death he was the manager of Barraud and Abraham's store in Feilding.

Jeremy Crispian **STANLEY**, a 1997 All Black, is a qualified doctor. When he and his All Black father Joe played in John Kirwan's testimonial match in 1994, it was the first time a father and son combination had played first-class rugby since the Nepias in 1950.

Joseph Tito **STANLEY**, an All Black from 1986 to 1991, played in 27 consecutive tests. Three other All Blacks — Ian Jones, Olo Brown and Walter Little — share the distinction of playing in New Zealand teams with both Stanleys, Joe and Jeremy.

Edgar Thomas 'Eddie' **STAPLETON** was an Australian international who was invited to play for the All Blacks during the Australian segment of their 1960 tour, when All Blacks Denis

Cameron and Steve Nesbit were injured. Stapleton was a cousin of 'Wild Bill' Cerutti.

John William 'Billy' **STEAD**, an All Black from 1903 to 1908, played in 42 All Black games and was never in the losing side. In 1905 he missed the Welsh international for reasons reported as anything from dysentery to a willingness to see the disappointed 'Simon' Mynott play. He was a rugby columnist for *New Zealand Truth* for several years.

Anthony Gordon 'Tony' **STEEL**, an All Black from 1966 to 1968, was elected a Member of Parliament in 1990 and 1996. A notable sprinter, he recorded a best time of 9.6 seconds for the 100 yards. He became headmaster of Hamilton Boys' High School.

John 'Jack' **STEEL**, an All Black from 1920 and 1925, later became the publican at the Governors Bay (Christchurch) and Golden Eagle (Greymouth) hotels. He was also a professional sprinter and a leading standardbred owner who had the top stake-earner of 1940–1941, Zincoli.

Leo Brian **STEELE**, a 1951 All Black, made the All Blacks while playing for Wellington, but ended his provincial rugby days playing for Horowhenua. In later times, Steele gained a media profile by becoming involved in fundraising events for telethons. He

lived in a hut at the top of a pole in 1978; in 1990 he lived in a caravan on scaffolding in a shopping centre car park. As recently as 2005 he walked 76 laps (on his 76th birthday) of Nelson Park, Hastings, to help raise money for victims of the Indian Ocean tsunami.

Edward Richard George 'Dick' **STEERE**, an All Black from 1928 to 1931, played as a lock in New Zealand's last 2-3-2 scrum and in their first 3-4-1 configuration. During a trial match to help select the 1929 All Blacks, Steere heeded the advice of his provincial coach and played in his own socks, white headgear and ran like hell when his team got the kick-off. Securing a lucky bounce, he dashed over for a try in the first few seconds of the trial — and made the team.

Paul Christopher **STEINMETZ**, a 2002 All Black, only just made the grade, coming on as a replacement against Wales, after having been whistled up as a reinforcement when Carlos Spencer and Keith Lowen were injured. And then he was an All Black for only three minutes, having been summoned in the 77th minute against Wales.

Lee **STENSNESS**, an All Black in 1993 and 1997, represented King Country Secondary Schools in earlier years. He later gained selection for New Zealand Universities and travelled to the World Student Games. He was nicknamed 'Stainless'.

Owen George **STEPHENS**, a 1968 All Black, was the third All Black, after Evan Jessep and Des Connor, to play test rugby both for and against New Zealand. He achieved this feat in 1974 when playing for Australia against New Zealand.

Ian Neal **STEVENS**, an All Black from 1972 to 1976, later played for the Diggers club in South Africa. While at Palmerston North Boys High he had played in combination with fellow All Black Bob Burgess. He teamed up with Mark Sayers on the 1972–1973 tour to Britain to become the team's comedians.

Donald Robert Louis **STEVEN-SON**, a 1926 All Black, became an obstetrician and gynaecologist. His second and third Christian names were in honour of the Scottish author Robert Louis Stevenson. As a moderate line-kicker when stationed at fullback, he often ran up the touchline to gain ground before being pushed out, rather than chance his boot. Under the rules of the day, his team were entitled to throw in to the line-out.

Allan James **STEWART**, an All Black in 1963 and 1964, locked the New Zealand test scrum with both Meads brothers. He was nicknamed 'Malthoid' and dropped out of the game at 23, an unusually young age for a tight forward to hang up his boots.

David **STEWART**, an 1894 New Zealand rep, was nicknamed 'Dick'. He played at a time when the South Canterbury union's rep programme amounted to one match per season.

Edward Barrie **STEWART**, a 1923 All Black, scored two tries in his only All Black outing — against New South Wales. In 1921 he had the distinction of playing against the Springboks for Otago while still a pupil at John McGlashan College.

James Douglas **STEWART**, a 1913 All Black, once scored four tries for Auckland against Southland. He was deemed to be one of the lucky All Blacks who, but for the fact that the leading players were out of the country on tour in North America, probably would not have gained national honours.

Kenneth William **STEWART**, an All Black from 1972 to 1979, made his All Black debut at the age of 19 against New York.

Ronald Terowie 'Ron' **STEWART**, an All Black from 1923 to 1930, also made his debut at the age of 19 — against New South Wales. While playing as a wing forward in the second test in South Africa in 1928, he packed down in the front row of the 2-3-2 scrum on the side from which the ball was being fed. As a result the term 'loosehead' evolved.

Vance Edmond **STEWART**, an All Black in 1976 and 1979, was selected for the 1977 All Black tour to France but had to withdraw after he injured his thumb. He won the Ranfurly Shield as coach of Canterbury in 1994 and was the inaugural Crusaders coach in 1996.

Leonard 'Jack' **STOHR**, an All Black in 1910 and 1913, was the first New Zealander to kick three penalty goals in a first-class match in New Zealand. He achieved this feat for Taranaki against Wanganui in 1909. It is also claimed that he once kicked a goal from a spot midway between halfway and his own 22 against Transvaal. He moved to South Africa in 1920 and became a chemist at Springs.

Edward James Taite 'Eddie' **STOKES**, a 1976 All Black centre three-quarter, weighed in at 92 kg. He was a member of the outstanding Bay of Plenty backline of the 1970s that included fellow All Blacks John Brake, Mark Taylor and Greg Rowlands.

Arthur Massey **STONE**, an All Black from 1981 to 1986, played provincial rugby for Waikato, Bay of Plenty and

Otago. He is sometimes referred to, light-heartedly, as 'Arfa Stone — the lightest All Black ever'. He scored a famous intercept try to win the Ranfurly Shield for Waikato against Auckland in 1980.

Percival Wright 'Percy' **STOREY**, an All Black in 1920 and 1921, played 12 games for New Zealand and scored 16 tries. During the First World War he was wounded at Passchendaele but recovered to play for the United Kingdom XV. He was a New Zealand selector in 1944.

Anthony Duncan 'Ant' **STRACHAN**, an All Black in 1992, 1993 and 1995, was a temporary replacement for Graeme Bachop in the 1995 World Cup final against South Africa. When summoned as a surprise choice for the 1992 All Blacks, he had been in the odd position of having played six rep seasons without being a first choice provincial player.

Samuel Cunningham 'Sam' **STRAHAN**, an All Black from 1967 to 1973, was not available for the 1971 series against the British Isles or the 1972–1973 British tour owing to farming commitments. He was educated at Huntley Preparatory School, Marton, and Wanganui Collegiate.

William Archibald 'Archie' **STRANG**, an All Black in 1928, 1930 and 1931, kicked the famous dropped goal that enabled New Zealand to beat South Africa 7-6 in the second test of the 1928 series. He had earlier had the unusual experience of captaining South Canterbury during a brief tour to the West Coast in his first year out of school.

John 'Clinton' **STRINGFELLOW**, a 1929 All Black, scored a dramatic intercept try in the third test against Australia in 1929. He played 107 games for Wairarapa, an outstanding achievement in provincial rugby in the 1920s and 1930s. He was strongly built (1.78 m and 79 kg), and was anything but a 'stringy fellow'.

Angus John **STUART**, a New Zealand representative in 1893, toured New Zealand with the 1888 British team and decided to stay. He was a Wellington railway porter in later life.

Kevin Charles **STUART**, a 1955 All Black, was the brother of All Black captain Bob Stuart. Despite a dislocated shoulder, Kevin stayed on the field in the Canterbury-South Africa match of 1956, and effected a try-saving tackle with his 'bad' shoulder that enabled Canterbury to win 9-6.

Robert Charles 'Bob' **STUART**, an All Black loose forward in 1949, 1953 and 1954, played once as a prop for New Zealand. He was a surprise choice as captain of the 1953–1954

All Blacks to Britain, rose to the position of New Zealand rep on the IRB, became an agricultural econ- omist and director of the Vocational Training Council, and was awarded the OBE in 1974 for services to agriculture and rugby.

Robert Locksdale 'Robbie' **STUART**, a 1977 All Black, was one of two Rob- ert Stuarts to play for New Zealand. He is one of the few lock forwards to replace a prop in a test match (Gary Knight against France), whereupon his recorded status changed to 'lock and front-row forward'.

John Lorraine 'Jack' **SULLIVAN**, an All Black from 1936 to 1938, once represented the Whangamomona sub- union. He also scored two fine tries for New Zealand against South Africa in the 1937 series and became chairman of the NZRFU. In the latter position his comment of 'no comment' almost defined a generation in terms of media-rugby union relationships.

Frank **SURMAN**, a New Zealand rep in 1896, was forced to leave the field during his only game for New Zealand against Queensland, after tripping over the wire designed to keep the crowd off the playing surface.

Stephen Dennis **SURRIDGE**, an All Black in 1997, played rugby for Cambridge University, was a national judo champion and is also an artist.

Alan Richard **SUTHERLAND**, an All Black from 1968 to 1976, did not play rugby at school. In 64 matches for New Zealand he scored 32 tries and kicked 17 conversions and three penalty goals. He later represented Rhodesia, married a Miss South Africa and set up a thoroughbred breeding establishment in South Africa, where he still lives.

Kenneth Sydney 'Snowy' **SVEN-SON**, an All Black from 1922 to 1926, scored a try in each of the four tests played by the Invincibles on their tour to Britain, France and Canada. He represented Wanganui, Buller, Wellington and Marlborough.

John Patterson **SWAIN**, a 1928 All Black, also played water polo for Wellington. Hence, perhaps, his nickname, 'Tuna'.

John Tita 'James' **SWINDLEY** was an 1894 New Zealand rep, and although it is not known where he was born, he is known to have died in Sumatra in 1918 as a result of a mining accident. He was the son of Major Frederick Swindley, who served with the Armed Constabulary in the Urewera invasion in 1869.

John Grey **TAIAROA** was an 1884 New Zealand rep, who drowned in a boating accident on Otago Harbour. Before his death he had been a Hawke's

Bay cricket rep and held the New Zealand record for the long jump.

Peina **TAITUHA**, a 1923 All Black, was also known as Taituha Peina and Taituha Peina Kingi. He was one of 37 players called upon by the New Zealand selectors for the 3-match series against New South Wales in 1923, enough for two and a half teams.

John Maurice **TANNER**, an All Black from 1950 to 1954, was first called into the All Blacks as a replacement for Ron Elvidge in the fourth test against the 1950 British Lions. It was a surprise selection, given that Tanner had not played for his province, Auckland, during the 1950 season.

Kerry John **TANNER**, an All Black from 1974 to 1976, suffered a debilitating blood disorder during the 1976 All Black tour to South Africa. Earlier his form took a turn for the better following a comment made by a maternity nurse when Tanner was assisting with settling his wife down to the business of giving birth. 'Which one of you is having the baby?' the nurse jibed, and Tanner's thoughts turned to losing weight and improving his fitness.

Saimone **TAUMOEPEAU**, a 2004–2005 All Black prop, scored a try in his first test against Italy. He was the only member of the 2004 All Blacks not to have played Super 12 rugby.

Glenn Lyndon **TAYLOR**, a Northland All Black in 1992 and 1996, appeared in 63 Super 12 matches for three different teams — the Chiefs, the Hurricanes and the Blues. He captained New Zealand A to Wales, France and Romania.

Henry Morgan **TAYLOR**, an All Black in 1913 and 1914, was selected as a halfback for the 1914 New Zealand tour to Australia. Following injuries he was converted into a wing threequarter and scored three tries in this position in the second test of the series. He also represented Canterbury at cricket.

John McLeod 'Jack' **TAYLOR**, an All Black in 1937 and 1938, played fullback in all three tests against the 1937 Springboks. Taylor was later elected a life member of the Wellington RFU.

Kenneth John **TAYLOR**, a 1980 All Black, played his only game for New Zealand against Fiji. Unusually, he also played soccer for his school's First XI.

Murray Barton **TAYLOR**, an All Black in 1976, 1979 and 1980, scored four tries and kicked four dropped goals for New Zealand. He was the first player from Hamilton's Fraser Tech club to become an All Black, and the first Waikato five-eighth to play test rugby.

Norman 'Mark' **TAYLOR**, an All Black from 1976 to 1978, played test rugby at second five-eighth and wing threequarter. He remained in Britain following the 1978 Grand Slam tour and played for the Wasps club and Middlesex while managing a cleaning company in London.

Reginald **TAYLOR**, a 1913 All Black, was killed in action in Belgium during the First World War at the age of 28. Before that he had been a vital member of the 1913 Taranaki team that claimed the Ranfurly Shield from Auckland.

Warwick Thomas **TAYLOR**, an All Black from 1983 to 1988, was the brother of Murray Taylor. Both were five-eighths. Warwick was regarded as a 'tradesman-like footballer', although it was his brother Murray, a plumber, who was the real-life tradesman.

Percy Laurence **TETZLAFF**, a 1947 All Black, has one of the more distinctive All Black names — and builds. Despite his short stature he had the torso and power of a six-footer.

Neil William **THIMBLEBY**, a 1970 All Black, has one of the more unique All Black surnames. He was a watersider.

Barry Trevor **THOMAS**, an All Black in 1962 and 1964 whose nickname was 'Bear', played provincial rugby for both Auckland and Wellington. His father-in-law, Sam Cameron, played for Taranaki and Wanganui.

Leslie 'Arthur' **THOMAS**, a 1925 All Black, became a Poverty Bay selector. He played for New Zealand in three matches on the 1925 tour of Australia and had the distinction of playing against the obscure E.J. 'Ted' Thorn's XV.

Barry Alan **THOMPSON**, a 1979 All Black, was educated at Oxford — Oxford Primary School, Canterbury, New Zealand, that is.

Hector Douglas 'Mona' **THOMSON**, an All Black in 1905, 1906 and 1908, scored six tries against British Columbia during the tour of the 1905–1906 Originals. He played provincial rugby for Wellington,

Auckland, Canterbury and Wanganui and later retired from his position as an under-secretary in the Immigration Department.

Brad Carnegie **THORN**, an All Black in 2003, was formerly an outstanding member of the Brisbane Broncos rugby league team in the Australian NRL. He caused a sensation in 2001, when, after gaining All Black selection, he declined the offer on the grounds that he was uncertain of his future in union and that he felt he had not yet justified his sudden elevation.

Grahame Stuart **THORNE**, an All Black from 1967 to 1970, played for New Zealand before representing his province, Auckland. A law student who became a bottlestore owner in South Africa and a TV sports commentator in New Zealand, Thorne

OH MY GOODNESS, A SHOCKING MOVE... HE SHOULD BE SENT OFF FOR THAT - THORNE HAS HAD HIS HAIR PERMED!

went on to grow grapes and olives in Blenheim. He is remembered for his unconventional, if temporary, permed hair.

Reuben David **THORNE**, an All Black from 1999 to 2004, was a member of the New Plymouth Boys High First XV that won the initial World First XVs tournament in 1992. He became an All Black captain despite missing out on any national age group sides. He is married to Andrew Mehrtens' sister Kate.

Neville Henry **THORNTON**, an All Black in 1947 and 1949, was a No. 8 forward who played in only the first test of the 1949 series in South Africa. In each of the other three tests a different player was used at the back of the scrum. He retired as principal of Papakura High School in 1977.

Neemia Stanley **TIALATA**, an All Black on the 2005 Grand Slam tour, attended the same college, Parkway, as Tana Umaga. They are the school's only All Blacks. His nickname is 'Nezza'.

Filogia Ian 'Filo' **TIATIA**, a 2000 All Black, played in two test matches and scored two tries. His brother Ace played for Samoa.

Frederick Joseph **TILYARD**, a 1923 All Black, scored a try in his only outing for New Zealand — against New South Wales. A stalwart of the Poneke club in Wellington, he served 28 years on the club's committee.

James Thomas 'Jimmy' **TILYARD**, an All Black in 1913 and 1920, was a brother of Frederick. Born in Tasmania, he represented Wellington at cricket in 1907–1908 as a teenager.

John Kahukura Raymond **TIMU**, an All Black from 1989 to 1994, switched to league and played for the Canterbury Bulldogs and London Broncos. A great surfing enthusiast, he now works as a builder in Wanaka.

Eric William Thomas **TINDILL**, an All Black in 1935, 1936 and 1938, also played cricket for New Zealand. Later he became an international rugby referee and an international cricket umpire. He is still in good health at the age of 95.

Hoeroa **TIOPIRA**, an 1893 All Black, represented Hawke's Bay from Te Aute College. He died in Taihape in 1930.

Isaiah **TOEAVA** was selected for the 2005 All Black tour of the UK on the strength of one NPC performance for Auckland. Born in Moto'otua and nicknamed 'Ice', his performances at the Under 19 World Cup tournament were monitored closely by the New Zealand selectors.

Ofisa Francis Junior **TONU'U**, an All Black in 1996, 1997 and 1998, is known as both Junior and Ofisa. He has recently featured as a TV comments man.

Lindsay James **TOWNSEND**, a 1955 All Black, played provincial rugby for Otago and North Auckland. In the mid-1950s Townsend was viewed as New Zealand's great halfback hope, but following a poor performance in the third test against the 1955 Australians, he never played for the All Blacks again. He later became a successful North Auckland selector-coach and during his tenure North Auckland won the Ranfurly Shield from Manawatu in 1978.

Christopher David **TREGASKIS**, an All Black in 1991, was 2.04 m tall and 118 kg — one of New Zealand's largest ever players. Despite his size he was unable to thrive and ended his first-class career playing for Marlborough, which was at that stage (1996) in the third division of the NPC.

Kelvin Robin **TREMAIN**, an All Black from 1959 to 1968 whose nick-name was 'Bunny', played provincial rugby for five provinces — Southland, Manawatu, Canterbury, Auckland and Hawke's Bay. He was regarded as one of the leading lights of the mighty 1960s All Blacks. His tragic passing at the age of 54 caused considerable national mourning. His

son Simon, also an accomplished flanker, became a National member of Parliament in the 2005 elections.

David **TREVATHAN**, a 1937 All Black, had a brother, Tommy Trevathan, who played rugby league for New Zealand. At one stage David was an employee of the Taieri and Peninsula milk factory.

Jack Manson **TUCK**, a 1929 All Black, died on board a launch off Whangaroa at the age of 60. He was a foundation member of the Harlequins Club.

Mose **TUIALI'I**, a 2004–2005 All Black No. 8, is 1.95 m tall. He scored a try with his first touch of the ball against Argentina in Hamilton in 2004.

Va'aiga Lealuga 'Inga' **TUIGA-MALA**, an All Black from 1989 to 1993, was known as 'Inga the winger'. He was also known as 'Mr Beep' after New Zealand coach Laurie Mains introduced the dreaded beep test in 1992, as a fitness recorder. Tuigamala was legendary as a player who enjoyed avoiding the 'hard yards' in training.

Sam **TUITUPOU**, a 2004 All Black second five-eighth, is 1.76 m tall. He once had a trial for the Canberra Raiders rugby league team in a pre-season game against the New Zealand

Warriors and although he was offered a contract, decided to stick with rugby union.

Robert Graham 'Bob' **TUNNI-CLIFF**, a 1923 All Black, played one game for New Zealand and scored one try. At 1.75 m and 75 kg, he was a small hooker who played all his provincial rugby for two small unions, Nelson and Buller.

John Steele 'Jock' **TURNBULL** went almost 50 years unrecognised as an All Black. However, good investigative work by *Men in Black* co-author Rod Chester revealed that Turnbull had appeared as a second-half replacement for Phillippe Cabot against New South Wales at Dunedin in 1921, a match the All Blacks lost 17-nil.

Richard Steven **TURNER**, a 1992 All Black, captained the Waikato Chiefs in the inaugural year of the Super 12 competition. His two All Black appearances were against a World XV in 1992, when the NZRFU controversially awarded full caps. Even though he never played against another country, Turner ranks among the official New Zealand internationals. Nicknamed 'Pod' because of his whale-like bulk, Turner is now a TV comments man.

Hubert Sydney 'Jum' **TURTILL**, a 1905 All Black, got his nickname while travelling as a chubby boy with his family from England. 'Jumbo' was abbreviated to 'Jum' in later years. He was killed by a shell explosion in France during the First World War, aged 38.

Timothy Moore **TWIGDEN**, an All Black in 1979 and 1980, won beach sprints in national surf life saving championships in 1973 and 1974. He was born in Taumarunui.

George Alfred **TYLER**, an All Black from 1903 to 1906, won several Auckland swimming titles and is reputed to have set an unofficial New Zealand and world record for the 100 yards straight swim. While touring with the 1905–1906 All Blacks, Tyler met and shook hands with King Edward VII and is said to have made the remark that he would never wash that hand again. Cartoonists picked up on the remark and when the team returned to New Zealand, Tyler was asked to display the famous hand that the King had shaken. He later turned to sports journalism with the *New Zealand Herald* and declared the departing 1924–1925 Invincibles to be the 'weakest team New Zealand has ever had'.

Daniel Knight **UDY**, an All Black in 1901 and 1903, played in the first official test match for New Zealand against Australia in 1903. His cousin, Hart Udy, toured Australia with the first New Zealand touring side in 1884.

Hart **UDY**, a New Zealand rep in 1884, was a blacksmith and wheelwright.

Jonathan Falefasa 'Tana' **UMAGA**, an All Black from 1997 to 2005, was born in Lower Hutt and could have played for Western Samoa. However, his rapid elevation to All Black status put paid to that, although his brother Mike played for Samoa. They opposed each other in a 1999 test.

Roger James **URBAHN**, an All Black in 1959 and 1960, was nicknamed 'Spider'. A journalist with the Taranaki *Daily News*, he co-wrote *The Fourth Springbok Tour of New Zealand* with Don Clarke.

Ronald Anthony **URLICH**, an All Black hooker in 1970, 1972 and 1973, was a surprise selection for the 1970 All Blacks, being unable to hold down a regular spot in the Auckland rep team. He eventually played 35 games for New Zealand.

Ian Neill **UTTLEY**, a 1963 All Black, played provincial rugby for Wellington, Auckland and Bay of Plenty. His father Ken played cricket for Otago, Auckland and South Island, and rugby for New Zealand Universities.

Geoffrey Thomas **VALLI**, a 1980 All Black, was born in Nightcaps.

Osaiasi 'Kupu' **VANISI**, a 1999 All Black, was the son of Vainikolo Vanisi, a wing who toured New Zealand with the 1969 Tongan national team — the first Tongan team to tour New Zealand.

Joeli **VIDIRI**, a 1998 All Black, suffered a serious kidney disease that ended his career in 2001. He scored 10 tries in each of the first three seasons of Super 12.

Patrick Bernard 'Pat' **VINCENT**, a 1956 All Black, later moved to the USA and eventually became governor of the USA Rugby Football Union. He had been a dancehall singer and recording artist who used to perform at the Riviera Cabaret in Christchurch in the 1950s, when he was captain of the Canterbury rugby team. He died suddenly at the age of 57 en route from Pittsburgh to San Francisco.

Ivan Matthew Henry **VODANO-VICH**, an All Black prop in 1955, scored a try in his first test — against Australia. He became a life member of the NZRFU and ran a menswear store in Wellington with fellow All Black Tom Morrison.

Frederick Henry 'Did' **VORRATH**, an All Black in 1935 and 1936, was made a life member of the Union club in Dunedin.

William Joseph 'Billy' **WALLACE**,

an All Black from 1903 to 1908, was the first New Zealander to score 500 first-class points. In 1908, he set up his own iron foundry.

Dion Allan George **WALLER**, a 2001 All Black, represented King Country, Wellington, Manawatu and the ill-fated hybrid team Central Vikings.

Patrick Timothy **WALSH**, an All Black from 1955 to 1964, played test rugby at fullback, wing threequarter, centre and second five-eighth, making his debut aged 19.

John **WALTER**, a 1925 All Black, was the youngest member of the 1925 New Zealand touring team to Australia, at 20, and became the top try-scorer amongst the forwards, with four. He was the uncle of 1967–1970 All Black Alan Smith.

Joseph Astbury 'Joe' **WARBRICK**, a New Zealand rep in 1884, was killed by an eruption from the Waimangu geyser. He had played for Auckland at the age of 15 and was the chief organiser/selector/captain of the 1888 New Zealand Native team.

Edward Percival 'Pat' **WARD**, a 1928 All Black, weighed 98 kg although he was only 1.75 m in height. He played 10 games for New Zealand, his only points coming from one penalty goal, kicked against Border in 1928.

Francis Gerald **WARD**, a 1921 All Black, was a Palmerston North doctor.

Ronald Henry **WARD**, an All Black in 1936 and 1937, was selected as a side-row forward for the first test against the 1937 Springboks, but was obliged to play most of the game on the wing when Donald Cobden was injured. Not for the only time in All Black history was a forward shunted to the wing disadvantaged, for Ward was dropped for the second test, although common sense prevailed when he was recalled for the third.

Alfred Clarence **WATERMAN**, a 1929 North Auckland All Black, played club rugby for six North Auckland clubs — Ohaeawai, Kaeo, P & T, Kaitaia, Old Boys and Whangarei City. He scored four tries against Newcastle at Newcastle, Australia.

Eric Leslie **WATKINS**, a 1905 All Black, later played league and was a member of the All Golds league team that toured England in 1907–1908.

James 'Donald' **WATSON**, a New Zealand rep in 1896, was educated at Watson's Academy (Edinburgh) and played for Edinburgh Academicals before emigrating to New Zealand.

William Donald 'Billy' **WATSON**, a New Zealand representative in 1893 and 1896, was one of four reinforcements dispatched to shore up the 1893 New Zealand team in Australia. One of the matches he played was against Western New South Wales Branch (Western Districts) at Bathurst. He later became a sheep dog trials judge.

Bruce Alexander **WATT**, an All Black first-five from 1962 to 1964, scored two tries on his test debut against Australia. He also kicked one of the most important dropped goals in All Black history — against Wales in 1963. He used to run on the spot in the aisle during Canterbury bus trips and the driver would let him know when he had reached the equivalent of 20 miles. He later ran marathons and, appropriately, became a postman.

James Michael 'Jim' **WATT**, a 1936 All Black, later became professor of pediatrics at Otago University.

James 'Russell' **WATT**, an All Black in 1957, 1958, 1960, 1961 and 1962, was a winger who 'reacted fiercely' to obstruction. He was ordered off and suspended after a club match, thereby missing selection for the All Blacks in the second test against the 1961 French team.

Murray Gordon **WATTS**, an All Black in 1979 and 1980, scored a try against France in 1979 in his first test.

Desmond Stanley **WEBB**, a 1959 All Black, was a solicitor who played in NZ Universities' win over the Springboks in 1956.

Peter Purves **WEBB**, an 1884 New Zealand rep, became Chief Audit Inspector.

Thomas Robert Dobson **WEBSTER**, a 1947 All Black, played provincial rugby for Otago, Wellington and Southland. He died at the age of 52 while serving as a Canterbury RFU management committee member.

Piri Awahou Tihou **WEEPU**, an All Black halfback in 2004 and 2005, is an accurate goal kicker. He startled traditionalists when first selected for the All Blacks by saying his greatest desire was to represent the Kiwis.

John 'Jock' **WELLS**, a 1936 All Black, was the president of the Wellington RFU in 1969.

William John Geddes 'Bill' **WELLS**, a New Zealand rep in 1897, was a farmer/sawmiller from Mount Messenger and one of four players selected as late replacements for the 1897 tour to Australia.

Arthur William 'Art' **WESNEY**, an All Black in 1938, was twice runner-up at the national diving championships in the mid-1930s. He also represented Southland at water polo and died at the age of 26 in wartime action at Sidi Rezegh, North Africa. He lost his life 13 days after playing for the New Zealand Army team against the South African Army equivalent.

Alfred Hubert 'Alf' **WEST**, an All Black from 1920 to 1925, was the victim of a gas attack during the First World War while serving as a gunner with the New Zealand Field Artillery. He died at the age of 41. His great-nephew, Graeme West, captained the Kiwis at league.

Lynley Herbert **WESTON**, a 1914 All Black, became the first captain of the newly formed North Auckland province in 1921. He was the first All Black from the Auckland club College Rifles.

Alan James **WHETTON**, an All Black from 1984 to 1991, appeared as a replacement in four tests, to commence his international career. In 1987 he scored five tries in successive matches during the inaugural Rugby World Cup. In all, he scored 26 tries for New Zealand.

Gary William **WHETTON**, an All Black from 1981 to 1991, broke Colin Meads' longstanding record of 55 tests, when he played against Canada in 1991. He and his brother Alan are the only twins to have played test rugby together for New Zealand.

Wilson James **WHINERAY**, an All Black from 1957 to 1965, played provincial rugby for Wairarapa, Mid-Canterbury, Manawatu, Canterbury, Waikato and Auckland. He became chairman of Carter Holt Harvey and the Hillary Commission and was knighted.

Andrew 'Son' **WHITE**, an All Black from 1921 to 1925, was a loose forward who was also a part-time goal kicker. On the Invincibles tour he played in 28 out of 38 games.

Hallard Leo 'Snow' **WHITE**, an All Black from 1953 to 1955, still holds the record for the number of appearances for Auckland — 195.

Richard Alexander 'Tiny' **WHITE**, an All Black from 1949 to 1956, played in 30 of the 36 matches undertaken by the 1953–1954 All Blacks to Britain. Later he served two terms as mayor of Gisborne. One of his sons, David, represented Canterbury, while another (Chris) became an outstanding international oarsman.

Roy Maxwell **WHITE**, an All Black in 1946 and 1947, was a New Zealand R-class yachting champion.

Graham John **WHITING**, an All Black in 1972 and 1973, later played league for the Maritime club.

Peter John **WHITING**, an All Black

lock from 1971 to 1976, scored tries in three successive tests against the 1972 Australians. He became a diamond merchant.

Craig David **WICKES** at 18 became the first schoolboy All Black — against Fiji in 1980. He was a replacement for Ken Taylor and just missed out on 15 minutes of fame. He enjoyed 14.

David Ross **WIGHTMAN**, a 1951 All Black, was a teacher of physical education before becoming an auctioneer.

Alexander James 'Ali' **WILLIAMS**, an All Black lock from 2002 to 2005, scored two tries against the 2005 British and Irish Lions. He was an age group rep for Auckland in soccer, tennis and cricket.

Alexander Leonard **WILLIAMS**, a 1922 and 1923 All Black, played for the South Island and New Zealand before fully representing his province, Otago. In 1921 he made a solitary provincial appearance as a substitute. He was one of the few All Blacks to make his New Zealand debut at Carterton, where New Zealand snuck home 12-11 against Wairarapa.

Bryan George 'Bee Gee' **WILLIAMS**, an All Black from 1970 to 1978, went on seven All Black tours. Following his first tour in 1970 he received over 1000 letters from South African admirers and set out to answer them

all. His sons Gavin and Paul have both played Super 12 and NPC rugby.

Claude Wright **WILLIAMS**, a 1938 All Black, played as a flanker, No. 8 and lock forward in his four games for New Zealand. He was believed to be in the 1939 team to South Africa, a tour cancelled because of the Second World War.

Graham Charles **WILLIAMS**, an All Black in 1967 and 1968, scored exactly 50 points for New Zealand — 16 tries and one conversion. He became assistant coach of New Zealand Colts.

Peter **WILLIAMS**, a 1913 All Black, gained selection for the 1914 All Black tour to Australia but was unable to travel. He made his All Black debut at the age of 29.

Raymond Norman **WILLIAMS**, a 1932 All Black, declared himself unfit for the tour to Australia after suffering a knee injury in the build-up game against Wellington. He had been declared fit to tour by the team doctor. A civil engineer who lived for 53 years in Zimbabwe, he moved to South Africa in 1937 and served with the South African Royal Engineers in Egypt in 1940.

Ronald Oscar **WILLIAMS**, an All Black in 1988 and 1989, never played a test match for New Zealand, although he did play test rugby for Fiji.

Michael 'Mick' **WILLIMENT**, an All Black from 1964 to 1967, never toured as an All Black. His nine matches were all home internationals. Williment was the unfortunate 31st player originally selected in the 1967 touring team to Britain and France, but who was discarded because only 30 should have been chosen.

Royce Kevin **WILLIS**, an All Black in 1998, 1999 and 2002, played a game for Bay of Plenty seniors while still at school.

Thomas Eion 'Tom' **WILLIS**, an All Black in 2001 and 2002, was the 700th All Black to play test rugby and had the distinction of captaining New Zealand in his first match — against Ireland. His father Eion hooked for Otago in 1953. Tom Willis captained his first senior team at the age of 18.

Charles 'Chas' **WILLOCKS**, an All Black in 1946, 1947 and 1949, suffered a badly cut eye on the 1947 New Zealand tour to Australia, the result of a punch by a team-mate. He also suffered a shoulder injury in the train crash in Bulawayo that affected the 1949 All Black tourists.

Stanley de Lar Poer 'Mick' **WILLOUGHBY** was a 1928 All Black. He and his brother Seymour played together for the North Island in 1928.

Murray Clifton **WILLS**, a 1967 All Black, played 132 games for his province, Taranaki.

Alexander **WILSON**, a New Zealand representative in 1897, was 'a good goal-kicker and a grafter'.

Alfred Leonard 'Len' **WILSON**, a 1951 All Black, was born in Dunfermline, Scotland.

Bevan William **WILSON**, an All Black in 1977, 1978 and 1979, successfully trained racehorses at Omakau.

Douglas Dawson 'Doug' **WILSON**, an All Black in 1953 and 1954, was a Canterbury and New Zealand Brabin Cup cricket representative.

Frank Reginald **WILSON**, a 1910 All Black, was injured in the first match of the All Blacks' 1910 tour to Australia and dropped out of the game. He later survived Gallipoli but became a casualty of the Battle of the Somme, dying at the age of 31.

Hector William 'Hec' **WILSON**, an All Black in 1949, 1950 and 1951, had the distinction of scoring a try when whistled up as a replacement prop for John Simpson in the fourth test against the 1950 British Lions.

Hedley 'Brett' **WILSON**, a 1983 All Black hooker, appeared with his fellow Counties All Black hooker

Andy Dalton in the same All Black trial team in 1984. Wilson turned out as a flanker.

Henry Clarke **WILSON**, an 1893 New Zealand representative, gained selection for New Zealand while playing club rugby for Athletic in Wellington, although he never represented that union. Because Canterbury was not affiliated to the NZRFU in 1893, he transferred to Wellington to gain selection for the 1893 tour to Australia.

Jeffrey William **WILSON**, an All Black from 1993 to 1999 and in 2001, nicknamed 'Goldie', played both rugby and cricket for New Zealand while still a teenager, and is married to New Zealand netball captain Adine Harper.

Nathaniel Arthur 'Ranji' **WILSON**, an All Black from 1908 to 1914, was regarded as the best New Zealand loose forward in the pre-First World War years. Although he was a sergeant with the New Zealand Army, because of his West Indian blood he was deemed to be 'coloured' and as such was barred from touring South Africa with the New Zealand Services team in 1919. He later became a New Zealand selector and helped pick the 1925 Invincibles.

Norman Leslie **WILSON**, an All Black in 1949 and 1951, later became a TV rugby comments man.

Richard George **WILSON**, an All Black from 1976 to 1980, scored five tries, 48 conversions, 51 penalty goals and one dropped goal in 25 matches for New Zealand. His father George played for Canterbury in 1949.

Robert J. 'Bob' **WILSON**, an 1884 New Zealand representative, was a 60 kg forward who replaced the originally selected Edward D'Auvergne in the 1884 New Zealand touring team to Australia. He is the only player to represent New Zealand without appearing for a rep team, although he did play for Queensland after moving to Australia.

Stuart Sinclair 'Stu' **WILSON**, an All Black from 1976 to 1983, captained New Zealand on their 1983 tour of England and Scotland from the wing position. He had earlier been a good golfer and one year lost the final of the Masterton Golf Club championships to his father.

Vivian Whitta **WILSON**, an All Black in 1920, was the Auckland Golf Club handicapper for 13 years. He was an elusive player and once, while playing for the All Blacks in Australia, he beat so many defenders that he became disorientated and started running around in circles, at which point all the players stopped to watch in fascination. 'Shut the bloody gate before the bugger bolts,' yelled out New Zealand forward Moke Belliss, at which point Wilson came to. He was also the player who scored the late try for Bay of Plenty in a Ranfurly Shield challenge against Hawke's Bay in 1922 that should have won the shield. The try was scored under the posts but the goal-kicker, afflicted with nerves, missed the conversion attempt.

George Denis 'Denny' **WISE**, a 1925 All Black, played for the Pirates Club in Dunedin. He was the top try-scorer on the All Blacks' 1925 tour of Australia.

Derren John Charles **WITCOMBE**, an All Black in 2005, was born in Tasmania. He has played cricket for North Auckland as a wicket-keeper/batsman.

Thomas 'Neil' **WOLFE**, an All Black in 1961, 1962, 1963 and 1968, played three tests against France in 1961 while still 19 and at 1.63 m in height. He later became managing director of a soft drink company in New Plymouth.

Morris Edwin 'Morrie' **WOOD**, a New Zealand rep in 1901 and an All Black in 1903 and 1904, played provincial rugby for Bush, Hawke's Bay, Wellington, Canterbury and Auckland. In 1904 he was the New Zealand long-jump champion.

Tony Dale **WOODCOCK**, an All Black from 2002 to 2005, has played in 17 tests, 16 of which have produced victories. He is a product of

New Zealand's age-group system. He schooled at Kaipara College and won All Black selection from the Helensville club.

Fred Akehurst **WOODMAN**, an All Black in 1980 and 1981, was one of three brothers who starred on the wing for North Auckland. His brother Kawhena also became an All Black, while their other brother Richard had to settle for rep honours. Fred made 114 appearances for his province.

Taui Ben 'Kawhena' **WOODMAN**, an All Black in 1984, made 126 appearances for Northland. A school-teacher, he is renowned in the north for his 12-egg Madeira cake.

Charles 'Arthur' **WOODS**, a 1953 and 1954 All Black from the Limehills Club in Southland, played 14 games for New Zealand and scored two points. The latter came when he kicked a conversion against Victoria (British Columbia) at the conclusion of the 1953–1954 tour.

Alan Hercules **WRIGHT**, a 1938 All Black, once scored four tries against Newcastle. 'Bumper' Wright, his father, played for Wellington.

Donald Hector **WRIGHT**, a 1925 All Black on the tour to Australia, was a surprise omission from the 1924–1925 tour to Britain. Several Aucklanders were so incensed they presented a petition to Parliament and met with the Deputy Prime Minister, Gordon Coates, in the hope that Wright's name could be added to the team list. Such pleadings were to no avail.

Terence John 'Terry' **WRIGHT**, an All Black from 1986 to 1992, scored 112 tries for Auckland, and 53 in Ranfurly Shield rugby. Auckland club Northcote's ground is named after his father, Harvey Wright.

William Alexander 'Bill' **WRIGHT**, a 1926 All Black, was one of two Auckland halfbacks named Wright who played for New Zealand in 1925–1926. The other was Donald Hector Wright. Bill Wright, reserve for Auckland, was summoned to replace Bill Dalley in the New Zealand team to play Auckland when it was discovered that injuries in the touring party left them short of a replacement halfback. (Jimmy Mill, the other halfback was also injured.) Given that Donald Hector Wright, the 1925 All Black, was still playing for Auckland, the reasonable comment was made that perhaps the selectors had got the 'wrong' Wright. Bill Wright's game for New Zealand against Auckland was his only All Black appearance and only his second game in first-class rugby.

THAT BLESSED KAWHENA WOODMAN HAS BEEN BAKING CAKES AGAIN!

©DARYL CRIMP

Edgar **WRIGLEY**, a 1905 All Black, was 19 years and 79 days of age when he played his only match for New Zealand. He was the youngest All Black until Jonah Lomu played against France in 1994. Wrigley switched to rugby league in 1907 and toured with the All Golds.

James Thomas 'Jim' **WYLIE**, a 1913 All Black, was born in Galatea and died in Palo Alto, USA. Something of a globetrotter, he made two consecutive tours to North America — for Australia in 1912, and for New Zealand in 1913.

Alexander John 'Grizz' **WYLLIE**, an All Black from 1970 to 1973, played 210 games over 17 seasons for his province Canterbury. He later coached Eastern Province and Transvaal in South Africa, Argentina and Clontarf in Ireland.

Tutekawa 'Tu' **WYLLIE**, a 1980 All Black, was elected the Member of Parliament for Southern Maori (Te Tai Tonga) in the 1996 General Election.

James Gladwyn **WYNYARD**, an All Black in 1935, 1936 and 1938, was born in Kihikihi and died at El Alamein, Egypt, during the Second World War aged 27. In 1934 he played rugby in the Waikato for a club called Waipa Suburbs.

William Thomas 'Tabby' **WYNYARD**, a New Zealand rep in 1893, once scored a try for New Zealand that was worth only two points, when playing against a Combined XV at Petone. The four tries he scored in Australia later in the year were worth three points each.

Victor Moses **YATES**, an All Black in 1961 and 1962, was a successful long-range goal-kicker for his province North Auckland. He switched to league in 1965, a code in which his brother John represented New Zealand.

Dennis **YOUNG**, an All Black hooker from 1956 to 1964, was the founder of the Canterbury Supporters Club and ended up working in the travel industry.

Francis Beresford 'Frank' **YOUNG**, an 1896 New Zealand rep against Queensland, was born in Tasmania. He was among the first players from the Wellington club Poneke to play for New Zealand.

Thirty of the best
All Blacks — in depth

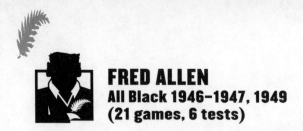

FRED ALLEN
All Black 1946–1947, 1949
(21 games, 6 tests)

What superstitions did you bring to rugby?
None — I came to rugby with an open and clear mind.

In what circumstances did you first learn you had been selected for the
All Blacks? Under the grandstand at Athletic Park after the final trial in 1946.

In what circumstances did you learn you were dropped from the All Blacks,
if you ever were? I was never dropped, but stood myself down from the third
and fourth tests in South Africa in 1949 to assist with the coaching.

What was the first car you ever owned? A 1935 Morris 8.

What home-made dish did you miss most when you were touring overseas?
Roast lamb with mint sauce.

What was your father's occupation?
He was a guard for the New Zealand Railways.

What town did your wife grow up in? Christchurch.

What was the best piece of sporting advice your father (or mother) ever
offered? There are no short cuts to the top in team games.

At what age did you play your first game? Eight.

What was the greatest game you ever played in?
The return game against New South Wales (at Sydney) in 1947.

On average, how many books do you read in a year?
Four or five, plus rugby biographies.

Which TV channel do you watch most? TV One and Sky Sport.

Did you play another sport after rugby?
Golf and squash, but I'm not playing now.

What is the most unusual thing you've achieved in your life?
Being the only undefeated coach in the history of All Black rugby.

Who was the most famous person you ever met?
The Queen (on three occasions).

Who is the most eccentric coach you ever played under? There wasn't one.

Who is the most eccentric team-mate you played alongside? No comment.

What was the most amazing comment you ever heard on a rugby field?
When Johnny Simpson hit Okey Geffin in South Africa in 1949, Okey said,
'But it wasn't me, John!'

What was your most embarrassing moment on the rugby field? At the age of
18 in 1938 marking Dave Trevathan in a Payne Trophy match. He drop-kicked
three goals against me within 15 minutes.

What's the smartest bet you ever made? I never bet on sport.

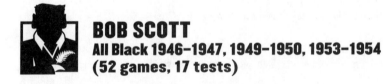

BOB SCOTT
All Black 1946–1947, 1949–1950, 1953–1954
(52 games, 17 tests)

What superstitions did you bring to rugby?
I always laced my boots the same way. At some stage of the 1953–1954 tour of
the UK I had to do up Morrie Dixon's boots the same way!

In what circumstances did you first learn you had been selected for the
All Blacks? Not sure now. I remember I was working for Milne and Choyce
and on the Monday morning reported to the personnel manager, to be told I
wouldn't be paid. I told him I couldn't afford to be away. It wasn't long before
Bob Milne summoned me to his office to inform me I would be paid.

In what circumstances did you learn you were dropped from the All Blacks,
if you ever were? Never was. Did the ego good in 1953 when the reverse
happened: I was asked to come out of retirement.

What was the first car you ever owned? An Austin.

What home-made dish did you miss most when you were touring overseas?
Roast dinner.

What was your father's occupation? He was a railway worker and tunneller.

What town did your wife grow up in? London.

What was the best piece of sporting advice your father (or mother) ever
offered? Neither parent was involved in sport and neither saw me play.
My father died when I was 13.

At what age did you play your first game? Eleven.

What was the greatest game you ever played in?
Two stand out — the All Blacks against the Lions at Auckland in 1950
and the Barbarians game at Cardiff in 1954.

On average, how many books do you read in a year? Twenty.

Which TV channel do you watch most? TV One.

Did you play another sport after rugby?
Golf (got down to a scratch handicap) and bowls. I'm still playing bowls.

What is the most unusual thing you've achieved in life?
Visiting Buckingham Palace, quite something for a barefoot school-kid from
the backblocks of King Country.

Who was the most famous person you ever met?
King George VI on the 1945–1946 Kiwis tour. I later met the Queen.

Who is the most eccentric coach you ever played under?
Norman McKenzie. He wasn't so much eccentric as unusual. I was injured
in the 1947 trial in Palmerston North. On the train to Wellington for the final
trial, he suggested I get as much Aussie currency together as possible.

Who is the most eccentric team-mate you played alongside?
Probably Jack Finlay of the Kiwis. He always apologised if he dropped a pass.

What was the most amazing comment you ever heard on a rugby field?
After fielding a high ball in the Christchurch test against the 1950 Lions in Christchurch, I was confronted by Billy Cleaver. We looked at each other and he said, 'Your move!'

What was your most embarrassing moment on the rugby field?
Against the Lions at Dunedin in 1950 when I went across to retrieve the ball near the corner flag, but nudged it over the goal line and Ken Jones scored a try.

What's the smartest bet you ever made?
A reporter named Day, who had played for England, questioned my ability to kick a goal from halfway. I took up the challenge and won a shilling!

JOHNNY SIMPSON
All Black 1947, 1949–1950
(30 games, 9 tests)

What superstitions did you bring to rugby?
It was always upsetting if I forgot to take my PK chewing gum to a game.

In what circumstances did you first learn you had been selected for the All Blacks? Heard it on the radio (in 1947), the day we moved from Ponsonby to Mairangi Bay.

In what circumstances did you learn you were dropped from the All Blacks, if you ever were? Never was.

What was the first car you ever owned? An Austin Cambridge.

What home-made dish did you miss most when you were touring overseas?
Roast lamb.

What was your father's occupation?
He was a ganger with New Zealand Railways.

What town did your wife grow up in? Wellington.

What was the best piece of sporting advice your father (or mother) ever offered? Keep onside and play fair.

At what age did you play your first game? Ten.

What was the greatest game you ever played in?
Defeating Wales at Cardiff Arms Park as a member of the 2nd NZEF Kiwis in 1945.

On average, how many books do you read in a year?
Because of failing eyesight, I listen to talking books from the Blind Foundation.

Which TV channel do you watch most? None.

Did you play another sport after rugby?
Lawn bowls (I was president of Bowls New Zealand in 1990–1991, accompanying the New Zealand team to Hong Kong, and am a life member of the Kapiti Coast centre).

What is the most unusual thing you've achieved in life?
Saved Glynn Tucker (who became keeper of the New Zealand Stud Book) from drowning in a water tank in Trieste during the war; survived a train crash south of Bulawayo, in which two passengers were killed, during the All Black tour of South Africa in 1949; rode a horse from Panmure to Bastion Point to attend Michael Savage's funeral in the 1930s. On the way home the horse bolted at Mt Wellington and I had to walk home to Panmure.

Who was the most famous person you ever met?
General Sir Bernard Freyberg, King George VI and Queen Elizabeth.

What was the most amazing comment you ever heard on a rugby field?
During the series in South Africa in 1949 my opponent, Chris Koch, suggested we go and have a cup of tea once the scrum was sorted out (by me!).

What was your most embarrassing moment on the rugby field?
Being ordered off in the 1947 North-South match in Invercargill. Leo Connelly protested to the referee on my behalf . . . and was sent off too. We walked off arm in arm.

What's the smartest bet you ever made?
I once struck a big double (Marie Brizard and Biltong).

RICHARD 'TINY' WHITE
All Black 1949–1956
(55 games, 23 tests)

What superstitions did you bring to rugby? None.

In what circumstances did you first learn you had been selected for the All Blacks? By telegram from the NZRFU (in 1949).

In what circumstances did you learn you were dropped from the All Blacks, if you ever were? Never was.

What was the first car you ever owned? An Austin 7, with a canvas roof.

What home-made dish did you miss most when you were touring overseas?
To be honest, I didn't miss New Zealand food because I enjoyed the English food so much, except for those dreadful Brussels sprouts that seemed to be served with most main meals.

What was your father's occupation? He was a sheep farmer.

What town did your wife grow up in? Gisborne.

What was the best piece of sporting advice your father (or mother) ever offered? After I was dropped from a primary school side in the 1930s because of my size, my father said, 'Don't worry, son, you will show them one day.'

At what age did you play your first game? Nine.

What was the greatest game you ever played in?
The Barbarians game at Cardiff in 1954.

On average, how many books do you read in a year? Five or six.

Which TV channel do you watch most? TV One.

Did you play another sport after rugby?
Circuit racing and fly-fishing (till death do us part!)

What is the most unusual thing you've achieved in life?
Being selected to tour Britain with the All Blacks in 1953.

Who was the most famous person you ever met? My parents.

Who is the most eccentric coach you ever played under? A Poverty Bay
coach who had us running into a tin fence. You soon learnt to come last!

Who is the most eccentric team-mate you played alongside? No comment.

What was the most amazing comment you ever heard on a rugby field?
In a Gisborne club game my team was becoming mightily frustrated
with the referee, who kept disallowing tries. Finally, in absolute frustration,
I said to him, 'You're not a referee's arsehole!' Instead of sending me off,
he replied, with much indignation, 'Yes, I am!' When we were playing
England at Twickenham, Kevin Skinner implored me to 'get lower on my arse'
with my push. We burst into laughter when, in identical circumstances, the
England captain later barked out, 'Get lower on my buttock, young fellow!'

What was your most embarrassing moment on the rugby field?
Nothing springs to mind.

What's the smartest bet you ever made? I don't gamble.

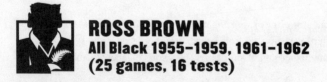

ROSS BROWN
All Black 1955–1959, 1961–1962
(25 games, 16 tests)

What superstitions did you bring to rugby? None.

*In what circumstances did you first learn you had been selected for the
All Blacks?* After getting off the bus after playing for Taranaki against
Waikato (in 1955).

In what circumstances did you learn you were dropped from the All Blacks, if you ever were? On the radio (in 1962).

What was the first car you ever owned? A Holden.

What home-made dish did you miss most when you were touring overseas?
Roast beef.

What was your father's occupation?
He was a timber merchant.

What town did your wife grow up in? Waitomo.

What was the best piece of sporting advice your father (or mother) ever offered? Tackle!

At what age did you play your first game? Ten.

What was the greatest game you ever played in?
The fourth test against the Springboks at Eden Park, 1956.

On average, how many books do you read in a year?
None — just the *Best Bets*!

Which TV channel do you watch most? TV One.

Did you play another sport after rugby?
Golf, cricket and bowls. I'm still playing bowls.

What is the most unusual thing you've achieved in your life?
Nothing springs to mind.

Who was the most famous person you ever met?
Princess Chichibu, patroness of the Japan RFU.

Who is the most eccentric coach you ever played under?
The late Jack Finlay.

Who is the most eccentric team-mate you played alongside? Can't say.

What was the most amazing comment you ever heard on a rugby field?
I was touch judge for a midweek All Black game in Australia and with the score 96-nil, the local captain said, 'Come on, boys, let's stop the century.'

What was your most embarrassing moment on the rugby field?
Dropping a pass from Kel Tremain near the posts and losing a certain try in a trial game at Wellington.

What's the smartest bet you ever made?
Having a good punt on Rogan Josh when he won the Melbourne Cup.

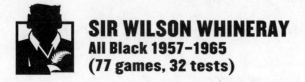

SIR WILSON WHINERAY
All Black 1957–1965
(77 games, 32 tests)

What superstitions did you bring to rugby? None.

In what circumstances did you first learn you had been selected for the All Blacks? The team was read out by NZRFU chairman Cuth Hogg in the function room at Athletic Park following the final trial in 1957.

In what circumstances did you learn you were dropped from the All Blacks, if you ever were? Pleased to say I eluded the selectors.

What was the first car you ever owned? A 1937 Chevrolet.

What home-made dish did you miss most when you were touring overseas?
Mainly the home-style Kiwi family foods — stew, mince and mashed potatoes.

What was your father's occupation? He was an accountant.

What town did your wife grow up in?
Palmerston North — we met when I was at Massey College.

What was the best piece of sporting advice your father (or mother) ever offered? From Dad: Never quit, always play out the full eighty minutes. From Mum: There are two games going on — one you play with the body, the other with your brains!

At what age did you play your first game? Five.

What was the greatest game you ever played in?
Tests would be against the Lions at Christchurch in 1959 and against
the Springboks at Auckland in 1965. Non-test, it would be New Zealand
Universities against the Springboks in 1956.

On average, how many books do you read in a year? Forty to fifty.

Which TV channel do you watch most?
Mixture of TV One, Sky Sport and the History channel.

Did you play another sport after rugby?
Golf and tennis. Back problems now impose limits.

What is the most unusual thing you've achieved in your life?
Being Commandant to the New Zealand SAS Group, 1997–2002.

Who was the most famous person you ever met?
Queen Elizabeth II and Nelson Mandela.

Who is the most eccentric coach you ever played under?
They're all eccentric. Before scrum machines were invented, Bill Corby
had a shoulder unit for the front row to push on fitted to a small truck chassis.
He sat in the driver seat shouting out and changing gear down to reverse!

Who is the most eccentric team-mate you played alongside?
My lips are sealed.

What was the most amazing comment you ever heard on a rugby field?
In a test against Australia, Peter Jones made a flying tackle at the Aussie
winger, missed and flattened the touch judge. The Wallaby front rower Ellis
said to Peter, 'You're out for life now, Peter, for flattening a match official.' The
referee heard the comment and said, 'Peter, tell him to f— off!'

What was your most embarrassing moment on the rugby field?
I guess losing the third test to the Springboks in Christchurch after we had
such a commanding lead at halftime. It didn't reflect well on the captain.

What's the smartest bet you ever made? Nothing stands out.

JOHN GRAHAM
All Black 1958, 1960–1964
(53 games, 22 tests)

What superstitions did you bring to rugby?
I always ran on to the field behind Kel Tremain and in front of Dennis Young. I always changed next to Kel Tremain.

In what circumstances did you first learn you had been selected for the All Blacks? Sitting at home, listening to the radio (in 1958) . . . 'D.J. Graham, Canterbury!'

In what circumstances did you learn you were dropped from the All Blacks, if you ever were? In 1958, I was informed by a team-mate, who had heard the team announced on the radio.

What was the first car you ever owned? A Morris Minor.

What home-made dish did you miss most when you were touring overseas?
Roast lamb, mint sauce, roast potatoes, onions and broad beans, and white sauce.

What was your father's occupation? He was a farmer at Putaruru.

What town did your wife grow up in? Ashburton.

What was the best piece of sporting advice your father (or mother) ever offered? Never be satisfied with less than your best.

At what age did you play your first game?
Eleven, for Lichfield Primary School.

What was the greatest game you ever played in?
All Blacks against South Africa at Newlands in 1960 — a special win against the old 'enemy'.

On average, how many books do you read in a year? Thirty-five to forty.

Which TV channel do you watch most?
TV3 News, Sky Sport, the History channel.

Did you play another sport after rugby?
Cricket, poorly. I'm no longer playing.

Who was the most famous person you ever met? Queen Elizabeth II.

What was the most amazing comment you ever heard on a rugby field?
Comments on the rugby field were very basic . . . never amazing.

What was your most embarrassing moment on the rugby field?
Being told in a club match in 1966 when I was struggling for form and did a
stupid thing, 'D.J., you're getting old and are past it'. I retired two weeks later!

What's the smartest bet you ever made? I've never been a gambler.

EARLE KIRTON
All Black 1963–1964, 1967–1970
(49 games, 13 tests)

What superstitions did you bring to rugby?
I never warmed up in the changing sheds and always went outside to gauge the
light, sun, wind, etc. I hated night games.

In what circumstances did you first learn you had been selected for the
All Blacks? Under the stand at Athletic Park following the final trials in 1963.
I didn't believe it when my name was read out.

In what circumstances did you learn you were dropped from the All Blacks,
if you ever were? I waited six games for an outing after the Newport loss in
1963. After 1964, I wasn't selected for New Zealand again until 1967.

What was the first car you ever owned? A Morris 12.

What home-made dish did you miss most when you were touring overseas?
Mum's trifle.

What was your father's occupation? He was a banker, then a property
developer and farmer.

What town did your wife grow up in? Christchurch and Wellington.

What was the best piece of sporting advice your father (or mother) ever offered? My father said, 'Just watch the ball into your hands and nurse it — then you have achieved 50 per cent of the skills needed.' My mother went to New Plymouth to watch Taranaki play Wales in 1969 and warned me that Phil Bennett was a more dangerous attacker than Barry John. When John was preferred for the test, she sent me a telegram saying, 'They've picked John — you lucky bugger!'

At what age did you play your first game? Five.

What was the greatest game you ever played in?
North Island against South Island at Christchurch in 1963.

On average, how many books do you read in a year? Ten.

Which TV channel do you watch most?
Sky Sport 1, Sky Sport 2, the Rugby Channel, and sometimes CNN.

Did you play another sport after rugby?
Tennis and a little golf, but I'm not playing now.

What is the most unusual thing you've achieved in your life?
After struggling to pass exams in New Zealand because I was so often out of the country, I sat the primary exam for a fellowship in orthodontics at the Royal College of Surgeons in London . . . and passed.

Who was the most famous person you ever met? The Queen.

Who is the most eccentric coach you ever played under?
Jack Finlay, who would pause in the middle of a team talk to tell you that his strawberries had been absolutely beautiful that season. A vague and wonderful person.

Who is the most eccentric team-mate you played alongside?
Chris Laidlaw was a great player who was very self-analytical. He would allow himself two mistakes a game at test level. Three mistakes and he'd consider he had only an average game; four was not acceptable. I'll never forget his provocative moment against Wales in 1967 when our magnificent

forwards, thanks to Ken Gray's effort in the front row, marched the Welsh
scrum back fully 25 metres. The crowd's singing stopped and eventually
they began to clap the All Blacks. As this was happening Laidlaw put his
hands in his pockets and said, 'Sorry, Edwards — not getting the ball today?'
I couldn't believe his audacity, although even in the tenseness of the situation
I chuckled.

What was the most amazing comment you ever heard on a rugby field?
During the French test in 1967 I was remonstrating with Claude Dourthe,
calling him a 'dirty bugger'. By means of sign language and several 'non,
nons' he was trying to plead innocence. Just then Bruce McLeod, our hooker,
was running past. 'You don't bloody talk to them,' he said. 'They don't
understand you — you just bloody whack them!' With that, he whacked
Dourthe and, without pausing, raced on to the next ruck!

What was your most embarrassing moment on the rugby field?
Trying to be a smart arse playing for Otago against Southland in the early
sixties and while racing round behind the posts to score the winning try,
dropped the ball.

What's the smartest bet you ever made?
After my unfortunate tour in 1963–1964, I announced that I would make it
back into the All Blacks. No one, including my team-mates, thought I had a
dog's show.

IAN MacRAE
All Black 1963–1964, 1966–1970
(45 games, 17 tests)

What superstitions did you bring to rugby? I always cleaned my own boots.

***In what circumstances did you first learn you had been selected for the
All Blacks?*** Under the old stand at Athletic Park before the tour of the UK
in 1963. Selected players were asked to assemble in a dungeon-like dressing
room, where my elbow suddenly blew up like a football. I was rushed to
hospital where the diagnosis was a broken blood vessel.

In what circumstances did you learn you were dropped from the All Blacks, if you ever were? On the radio.

What was the first car you ever owned? A 1948 Morris 8.

What home-made dish did you miss most when you were touring overseas?
Our own home-cooked fish and chips.

What was your father's occupation?
He was an engine driver in the Ohai mines.

What town did your wife grow up in? Loburn, North Canterbury.

What was the best piece of sporting advice your father (or mother) ever offered? Play fair.

At what age did you play your first game? Seven.

What was the greatest game you ever played in?
All Blacks against France in Paris, in 1967.

On average, how many books do you read in a year? Six.

Which TV channel do you watch most? Sky Sport.

Did you play another sport after rugby?
Tennis and golf. I'm still playing both (golf on an 18 handicap).

What is the most unusual thing you've achieved in your life?
Installing a new motor in my Morris Minor with only a manual for assistance.

Who was the most famous person you ever met?
Pioneering heart surgeon Christian Barnard.

Who is the most eccentric coach you ever played under?
Jack Finlay, who took the Colts to Australia in 1964. During a team talk, he pulled out the *Best Bets* and started talking racing. He demanded the team sang on the bus and in the shed prior to games.

Who is the most eccentric team-mate you played alongside?
Jazz Muller, a great practical joker who bought items at every joke shop wherever we were. He also slept in his first All Black jersey.

What was the most amazing comment you ever heard on a rugby field?
'You're off!' — referee Kevin Kelleher to Colin Meads in the Scottish international at Murrayfield in 1967.

What was your most embarrassing moment on the rugby field?
After a charity game at Oamaru in the early sixties, when I hadn't had time to clean my boots. I copped a real blast from Fred Allen after the game.

What's the smartest bet you ever made?
Backing Mac's Own on my wife's instructions at Hastings one day. It won and paid £80!

SIR BRIAN LOCHORE
All Black 1963–1971
(68 games, 25 tests)

What superstitions did you bring to rugby? None.

In what circumstances did you first learn you had been selected for the All Blacks? Under the grandstand at Athletic Park, after a trial (in 1963) in which I played No. 8, a position I had never played in my life.

In what circumstances did you learn you were dropped from the All Blacks, if you ever were? Fortunately, I never was.

What was the first car you ever owned? A 1934 V8 coupe.

What home-made dish did you miss most when you were touring overseas?
Mashed vegetables.

What was your father's occupation? He was a grocer, then a farmer.

What town did your wife grow up in? Masterton.

What was the best piece of sporting advice your father (or mother) ever offered? Always do your best.

At what age did you play your first game? Six.

What was the greatest game you ever played in?
All Blacks against France at Paris in 1967.

On average, how many books do you read in a year? Two or three.

Which TV channel do you watch most? TV One.

Did you play another sport after rugby?
Tennis, squash and golf. I'm still playing golf.

What is the most unusual thing you've achieved in your life?
Running a college.

Who was the most famous person you ever met? The Queen.

Who is the most eccentric coach you ever played under?
Ivan Vodanovich — a great guy who loved the long grind.

Who is the most eccentric team-mate you played alongside? No comment.

What was the most amazing comment you ever heard on a rugby field?
Kel Tremain saying we could achieve a pushover try against Wales in 1967 when we had just pushed them over the 22.

What was your most embarrassing moment on the rugby field?
Giving away an intercept try against the Springboks in the first test of the 1970 series.

What's the smartest bet you ever made? I don't bet.

FERGIE McCORMICK
All Black 1965, 1967–1971
(44 games, 16 tests)

What superstitions did you bring to rugby? I made sure my gear was always packed the same way. And I always put the right boot on first.

In what circumstances did you first learn you had been selected for the All Blacks? I heard it on the ferry coming back from Wellington after a rep game at Athletic Park (in 1965).

In what circumstances did you learn you were dropped from the All Blacks, if you ever were? On the radio (after the first test of the 1971 Lions series).

What was the first car you ever owned?
A Model A Ford.

What home-made dish did you miss most when you were touring overseas?
Home roasts, of course.

What was your father's occupation?
He was a farm worker, a cooper and a freezing worker.

What town or country did your wife grow up in?
Christchurch (first wife), Australia (second wife).

What was the best piece of sporting advice your father (or mother) ever offered? Always try your best.

At what age did you play your first game? Eight.

What was the greatest game you ever played in?
Probably the Barbarians game at Cardiff in 1967.

On average, how many books do you read in a year?
I used to read books, but TV steals that time now.

Which TV channel do you watch most? TV3.

Did you play another sport after rugby?
I played rugby till I was 40, then golf.

What is the most unusual thing you've achieved in your life?
Can't really say.

Who was the most famous person you ever met? The Queen.

Who is the most eccentric coach you ever played under? Ivan Vodanovich.
He had everyone running up that bloody sand hill at East London.

Who is the most eccentric team-mate you played alongside? Earle Kirton.

What was the most amazing comment you ever heard on a rugby field?
After I got caught up in a ruck in a North-South match at Hamilton and
got a bit stroppy, Colin Meads said, 'If you come back in here, you little
bugger, I'll fix you for good.' 'Don't worry, Pinetree,' I replied, 'I'm never
coming back in here!' Another time, with the crowd going wild because I'd
high-tackled someone, referee Tom Doocey said, 'I couldn't see what you did,
so I'm penalising you for swearing.'

What was your most embarrassing moment on the rugby field?
There are a couple — tripping over a child at halftime and knocking his
autograph book out of his hand; missing goals from straight in front for
Canterbury against Scotland.

What's the smartest bet you ever made?
An all-up that paid a handsome amount.

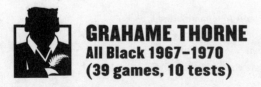

GRAHAME THORNE
All Black 1967–1970
(39 games, 10 tests)

What superstitions did you bring to rugby?
I always wore the same shirt on match days . . . until it wore out!
In cricket, I always put the left pad on first.

In what circumstances did you first learn you had been selected for the All Blacks? Under the old grandstand at Athletic Park before PC set in and nobody could be hurt! I was the bolter in 1967.

In what circumstances did you learn you were dropped from the All Blacks, if you ever were? Me? Dropped!

What was the first car you ever owned? An MG TF 1500 — at 21!

What home-made dish did you miss most when you were touring overseas? Pavlova.

What was your father's occupation? He was a photographer.

What town did your wife grow up in? Kampala, Uganda.

What was the best piece of sporting advice your father (or mother) ever offered? When the ugly ones start looking good, stop drinking.

At what age did you play your first game? Seven.

What was the greatest game you ever played in?
All Blacks against Wales, first test at Lancaster Park, 1969, and All Blacks against the Junior Boks at Potchefstroom in 1970 (when I took the kicks and saved the day).

On average, how many books do you read in a year? Sixteen.

Which TV channel do you watch most? TV One.

Did you play another sport after rugby?
I played cricket before rugby and golf (badly) after it.

What is the most unusual thing you've achieved in your life?
Perming my hair (and being reminded of it 23 years later!).

Who was the most famous person you ever met? Muhammad Ali.

Who is the most eccentric coach you ever played under?
Barrie Hutchinson. He used to quote Shakespeare's Hamlet and other literary

figures. He would say things like 'Now is the time for all University players to come out of the hills and attack the field of Eden Park!'

Who is the most eccentric team-mate you played alongside?
University Lawyers in 1966. I was 19, they were all lawyers and they dropped me for the final because I didn't turn up to practice. They lost.

What was the most amazing comment you ever heard on a rugby field?
I was playing, not listening.

What was your most embarrassing moment on the rugby field?
Diving for a try at the age of seven and realising it was the 25-yard line.

What's the smartest bet you ever made? Marrying Briony.

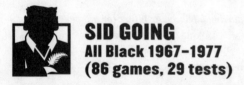

SID GOING
All Black 1967–1977
(86 games, 29 tests)

What superstitions did you bring to rugby? None.

In what circumstances did you first learn you had been selected for the All Blacks? Under the grandstand at Athletic Park (in 1967).

In what circumstances did you learn you were dropped from the All Blacks, if you ever were? Heard it on the radio (in 1977).

What was the first car you ever owned? A VW Beetle.

What home-made dish did you miss most when you were touring overseas?
Mutton roast.

What was your father's occupation? He was a farmer.

What town did your wife grow up in? Whangarei.

What was the best piece of sporting advice your father (or mother) ever offered? Play hard and use your skills.

At what age did you play your first game? Four or five.

What was the greatest game you ever played in?
The third test against France at Eden Park in 1968 and Northland's Ranfurly Shield win against Auckland, also at Eden Park, in 1971.

On average, how many books do you read in a year? One.

Which TV channel do you watch most? Sky Sport.

Did you play another sport after rugby?
Tennis and water-skiing . . . till the joints packed up!

What is the most unusual thing you've achieved in your life?
Surviving a shoot-out in San Francisco on my first All Black tour in 1967. Some guy drew a gun and started firing. A group of us, including coach Fred Allen, dived for cover as the victim collapsed in the gutter in a pool of blood. We felt like we'd walked into a movie scene.

Who was the most famous person you ever met?
Muhammad Ali (and Ian Kirkpatrick).

Who is the most eccentric coach you ever played under?
Ivan Vodanovich. He made us run around the field for warm-ups for hours, especially when a crowd was watching.

Who is the most eccentric team-mate you played alongside?
I can think of a few eccentric referees.

What was the most amazing comment you ever heard on a rugby field?
'Now put it in straight' was Air Commodore Larry Lamb's comment to me before the first scrum against Newport in 1972. I did, but he penalised me, and kept penalising me for supposedly crooked feeds. In the finish, I swung round and said, 'Here, you put it in!'

What was your most embarrassing moment on the rugby field?
Having a crucial penalty kick wiped out by referee Gert Bezuidenhout after the ball fell over three times — against the Springboks at Newlands in 1976. That decision so affected my confidence as a kicker I never landed another goal on tour. My most embarrassing off-field moment came when a Maori

elder addressed the Northern Maori team at a pa in Maori. As the captain, I was expected to translate the speech into English for my players. But I don't speak Maori. Jim Maniapoto came to my rescue.

What's the smartest bet you ever made? I've never bet.

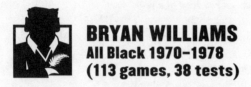

BRYAN WILLIAMS
All Black 1970–1978
(113 games, 38 tests)

What superstitions did you bring to rugby?
I wore coloured underwear, mainly black or blue.

In what circumstances did you first learn you had been selected for the All Blacks? After the final trial at Wellington in 1970. I had bruised my right hand and everyone wanted to come and shake it. It hurt like blazes.

In what circumstances did you learn you were dropped from the All Blacks, if you ever were? In the loss to Munster in 1978, I had a strained hamstring and the other one started playing up. I was about to go off when Bruce Robertson left the field. I stayed on and was promptly dropped from the test team.

What was the first car you ever owned?
An Austin A35 called Peanut. When I visited schools, kids were intrigued why I didn't have a big, flash car. We were amateurs and I was still a student.

What home-made dish did you miss most when you were touring overseas?
Chicken cooked in coconut cream.

What was your father's occupation?
He was a plumber and drainlayer (he had me digging drains during the school holidays).

What town did your wife grow up in?
Moerewa, Bay of Islands (where we first met).

What was the best piece of sporting advice your father (or mother) ever offered? Keep your feet on the ground and don't get big-headed. All Blacks have to do the dishes, too.

At what age did you play your first game? League at five, rugby at ten.

What was the greatest game you ever played in?
All Blacks against the Barbarians in 1973 — the most famous but not the most fondly remembered because of our errors and the fact we lost. I have happier memories of Auckland's Ranfurly Shield wins over Canterbury in 1971 and Wellington in 1974 and the All Blacks-Barbarians game at Twickenham in 1974.

On average, how many books do you read in a year?
Two or three, but lots of magazines.

Which TV channel do you watch most?
TV One, the Rugby Channel and Juice.

Did you play another sport after rugby? Tennis, golf and squash. I'm still playing golf often and tennis spasmodically. And still working out at the gym.

What is the most unusual thing you've achieved in your life?
Producing four children who have all been head prefects of large state schools — Mt Albert Grammar (two) and Auckland Girls Grammar (two).

Who was the most famous person you ever met?
Muhammad Ali and the Queen.

Who is the most eccentric coach you ever played under? None of note.

Who is the most eccentric team-mate you played alongside?
Kit Fawcett, who claimed in South Africa in 1976 that the team 'would score more off the field than on'.

What was the most amazing comment you ever heard on a rugby field?
Grahame Thorne said, 'Now you know what it was like to play outside you last year, Beegee' when I asked him if he could give me some ball. He constantly stepped off his left foot away from me, as I had done the year before.

What was your most embarrassing moment on the rugby field?
Trying to push Brian Ford into touch in the inter-island game in 1975.
He teetered along the sideline, recovered and ran 75 metres to score.
We lost the game. I had nowhere to hide.

What's the smartest bet you ever made? Never did.

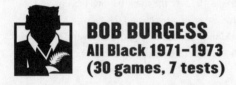

BOB BURGESS
All Black 1971–1973
(30 games, 7 tests)

What superstitions did you bring to rugby? That to get into the All Blacks
would require me running 100 miles a week.

In what circumstances did you first learn you had been selected for the
All Blacks? On the car radio coming back from beating Feilding (in 1971),
in the company of Judy and Lindsay Frazer of the Massey University
rugby club.

In what circumstances did you learn you were dropped from the All Blacks,
if you ever were? I withdrew to finish my MSc, then went to France to play
club rugby.

What was the first car you ever owned? A 1952 Ford Prefect.

What home-made dish did you miss most when you were touring overseas?
(1) My girlfriend and (2) roast potatoes.

What was your father's occupation?
He was a farm adviser with Department of Agriculture.

What town did your wife grow up in? Patea.

What was the best piece of sporting advice your father (or mother) ever
offered? Wash your own gear (from my mother).

At what age did you play your first game? Seven.

What was the greatest game you ever played in?
All Blacks against the Barbarians at Cardiff in 1973.

On average, how many books do you read in a year? Twenty-plus.

Which TV channel do you watch most? TV One.

Did you play another sport after rugby?
Tennis — weekly games with Chris Laidlaw and others.

What is the most unusual thing you've achieved in your life?
Earning a Ph.D.

Who was the most famous person you ever met?
(1) Spike Milligan; (2) Queen Elizabeth II.

Who is the most eccentric coach you ever played under?
Ian Colquhoun (1964–1966). He took us on annual pre-season runs over
Saddle Road (Ashhurst-Woodville) and along the Himitangi sand dunes.

Who is the most eccentric team-mate you played alongside?
Grant Batty. 'We're not going to get in, so let's have fun,' he said before the
North Island (early) trial in 1971.

What was the most amazing comment you ever heard on a rugby field?
'Gardes-toi, avec tes chaussures' (Take off your boots to defend yourself), as
we were leaving the field after winning an away game in the French national
competition in 1973–1974.

What was your most embarrassing moment on the rugby field?
Being knocked out by team-mate Jazz Muller in the third Lions test in 1971.

What's the smartest bet you ever made?
Saying that I'd come to France for their red wine (in an interview with
L'Equipe, 1973).

LAURIE MAINS
All Black 1971, 1976
(15 games, 4 tests)

What superstitions did you bring to rugby?
I always packed my gear and cleaned my boots the same way before every game.

In what circumstances did you first learn you had been selected for the All Blacks? Charlie Saxton rang me at home.

In what circumstances did you learn you were dropped from the All Blacks, if you ever were? I didn't see my name in the team published in the local paper.

What was the first car you ever owned? A Vauxhall.

What homemade dish did you miss most when you were touring overseas?
Roasts.

What was your father's occupation? He was a painter and decorator.

What town did your wife grow up in? Pretoria.

What was the best piece of sporting advice your father (or mother) ever offered? Just do your best, son, and enjoy it.

At what age did you play your first game? Six.

What was the greatest game you ever played in?
The second Lions test at Lancaster Park, Christchurch, in 1971.

On average, how many books do you read in a year? Two or three.

Which TV channel do you watch most? TV3 and Sky Sport.

Did you play another sport after rugby? Golf, and yes, I'm still playing.

What is the most unusual thing you've achieved in your life?
Coached Otago in more than 100 games after playing more than 100 games for the team.

Who was the most famous person you ever met?
Queen Elizabeth and Nelson Mandela.

Who is the most eccentric coach you ever played under?
I don't think I had one eccentric coach.

Who is the most eccentric team-mate you played alongside? Pass.

What was the most amazing comment you ever heard on a rugby field?
To a referee, 'Can I be penalised for thinking?' The answer was no. 'Then I think you are a prick!'

What was your most embarrassing moment on the rugby field?
Nothing stands out.

What's the smartest bet you ever made?
That the 2005 British Lions would be no good.

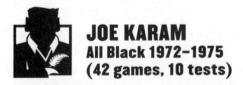

JOE KARAM
All Black 1972–1975
(42 games, 10 tests)

What superstitions did you bring to rugby? None.

In what circumstances did you first learn you had been selected for the All Blacks? Under the grandstand at Athletic Park after the final trial in 1972.

In what circumstances did you learn you were dropped from the All Blacks, if you ever were? Never was.

What was the first car you ever owned? A VW Beetle.

What home-made dish did you miss most when you were touring overseas?
Roast lamb (from the farm) with mint sauce, and fresh vegetables out of the garden.

What was your father's occupation? He was a farmer.

What town did your wife grow up in? Auckland.

What was the best piece of sporting advice your father (or mother) ever offered? Keep your eye on the ball.

At what age did you play your first game? Seven.

What was the greatest game you ever played in?
All Blacks against Wales at Cardiff in 1972 (we just got there, 19-16).

On average, how many books do you read in a year? One hundred.

Which TV channel do you watch most? Sky Sport and Sky Movies.

Did you play another sport after rugby? Tennis — and I'm still going.

What is the most unusual thing you've achieved in your life?
Becoming involved in a high-profile, hugely controversial crime investigation on behalf of David Bain.

Who was the most famous person you ever met? The Queen.

Who is the most eccentric coach you ever played under?
J.J. Stewart. He had us practise the up-the-jumper move and another one where the forwards threw Batty over the line-out holding the ball.

Who is the most eccentric team-mate you played alongside? No comment.

What was the most amazing comment you ever heard on a rugby field?
After I'd kicked off for the second half, Jazz Muller said, 'He's offside, ref.'
Ken Gray said, 'Take no notice, ref — he's forgotten we've changed ends!'

What was your most embarrassing moment on the rugby field?
Missing a conversion from in front of the posts against Fiji at the end of the 1974 Australia-Fiji tour. They nearly beat us.

What's the smartest bet you ever made?
Backing Muhammad Ali to beat George Foreman (the Rumble in the Jungle) with all my team-mates. The fight took place while we were in Singapore en route to Ireland in 1974.

BRUCE ROBERTSON
All Black 1972–1974, 1976–1981
(102 games, 34 tests)

What superstitions did you bring to rugby?
I tried to replicate the things I'd done when we'd won previous games.

In what circumstances did you first learn you had been selected for the All Blacks? I heard it from a person at a fish and chip shop in Gisborne.

In what circumstances did you learn you were dropped from the All Blacks, if you ever were? I was at a party at Peter Goldsmith's and they told me I'd missed out. They were all very apologetic!

What was the first car you ever owned? A Ford Anglia.

What home-made dish did you miss most when you were touring overseas?
Mum's chocolate chips.

What was your father's occupation?
He was a Post Office worker at Hastings.

What town did your wife grow up in? Hokianga, then Papakura.

What was the best piece of sporting advice your father (or mother) ever offered? Enjoy yourself and try your hardest.

At what age did you play your first game?
Five (as a prop for Mahora Primary).

What was the greatest game you ever played in?
The Welsh centenary test at Cardiff in 1980. It was my 100th game, and we won.

On average, how many books do you read in a year?
Two or three.

Which TV channel do you watch most? Sky Sport.

Did you play another sport after rugby?
Basketball (and became manager of the Manurewa rep side) and tennis
socially.

What is the most unusual thing you've achieved in your life?
Passing my music exams at Teachers College.

Who was the most famous person you ever met?
The Queen, Spike Milligan and Muhammad Ali.

Who is the most eccentric coach you ever played under? No comment.

Who is the most eccentric team-mate you played alongside?
Not exactly eccentric, but Stu Wilson provided plenty of laughs. He and
Bernie Fraser took photos of each other at halftime during a game in Fiji.

What was the most amazing comment you ever heard on a rugby field? In
a game between Counties and Wellington, Counties was on attack and Stu
Wilson was standing by the goalposts. He then hid himself behind the goalpost
and said, 'Now you see me, now you don't.'

What was your most embarrassing moment on the rugby field?
Probably during the Welsh test in 1978 when I made a shocker of a pass
to Stu Wilson.

What's the smartest bet you ever made?
I bet my best mate I would date Nellie before he did. Thirty years later,
we're still going.

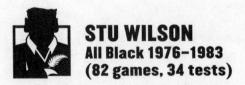

STU WILSON
All Black 1976–1983
(82 games, 34 tests)

What superstitions did you bring to rugby?
Before every training run and game, I always put on my gear from top to
bottom, i.e. jersey first, shorts, socks and then the boots, with the left boot first
and right boot last.

In what circumstances did you first learn you had been selected for the All Blacks? After the 1976 NPC game against Otago at Dunedin the Wellington team was staying at the Beach Hotel. I was in the men's toilet taking a tinkle when the Wellington manager came in and said, 'You're in the All Blacks!' I didn't know whether to shake his hand or piddle over his trousers.

In what circumstances did you learn you were dropped from the All Blacks, if you ever were? Never was.

What was the first car you ever owned? A VW Beetle.

What homemade dish did you miss most when you were touring overseas?
Roast lamb with mint sauce.

What was your father's occupation?
He was the manager of a stock and station company.

What was the best piece of sporting advice your father (or mother) ever offered? They said it would not be easy. They just said it would be worth it.

At what age did you play your first game? Six.

What was the greatest game you ever played in?
The All Blacks against the Springboks — the 'flour bomb' test — at Eden Park in 1981.

On average, how many books do you read in a year? About a dozen.

Which TV channel do you watch most? Sky's MGM movie channel.

Did you play another sport after rugby?
Golf. I hack around badly on a nine handicap.

What is the most unusual thing you've achieved in your life?
Playing my father in the senior men's golf final at the Lansdowne Club in Masterton when I was still at school. I lost the 36-hole final 3 and 2.

Who was the most famous person you ever met?
Her Majesty the Queen . . . at her house.

Who is the most eccentric coach you ever played under?
Eric Watson, who allowed Malcolm Hood, the All Blacks physio,
to take a warm-up, but instead of using rugby balls we used bricks.
Imagine kicking one!

Who is the most eccentric team-mate you played alongside?
Nicky Allen. On the morning of the Welsh centennial test in 1980, when we
were rooming together, I found him standing naked in front of the bathroom
mirror, oil all over his body, posing like a body builder. I asked him if he
was nervous. He replied, 'What do you think?'

What was the most amazing comment you ever heard on a rugby field?
Wellington captain Paul Quinn had been in the ear of a referee all day, until
finally the referee erupted: 'Quinn, who's refereeing this game, you or me?'
Paul smiled benignly and said, 'Neither of us.'

What was your most embarrassing moment on the rugby field?
Hitting Stan Pilecki, the Wallaby prop, in the back of the head during a test
at the Sydney Cricket Ground. The problem was Stan never felt it and I broke
two bones in my hand.

What's the smartest bet you ever made?
Putting $100 on the All Blacks to beat the 2005 Lions 3-nil in the test series at
$2.75.

DAVE LOVERIDGE
All Black 1977–1983, 1985
(54 games, 24 tests)

What superstitions did you bring to rugby?
I always put my left boot on first. It seemed to work most times.

*In what circumstances did you first learn you had been selected for the
All Blacks?* Heard it on the radio at an after-match function (in 1978).

*In what circumstances did you learn you were dropped from the All Blacks,
if you ever were?* Never was.

What was the first car you ever owned? A Ford Anglia.

What home-made dish did you miss most when you were touring overseas?
Pork roast.

What was your father's occupation? He was a farmer.

What town did your wife grow up in?
Takapuna in North Shore City.

***What was the best piece of sporting advice your father (or mother) ever
offered?*** Don't ever give up.

At what age did you play your first game? Five or six.

What was the greatest game you ever played in?
The Welsh centenary test at Cardiff in 1980.

On average, how many books do you read in a year? One or two.

Which TV channel do you watch most? TV One and Sky Sport.

Did you play another sport after rugby?
Cricket, till the body gave out.

What is the most unusual thing you've achieved in your life?
Ran a marathon for a bet, being well overweight when I took the bet.

Who was the most famous person you ever met? The Queen.

Who is the most eccentric coach you ever played under?
Eric Watson, who reckoned the only reason he went on the field at halftime
was to turn the forwards around.

Who is the most eccentric team-mate you played alongside? Pass.

What was the most amazing comment you ever heard on a rugby field?
Referee Roger Quittenton to Mark Donaldson, after Donaldson had
hit an opponent when the All Blacks were playing Glasgow in 1979,
'If you so much as fart out of tune, you're off!'

What was your most embarrassing moment on the rugby field?
Getting knocked out when trying to stop Ray Mordt scoring a try
in the third Springbok test in 1981.

What's the smartest bet you ever made?
Bet I could race the fastest player in our team. He won but I still raced him.

ALLAN HEWSON
All Black 1979, 1980–1984
(34 games, 19 tests)

What superstitions did you bring to rugby?
Only that I always had baked beans for Saturday lunch before every game.

In what circumstances did you first learn you had been selected for the
All Blacks? Russ Thomas (All Blacks manager) told Bernie Fraser and
me we had been selected for the 1979 tour of the UK, on a plane going to
Christchurch.

In what circumstances did you learn you were dropped from the All Blacks,
if you ever were? While watching TV in the Angus Inn Sports Bar with
a mate.

What was the first car you ever owned? A Mini Minor.

What home-made dish did you miss most when you were touring overseas?
Roast lamb.

What was your father's occupation? He was a headmaster.

What town did your wife grow up in?
Lower Hutt (but she supported Petone!).

What was the best piece of sporting advice your father (or mother) ever
offered? You will never get paid to play sport!

At what age did you play your first game? Five.

What was the greatest game you ever played in?
I don't know about the greatest but the most bizarre obviously was the 1981 Springbok test at Eden Park, when we were buzzed by the Cessna and I kicked the winning goal.

On average, how many books do you read in a year? Six.

Which TV channel do you watch most? Sky Sport.

Did you play another sport after rugby?
Played senior cricket for 25 years. Now into golf.

What is the most unusual thing you've achieved in your life?
Being married for 30 years.

Who was the most famous person you ever met?
Bob Scott and George Nepia — my fullback heroes.

Who is the most eccentric coach you ever played under?
Earle Kirton, famous for the wine and the scarf.

Who is the most eccentric team-mate you played alongside?
Stu Wilson. Too many examples to give.

What was the most amazing comment you ever heard on a rugby field?
There are two examples, actually: Stu Wilson, when at the bottom of a ruck, asking the Auckland forwards if they could tell him the time; and Stu Wilson asking Gary Cunningham to hurry up and score so he could see what the other side of halfway looked like.

What was your most embarrassing moment on the rugby field?
Drinking sherry at halftime during a club match in my early days. I was told I was meant to spit it out!

What's the smartest bet you ever made?
I selected a horse for my grandfather when I was 11 and he gave me the money when it won.

MURRAY MEXTED
All Black 1979–1985
(72 games, 34 tests)

What superstitions did you bring to rugby? I didn't have any.

*In what circumstances did you first learn you had been selected for the
All Blacks?* I sat in a PA Vauxhall outside the Wellington Football Club lounge
(in 1979), listening to the team announcement on the 6 o'clock news.
I heard my name and returned to the bar.

*In what circumstances did you learn you were dropped from the All Blacks,
if you ever were?* Fortunately, I was never dropped.

What was the first car you ever owned? A 1957 Morris Minor.

What home-made dish did you miss most when you were touring overseas?
Roast lamb.

What was your father's occupation?
He was a motor company proprietor.

What town did your wife grow up in? Auckland.

*What was the best piece of sporting advice your father (or mother) ever
offered?* Dad said to me once, 'Murray, as the level gets higher, you play
better, so you'll be okay.' That sort of advice gives you an inner confidence
and security, which I owe to both parents.

At what age did you play your first game? Six.

What was the greatest game you ever played in?
The Springbok 'flour bomb' test of 1981 at Eden Park.

On average, how many books do you read in a year?
One, and thousands of articles.

Which TV channel do you watch most? J2 music channel.

Did you play another sport after rugby?
Surfing, and I'll still be surfing when I'm 100.

What is the most unusual thing you've achieved in your life?
I couldn't possibly put that in writing.

Who was the most famous person you ever met? Prince Charles.

Who is the most eccentric coach you ever played under?
Bryce Rope, a delightful character who used to talk about
the 'hinge' of a door when discussing how a team should operate.
The top hinge was the loose forwards, the middle hinge the tight forwards
and the bottom hinge the backs. We are all still trying to work it out. All I
remember is that after each match we used to toast 'The Hinge'.

Who is the most eccentric team-mate you played alongside?
Stu Wilson, because he had absolutely no game plan or idea what he or the
team was going to do next. All he wanted was the ball, which is why we
nicknamed him 'Gizza'.

What was the most amazing comment you ever heard on a rugby field?
Stu Wilson asking an opponent 'Where's the party tonight?' at a particularly
aggressive moment in a test match against Australia.

What was your most embarrassing moment on the rugby field?
Can't think of one.

What's the smartest bet you ever made?
Don't think I've ever made a smart bet.

JOCK HOBBS
All Black 1983–1986
(39 games, 21 tests)

What superstitions did you bring to rugby?
I had routines rather than superstitions. For Canterbury, the loose forward trio
wore pink woollen vests given to us by team-mate Don Hayes on match day.

In what circumstances did you first learn you had been selected for the All Blacks? Via the live television announcement whilst at the Christchurch RFU clubrooms (in 1983).

In what circumstances did you learn you were dropped from the All Blacks, if you ever were? I retired due to injury.

What was the first car you ever owned? A red Mini van.

What was your father's occupation? He was a judge.

What town did your wife grow up in? Cheviot, North Canterbury.

What was the best piece of sporting advice your father (or mother) ever offered? My father, before offering any rugby advice, would always begin, 'I know nothing about rugby . . .' He was right!

At what age did you play your first game? Five.

What was the greatest game you ever played in?
Canterbury against Auckland in the epic Ranfurly Shield match of 1985; the All Blacks against the Lions, fourth test of the 1983 series.

On average, how many books do you read in a year? Twenty.

Which TV channel do you watch most? TV One.

Did you play another sport after rugby?
Social tennis and golf, but not any longer.

What is the most unusual thing you've achieved in your life?
Crutching 100 ewes in one day.

Who was the most famous person you ever met? Prince William.

Who is the most eccentric coach you ever played under?
'Peg' Wairau, of the Christchurch senior team. He organised line-out practices without the ball. He questioned the lock, 'Why haven't you jumped?' 'Because he hasn't thrown the ball in yet!'

Who is the most eccentric team-mate you played alongside?
Stu Wilson and Bernie Fraser — anything could happen at any time, and usually did.

What was the most amazing comment you ever heard on a rugby field?
An on-field, halftime team talk from Alex Wyllie. 'You're all bloody useless,' — and he walked off.

What was your most embarrassing moment on the rugby field?
Joining the wrong scrum after another concussion.

What's the smartest best you ever made? To marry Nicky Deans.

GRANT FOX
All Black 1984–1993
(78 games, 46 tests)

What superstitions did you bring to rugby?
I always put my right boot on last.

In what circumstances did you first learn you had been selected for the All Blacks? I heard it on the radio (in 1984).

In what circumstances did you learn you were dropped from the All Blacks, if you ever were? The coach (Laurie Mains) told me before the World XV series in 1992.

What was the first car you ever owned? A VW.

What home-made dish did you miss most when you were touring overseas?
Roast lamb.

What was your father's occupation?
He was a farmer, then a kiwi fruit orchardist.

What town did your wife grow up in? Auckland.

***What was the best piece of sporting advice your father (or mother) ever
offered?*** Practice leads to precision.

At what age did you play your first game? Six.

What was the greatest game you ever played in?
The 1987 World Cup final against France at Eden Park.

On average, how many books do you read in a year? Lucky if it's one.

Which TV channel do you watch most? Sky Sport.

Did you play another sport after rugby? Golf, and I'm still at it.

What is the most unusual thing you've achieved in your life?
Scoring two eagles in the one round of golf (on a par 4 and a par 5).

Who was the most famous person you ever met? The Queen.

Who is the most eccentric coach you ever played under?
None of them were eccentric.

Who is the most eccentric team-mate you played alongside?
Undoubtedly the bunch of hard-case players who were in the University senior
team of the early 1980s, including Greg Denholm, John Drake and Phil Halse.
They used to wisecrack their way through most games. Halse once asked the
referee if he could penalise him for thinking. The ref said no, so Halse said to
him, 'Well, I think you're a prick!'

What was the most amazing comment you ever heard on a rugby field?
At the conclusion of the first test in Sydney in 1992, which the All Blacks lost
after I'd missed a late shot at goal, I was sitting disconsolately on the ground
with my head in my hands when David Campese came up. 'Are you all right?'
he asked. 'What the hell do you think!' I snapped back. In a club game at
Eden Park, I remember our University No 8. John McDermott calling 'Mine!'
as a kick wafted towards him. But as the wind carried it over his head, he
suddenly changed tack: 'Oh, no, yours!'

What was your most embarrassing moment on the rugby field?
Playing against Manawatu in 1984, I was sick of being late-tackled. After one

more, I got up and took a swing at the perpetrator, missed and swung myself right off my feet!

What's the smartest bet you ever made? I don't gamble.

IAN JONES
All Black 1989–1999
(105 games, 79 tests)

What superstitions did you bring to rugby?
I always sat in the same spot in the changing room. And I put shin pads, socks and boots on my right leg first.

In what circumstances did you first learn you had been selected for the All Blacks? Watching the 6 o'clock TV news at home (in 1989).

In what circumstances did you learn you were dropped from the All Blacks, if you ever were? Heard it on the news on a Sunday afternoon.

What was the first car you ever owned? I had a third-share in a Humber 80.

What home-made dish did you miss most when you were touring overseas?
Raw fish salad.

What was your father's occupation? He was a service station proprietor.

What town did your wife grow up in? Whangarei.

What was the best piece of sporting advice your father (or mother) ever offered? Work hard (from Mum).

At what age did you play your first game? Five, for Kamo.

What was the greatest game you ever played in?
The 1995 World Cup final against the Springboks at Ellis Park.

On average, how many books do you read in a year?
Twenty to twenty-five.

Which TV channel do you watch most? I'm a channel surfer.

Did you play another sport after rugby? No.

What is the most unusual thing you've achieved in your life? Not unusual, but my best achievement is being a father to Flynn, Mia and Noah.

Who was the most famous person you ever met? The Queen.

Who is the most eccentric coach you ever played under?
I didn't have any eccentric coaches.

Who is the most eccentric team-mate you played alongside? I think I was.

What was the most amazing comment you ever heard on a rugby field?
During a North Auckland-Otago NPC game, while playing with a broken nose (that I thought nobody knew about), an Otago forward ran past and said, 'How's the nose?' Put me right off!

What was your most embarrassing moment on the rugby field?
Don't remember embarrassing myself on the field. Plenty of times off it, though.

What's the smartest bet you ever made?
Playing the last three years of my career in England.

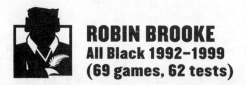

ROBIN BROOKE
All Black 1992–1999
(69 games, 62 tests)

What superstitions did you bring to rugby?
None, but many I've played with certainly did have. In Italy, they would put their socks on before their speedos, and, oh boy, did they rate themselves nude!

In what circumstances did you first learn you had been selected for the All Blacks? Out of the blue, I was visiting brother Zinzan in hospital (in 1992). I'd taken him a 14-inch TV to watch. We set it up and, on his insistence, I stayed to watch the 6 o'clock news and sport. When they read my name out I was totally floored.

In what circumstances did you learn you were dropped from the All Blacks, if you ever were? It was after the 1999 World Cup. I knew what was coming, so it didn't hit me hard.

What was the first car you ever owned? A Toyota Corolla.

What home-made dish did you miss most when you were touring overseas? Mum's mince pie made with real lard!

What was your father's occupation?
He was a farmer, taxi driver, comedian and all-round good bugger.

What town did your wife grow up in? Titirangi, in Auckland.

What was the best piece of sporting advice your father (or mother) ever offered? Never start a fight, but if one breaks out, finish it (from Dad). You can be anything you want to be (from Mum).

At what age did you play your first game? Five.

What was the greatest game you ever played in?
Even though we lost, it would have to be the World Cup final against South Africa at Ellis Park in 1995.

On average, how many books do you read in a year? Twenty.

Which TV channel do you watch most?
Entertainment, when my wife has the remote; channel 42 when she puts it down.

Did you play another sport after rugby?
Golf, and I hope to keep playing it till I need both hips replaced.

What is the most unusual thing you've achieved in your life?
Participating in the World Cup of elephant polo in Thailand in 2005.

Who was the most famous person you ever met?
Lady Di. I told her I was a shark hunter, and she believed me.

Who is the most eccentric coach you ever played under?
Gianni from Italy, the most passionate, full-of-himself person I ever met. He was so eccentric, the team held a meeting during one of his team talks, and sacked him, mid-season!

Who is the most eccentric team-mate you played alongside?
Andrew Mehrtens — intelligent, funny, energetic. When he's awake, he's talking and cracking jokes on and off the field. His batteries definitely last longer.

What was the most amazing comment you ever heard on a rugby field?
Nothing springs to mind.

What was your most embarrassing moment on the rugby field?
When Sean Fitzpatrick hit a ruck hard, clobbering me with his hard head and bursting my ear drum. It affected my balance. I was missing kick-offs by two metres for the rest of the game.

What's the smartest bet you ever made?
Not to be lured into bets when drinking with Olo Brown. No one would ever have bet against him.

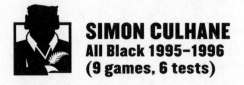

SIMON CULHANE
All Black 1995–1996
(9 games, 6 tests)

What superstitions did you bring to rugby? I had to have my match-day undies.

In what circumstances did you first learn you had been selected for the All Blacks? The squad was named (in 1995) after the final trial in Whangarei. It was nerve-wracking.

In what circumstances did you learn you were dropped from the All Blacks, if you ever were? Whilst on tour in Britain in 1997 with the Otago Highlanders.

What was the first car you ever owned? A Subaru 1600 DL.

What home-made dish did you miss most when you were touring overseas?
A good mince pie.

What was your father's occupation? He was a petrol tanker driver.

What town did your wife grow up in? Invercargill.

What was the best piece of sporting advice your father (or mother) ever offered? Be humble whether you win or lose.

At what age did you play your first game? Six.

What was the greatest game you ever played in?
The two tests against the Springboks, at Durban and Pretoria, that set up the All Blacks' first series win on South African soil in 1996.

On average, how many books do you read in a year? Six.

Which TV channel do you watch most? Sky Sport.

Did you play another sport after rugby? A little cricket, but not any longer.

What is the most unusual thing you've achieved in your life?
Being part of an All Black team that won a World Cup game 145-17!

Who was the most famous person you ever met? Nelson Mandela.

Who is the most eccentric coach you ever played under?
Gordon Hunter — some of his team talks were definitely from left field.

Who is the most eccentric team-mate you played alongside?
It would have to be Marc Ellis, who was always putting his foot in it.

What was the most amazing comment you ever heard on a rugby field?
Zinzan Brooke asking one of the Southland forwards if his sprigs were plastic, after he'd been dealt to.

What was your most embarrassing moment on the rugby field?
Missing an important easy kick.

What's the smartest bet you ever made? I'm not a punter.

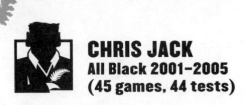

CHRIS JACK
All Black 2001–2005
(45 games, 44 tests)

What superstitions did you bring to rugby?
I always try to wear the same pair of undies, which in 2005 were a blue pair, and I always warm up in my jersey.

In what circumstances did you first learn you had been selected for the All Blacks? My Aunty Jennifer left a message on my cellphone as I was in a meeting when the team was announced (in 2001).

In what circumstances did you learn you were dropped from the All Blacks, if you ever were? Haven't suffered that fate yet, but I'm always nervous about phone calls before the team is announced.

What was the first car you ever owned? A 1971 lime green Holden Kingswood.

What home-made dish did you miss most when you were touring overseas? Mashed potatoes.

What was your father's occupation? He worked in the wool industry.

What town did your wife grow up in? Christchurch.

What was the best piece of sporting advice your father (or mother) ever offered? Go hard, son.

At what age did you play your first game? Ten.

What was the greatest game you ever played in?
The Welsh test at Cardiff in 2004, when we held on by a point, and the Bledisloe Cup game in Sydney in 2005 when we came from 0-13 down to win 30-13.

On average, how many books do you read in a year? Three or four.

Which TV channel do you watch most? TV2.

Did you play another sport after rugby? Haven't had to worry about this yet.

What is the most unusual thing you've achieved in your life?
As a teenager, painting a Mazda to look like a *Dukes of Hazzard* car and entering it in a rally.

Who was the most famous person you ever met?
Prince William and Nelson Mandela.

Who is the most eccentric coach you ever played under?
A Frenchman called Arkley, who just kept passing the ball about. No one understood what he was saying.

Who is the most eccentric team-mate you played alongside?
Norm Maxwell — he kept his wardrobe in the boot of his car.

What was the most amazing comment you ever heard on a rugby field?
After we drew a match nil-all once, a team-mate reckoned the outcome was like kissing your sister.

What was your most embarrassing moment on the rugby field?
Giving the crowd in Paris an interesting view when somehow my shorts came down in a maul.

What's the smartest bet you ever made? Not into gambling.

RICHIE McCAW
All Black 2001–2005
(33 games, 33 tests)

What superstitions did you bring to rugby?
None really, except I never vary my warm-up routine.

In what circumstances did you first learn you had been selected for the All Blacks? Listening to the radio with my family.

In what circumstances did you learn you were dropped from the All Blacks, if you ever were? Fortunately, I haven't been, yet.

What was the first car you ever owned? A Mazda 323.

What home-made dish did you miss most when you were touring overseas?
Home-cooked roast.

What was your father's occupation? He's a farmer.

What town did your wife grow up in? Not married.

What was the best piece of sporting advice your father (or mother) ever offered? Have a go, and let there be no 'what ifs?'.

At what age did you play your first game? Eight.

What was the greatest game you ever played in?
My All Black test debut (against Ireland at Dublin in 2001) when I was just 20.

On average, how many books do you read in a year? Ten to fifteen.

Which TV channel do you watch most? TV One.

Did you play another sport after rugby? Have not finished playing rugby yet.

What is the most unusual thing you have achieved in your life?
I learnt to play the bagpipes.

Who is the most famous person you ever met? Prince William.

Who is the most eccentric team-mate you played alongside?
Norm Maxwell, who once turned up for a big match with two left boots.
On another occasion, having forgotten his dress shoes, he took the studs off
his rugby boots and wore them to a formal function.

What was the most amazing comment you ever heard on a rugby field?
The most annoying was George Gregan reminding us we'd have to wait
another four years when the Wallabies were beating us in the 2003 World Cup
semi-final in Sydney. There was nothing we could say back.

What was your most embarrassing moment on the rugby field?
Trying to go head to head with Bulls prop Richard Bands and being KO'd.

What's the smartest bet you ever made?
Leaving Otago when I finished school.

AARON MAUGER
All Black 2001–2005
(31 games, 30 tests)

What superstitions did you bring to rugby?
From 1999 to 2003 I wore the same pair of green Speedos underwear for every game, until they were stolen by my brother Nathan, who wore them for the rest of the season.

In what circumstances did you first learn you had been selected for the All Blacks? Joe Maddock and Leon MacDonald knocked on my door 10 minutes after the team was announced for the 2001 tour.

In what circumstances did you learn you were dropped from the All Blacks, if you ever were? Have only ever missed selection through injury.

What was the first car you ever owned? A Mazda Eunos.

What home-made dish did you miss most when you were touring overseas?
Bacon and sausage pasta.

What was your father's occupation? He's a builder.

What town did your wife grow up in? Blenheim.

What was the best piece of sporting advice your father (or mother) ever offered? The bigger they are, the harder they fall (from Dad). Never give up (from Mum).

At what age did you play your first game? Five.

What was the greatest game you ever played in?
Crusaders against the Waratahs at Jade Stadium, 2002 (we won 96-19) and the Canterbury-Wellington Ranfurly Shield game in 2001.

On average, how many books do you read in a year? Six.

Which TV channel do you watch most? TV3 News and Sky Movies.

Did you play another sport after rugby? Not finished playing rugby yet.

What is the most unusual thing you've achieved in your life?
This information cannot be disclosed.

Who was the most famous person you ever met?
Princess Anne and Maurice Green.

Who is the most eccentric coach you ever played under? No comment.

Who is the most eccentric team-mate you played alongside?
Norm Maxwell . . . a wonderful character.

What was the most amazing comment you ever heard on a rugby field?
A South African player made a comment to me in 2003 that sounded
impressive, but as he was speaking Afrikaans, I couldn't understand it!

What was your most embarrassing moment on the rugby field?
Missing a kick pretty much in front of the posts against the Highlanders in
2000.

What's the smartest bet you ever made? Collecting $7000 for a $16 easy-bet.

The ultimate
All Black
pub quiz

Q. During their Australian tour, the 1920 All Blacks played a match at Taree against which, possibly wet, team?

– Manning River District.

Q. The 1925 All Blacks to Australia played a match against E.J. Thorn's XV at Manly. Who was E.J. Thorn and what position did he hold?

– E.J. Thorn was Ted Thorn, president of the Manly club.

Q. Which team did the All Blacks play at Toowomba during their 1932 tour of Australia?

– Darling Downs.

Q. The 1935–1936 All Blacks toured Canada on their way back from a tour of Britain. Which two teams did they play in Canada, and where?

– Vancouver at Vancouver and Victoria at Victoria.

Q. The 1949 All Blacks tour of South Africa produced some interesting doubles. Which two teams did the tourists meet twice on the tour, and what were the results (win, lose or draw)?

– They played the province of Border twice and Rhodesia twice. The All Blacks failed to win any of these games, losing to and drawing with Border, and doing the same against Rhodesia.

Q. Which Australian team gave the 1925 All Blacks their only defeat?

– New South Wales Second XV.

Q. The 1953–1954 All Blacks, toured Britain, France and North America. They played two matches in France — who were these games against and what were the results?

– They played South West France at Bordeaux and France in Paris, and lost both games.

Q. In which town with a religious connection did the 1970 All Blacks play the Paul Roos Team?

– Bethlehem (in South Africa).

Q. The 1976 All Black tourists to Argentina played a game against one other South American country. Which country, and in what city?

– Uruguay at Montevideo.

Q. What holiday destination was the venue for the 1984 All Blacks' game against Queensland Country?

– Surfers Paradise.

Q. The 1984 All Black tourists to Fiji played two geographical XVs. What were they?

– A Western XV and an Eastern XV.

Q. In 1988 the All Blacks played a club side when touring Australia. Which club?

– Sydney club Randwick.

Q. The 1995 World Cup All Blacks' executive team featured four former All Blacks. Who were they and what roles did they have?

– Laurie Mains (coach), Earle Kirton (assistant coach), Brian Lochore (campaign manager) and Colin Meads (manager).

Q. Name the coach, two assistant coaches and manager of the 1996 All Blacks that toured Australia and South Africa and identify which of them were All Blacks themselves.

– Coach John Hart, assistant coaches Gordon Hunter and Ross Cooper, manager Mike Banks. None were former All Blacks.

Q. New Zealand's first ever game at home was played against New South Wales at Christchurch in 1894. What was the outcome?

– New South Wales won 8–6.

Q. Queensland first toured New Zealand in 1896, and played one game against New Zealand at Wellington. What was the result?

– New Zealand won 9–nil.

Q. Australia first toured New Zealand in 1905, and played one test against New Zealand while the Originals were on their way to Britain. Who won?

– New Zealand won 14–3.

Q. Which unusual British team toured New Zealand in 1908?

– The Anglo-Welsh, minus Scotsmen and Irishmen.

Q. There are eight occasions in which the All Blacks have lost a test match to the touring Australians, yet still managed to win the series. Name four of the years in which this happened.

– 1913, 1952, 1955, 1958, 1964, 1978, 1982 and 1990.

Q. The All Blacks have won test matches 10-9 on three occasions. Name the losing team and the year.

− British Isles in 1977, France in 1984 and Australia in 1985.

Q. The All Blacks have been involved in five test matches with a score of 13-12. Name the two opposition teams involved and state how many of these five games were won by the All Blacks.

− The two opposition teams are Australia and Wales. New Zealand has won 13-12 on three occasions: the second test against Australia in 1986; the first test against Australia in 1978 and the test against Wales in 1978. New Zealand lost 12-13 in the first test against Australia in 1986 and also against Wales in 1935.

Q. Earle Kirton had a rather inauspicious start to his All Black career. What did he do?

− He dropped the first pass he received as an All Black − against Newport.

Q. What dietary sin did Earle Kirton commit before taking the field for the All Blacks against an Under 24 selection in Vancouver?

− He ate a hot dog 30 minutes before the game. Neither he nor the team played well.

Q. Public address system announcements today normally acknowledge sponsors, but during the 1963 match between Aberavon and Neath and the All Blacks, something very different was advertised. What was it?

− A chrysanthemum show.

Q. What medical treatment did Stan Meads require at Oxford during the All Blacks' 1963–1964 tour?

− He had to have a carbuncle lanced.

Q. As well as appearing for the All Blacks during the team's 1963–1964 tour, Waka Nathan also appeared on Welsh TV. Doing what?

− He sang and played guitar.

Q. On the 1963–1964 All Blacks tour, Derek Arnold scored three tries while playing out on the wing against Glasgow and Edinburgh at Glasgow. What was unusual about this?

— He'd been moved to that position from second-five because he was injured.

Q. Two All Black locks on the 1963–1964 tour to Britain, France and Canada suffered from appendicitis. Who were they?

— Stan Meads and Ron Horsley.

Q. What three items of apparel did Kevin 'Monkey' Briscoe wear when acting as the Judge of the Court during All Black mock court sessions?

— A full-bottomed wig, white sheet and spectacles.

Q. What was All Black Paul Little's occupation?

— He was a barber and used to cut the All Blacks' hair when they were on tour.

Q. Paul Little's nickname was 'Okey'. What was it short for?

— 'Pinocchio'.

Q. What act of support from a fan during the trial match at Wellington is said to have advanced Brian Lochore's All Black prospects?

— A lone voice in the crowd bellowing out 'Lochore, Lochore' throughout the game.

Q. When Jonah Lomu ran over Mike Catt in 1995 to score against England he was the second All Black to treat an English opponent like this. Who was the first, and who was his victim?

— Colin Meads ran over the top of England fullback John Willcox in 1964 on his way to scoring a vital try.

Q. What unusual footwear did Dennis Young, the champion All Black hooker of the 1960s, wear on the field?

— He wore boots made of kangaroo hide, without heels, to help him hook the ball more swiftly.

Q. What act by Ralph Caulton led to the All Blacks losing to South African Combined Services in 1960?

— A wild fly kick.

Q. What swimming record did Chris Laidlaw once hold?

— The national junior men's 50 yard butterfly.

THE BOOTS ARE MADE OF 'ROO SKIN!!

© DARYL CRIMP

Q. At what two other sports did Laidlaw represent Otago before making his mark as a rugby player?

– Basketball (he was an Otago junior rep) and surfing (he represented Otago in the national surf lifesaving champs in Wellington after winning the Otago surf race title).

Q. Who was the first All Black to make two full-scale tours of the British Isles and in what years?

– Ian Clarke— in 1953–1954 and 1963–1964.

Q. What was unusual about the seven tries scored by the 1963–1964 All Blacks in their 39-3 victory over British Columbia?

– All were scored by forwards.

Q. Which occupation had the greatest representation in the 1963-1964 All Black tourists to Britain, France and Canada?

– Farming. There were eight farmers in the squad.

Q. Dropped goals were a feature of the All Blacks' 1963–1964 tour to Britain, France and Canada. How many were kicked in total

and which two players kicked
the most?

– There were 19 kicked in
total. Both Don Clarke and
Mac Herewini kicked five
dropped goals.

Q. Who were the two fullbacks
in the 1976 All Black touring
team to South Africa who had
represented Otago?

– Laurie Mains and Kit
Fawcett, both from Otago.

Q. Which two sets of brothers
travelled with the All Blacks
to France in 1990?

– Rob and Steve Gordon,
and Gary and Alan
Whetton.

Q. Which two sets of brothers
travelled with the All Blacks
to Britain and France in
1963–1964?

– Don and Ian Clarke, and
Colin and Stan Meads.

Q. Name the Australian invitation
player who appeared for the 1960
All Blacks against Queensland
on a day when the All Black
touring party was committed
to playing two games and had
injuries in the ranks.

– Maurice Graham.

Q. How many All Black trial
matches were held in 1948, prior
to the selection of the 1949 team
to tour South Africa?

– Sixteen.

Q. What medical misadventure kept
'Opai' Asher from playing rugby
for two years?

– He suffered a serious leg
injury while on duty as a
fire brigade officer in 1904.

Q. How many test matches did
brothers Graeme and Stephen
Bachop play together in 1994?

– Four.

Q. Who was the first New Zealand
rep rugby player to die?

– William Millton, who died
from typhoid in 1887.

Q. In what year was the first direct
telecast of an All Black test;
where was it and who were the
opposition?

– The first game to be
televised live was the third
test against Australia
at Eden Park in 1972.

Q. Which government cancelled the
scheduled 1973 South African
tour of New Zealand?

– The Labour Government.

Q. Against which team did the All Blacks play their first match of the professional era?

— Italy A in Sicily in 1995.

Q. Against which team did the All Blacks play their first test match of the professional era?

— Italy, also in 1995.

Q. How many times was Colin Meads dropped from the All Blacks?

— Twice.

Q. How many times was Kelvin Tremain dropped from the All Blacks?

— Twice, the second time (1969) permanently.

Q. The 1921 series against the Springboks saw the playing status of Teddy Roberts, generally regarded as New Zealand's best back, change at each of the three tests. What status did he hold for each game?

— He was not selected for the first test, was in the playing line-up for the second and was captain for the third.

Q. Who is the youngest player to be dropped from the All Blacks?

— Jonah Lomu, who was 19 when he was dropped after the two-match series against France in 1994.

Q. What was unusual about 1976 All Black replacement Perry Harris' test debut?

— He had never before even seen the All Blacks play.

Q. What was unusual about Brian Lochore's recall for the vital third test against the 1971 Lions?

— He had retired. And he was asked to play out of position, as a lock.

Q. Fifteen new caps have played for the All Blacks against Australia twice. In what years, and why?

— In 1903, because it was the All Blacks first ever test, and in 1946, because of the effects of the Second World War.

Q. How many new caps played South Africa in 1921 and why?

— Fourteen, because of the effects of the First World War.

Q. Why did 13 new caps appear against Australia in 1949?

— The 'top 30' were on duty touring South Africa.

Q. How many new caps appeared in the 'Baby Blacks', in 1986, when most of the top players were under suspension following the Cavaliers' tour to South Africa?

– Ten.

Q. Colin Meads suffered what medical problem after captaining the All Blacks in the 1971 series against the Lions?

– A serious back injury from a motor accident.

Q. What was unusual about Duncan Robertson's two tests against South Africa in 1976?

– He played at fullback, not his usual first-five.

Q. At what position did fullback Tony Davies play in the deciding fourth test against South Africa in 1960?

– First-five.

Q. Marc Ellis made his test debut against Scotland in 1993. In which position did he operate?

– First-five.

Q. In what position was Leon MacDonald selected for the 2003 World Cup squad?

– Fullback.

Q. In what position did Brian McKechnie, selected as a first-five, appear in the two tests against France at Toulouse and Paris in 1977?

– Fullback.

Q. It was third time lucky for David Kirk in 1987, when he was given the captaincy of the New Zealand World Cup squad. Who had been the two preferred captains?

– Jock Hobbs and Andy Dalton.

Q. What do the following nine players — Ken Bloxham, Grant Perry, Tony Kreft, Roger Boon, Lindsay Clark, Sandy McNicol, Brian Hegarty, Peter Hurley and Perry Harris — have in common?

– They were all called up as replacements during the course of All Black tours. Neither Hegarty nor Hurley got to take the field.

Q. Aside from the similarity in their names, what do Stuart Conn (Auckland) and Stewart Cron (Canterbury) have in common?

– They were both loose forwards, and both played for the All Blacks in the same year — 1976.

179

Q. Name the player who twice turned down an invitation to travel as an All Black replacement.

– Greg Denholm, who declined both offers because of his business commitments.

Q. When did New Zealand first lose a test series, and to whom?

– In 1929, when they lost three tests to Australia.

Q. Which All Black team created a sensation by losing two tests on the same day?

– In 1949 the All Blacks lost two tests on 3 September — at Wellington and Durban.

Q. How many test tries did Joe Rokocoko score in the 2003 season?

– Seventeen (in 12 tests).

Q. Who was the first All Black to land six penalty goals in a test?

– Don Clarke, against the British Lions at Carisbrook in 1959.

Q. How many times did Grant Fox kick six penalty goals in All Black tests?

– Three times, against Argentina, Scotland and France. He also kicked seven penalty goals against Samoa.

Q. How many times did Andrew Mehrtens kick six penalty goals in All Black tests? And what was the maximum number of penalties Mehrtens scored in an All Black game?

– Four times, against Australia, Ireland, South Africa and Scotland. The maximum number he kicked in any one game was nine, which he did twice, against Australia and France.

Q. Jimmy Hunter played in 24 matches on the 1905–1906 All Blacks tour of the British Isles. How many tries did he score — 24, 29, 39 or 44?

– Forty-four (including two bags of five tries, one against Northumberland and the other against Oxford University).

Q. Which front-rower scored two tries for the All Blacks in their 19-nil victory over Wales in 1924?

– William Richard 'Bull' Irvine.

Q. Four Welsh clubs have beaten the All Blacks. Which clubs, and when?

– Swansea beat the 1935-1936 All Blacks 11-3; Cardiff beat the 1953-1954 All Blacks 8-3; Newport beat the 1963-1964 All Blacks 3-nil; and Llanelli beat the 1972-1973 All Blacks 9-3.

Q. When the 1905 All Blacks beat Swansea 4-3, Swansea scored a penalty goal. What did the All Blacks score?

– A dropped goal (by Billy Wallace).

Q. What was the name of the Newport player who dropkicked the winning goal for Newport against the 1963–1964 All Blacks?

– Dick Uzzell, who was badly injured in a car accident some months after the game.

Q. Who was the unexpected heavyweight halfback who travelled with the 1949 All Blacks to South Africa?

– William 'Bill' Conrad, who at 12 st 13 lb was the heaviest of the 15 backs who toured.

Q. What act nearly scuppered Henry Atkinson's chances of making the 1913 All Black team?

− He was the subject of a malicious letter to the NZRFU stating that he was unavailable for the tour to North America.

Q. How many of 1928–1931 All Black Walter Batty's brothers played club rugby in Auckland?

− Five.

Q. The 1958 All Blacks beat the visiting Australian team in the first test 25-3. How many tries did they score, how many were converted, and by whom?

− They scored seven tries, but only two were converted − by Don Clarke.

Q. Despite participating in the 25-3 thrashing of the 1958 Australians, two debut All Blacks were dropped after that game, never to represent their country again. Who were they?

− Mick Cossey of Counties and Tom Coughlan of South Canterbury.

Q. Which Welsh player appeared at centre for Swansea against the 1953–1954 All Blacks and as a No. 8 for the British Lions in New Zealand in 1959?

− John Faull.

Q. Don Clarke kicked six penalty goals in the first test against the 1959 British Lions, but how many did he land in the second test?

− None.

Q. What advice was Steve Nesbit, a running first-five with the 1960 All Blacks, given prior to the second test in South Africa?

− He was told categorically not to run the ball.

Q. The first test between New Zealand and France in 1961 could conceivably be classified as the 'sibling' test. Two sets of brothers lined up for the All Blacks and a further set for France. Name them.

− Don and Ian Clarke, and Colin and Stan Meads for the All Blacks; and Andre and Guy Boniface for France.

Q. Five new caps played in the first test against France at Auckland in 1961 — Don McKay, Neil Wolfe, Des Connor, Victor Yates and Stan Meads. One of them marked the occasion with a try. Which one?

− Don McKay.

Q. What was unusual about the two penalty goals landed by Jim Lenehan during the game between the 1962 All Blacks and New South Wales, won 12-11 by NSW?

— He dropkicked them.

Q. The All Blacks have won two tests by the score of 3-nil. Against which teams, when and who kicked the winning penalty goals?

— In 1954 against Scotland at Murrayfield when Bob Scott kicked the penalty goal and in 1962 against Australia at Carisbrook when Don Clarke kicked the goal.

Q. What was unusual about the All Blacks' 36-3 score in the 1963–1964 tour finale against the Barbarians in Britain?

— All the points were actually scored by All Blacks. The Barbarians' 3 points came from a goal from a mark by Ian Clarke, who was a guest player for the Barbarians.

Q. How many All Black trials were there prior to the naming of the test team to play the 1964 Australians and how many the following year?

— There were no trials for the 1964 team, but six trials were held in 1965.

Q. What was unusual about the All Black forwards who played the 1965 Springbok tourists?

— The same eight forwards played in all four tests — Brian Lochore, Dick Conway, Kel Tremain, Colin Meads, Stan Meads, Ken Gray, Bruce McLeod and Wilson Whineray.

Q. Of which All Black opponent was it once said, 'He has educated hips'?

— Jack Matthews, who played for the 1950 British Lions against the All Blacks.

Q. Which noted All Black opponent from 1950 subsequently went on to become a doctor-missionary in Africa?

— Jack Kyle, of the British Lions.

Q. Name the three halfbacks in the 1950 British Lions touring team to New Zealand.

— Gordon Rimmer, Rex Willis and Gus Black.

Q. Which 1950 British Lion returned to live in New Zealand and after playing very well for Wellington went close to making the 1953–1954 All Blacks?

— Don Hayward.

Q. Who made the tackle that prevented Bleddyn Williams scoring what could have been a match-winning try in the fourth test of the 1950 series between the All Blacks and the Lions?

— Prop Kevin Skinner.

Q. Name the two Taranaki players selected at fullback for the All Blacks in successive years.

— Maurice Cockerill in 1951 and Noel Bowden in 1952.

Q. The 1953–1954 All Blacks lost to South West France by a last-minute penalty goal. What was the infringement?

— The French referee claimed that Vince Bevan had not fed the ball straight to a scrum. The fact that the ball had not actually left Bevan's hands when the ruling was made was deemed irrelevant.

Q. What do the seven five-eighths and centres who toured with the 1953–1954 All Blacks have in common?

— None of them ever played for the All Blacks again. Jim Fitzgerald, John Tanner, Brian Fitzpatrick, Colin Loader, Doug Wilson and Guy Bowers were discarded and Laurie Haig retired.

Q. Name two All Black forwards with the nickname 'Tiny'.

— 'Tiny' White and 'Tiny' Hill, who played in the same pack of New Zealand forwards in 1956.

Q. How many players left the field (most of them temporarily) during the first test of the 1956 series between New Zealand and South Africa?

— Seven.

Q. Nev MacEwan played in three positions for the All Blacks in test matches. What were they?

— Lock (where he played most of his career), No. 8 (for his test debut in the second test against the 1956 Springboks) and prop, during the course of the 1960 All Black tour to South Africa.

184

Q. Name the halfback who played for North-West Cape against the 1970 All Blacks in South Africa.

— Wobbles Ravenscroft.

Q. Trevor Wiggill appeared at hooker against the 1970 All Blacks in South Africa for which team?

— Border.

Q. What song did Grahame Thorne sing with leading South African entertainer Min Shaw during a social function on the 1970 All Black Tour?

— 'Raindrops Keep Falling on my head'.

Q. What happened at the end of the match between the All Blacks and Griqualand West in 1970?

— A riot erupted in the crowd.

Q. How many cans of beer were consumed by the 1970 touring All Blacks in South Africa at one drinking session?

— Six hundred.

Q. A pharmacist named 'Chummy' Jankielsohn coached which provincial team against the 1970 All Blacks?

— North-West Cape.

Q. What did All Black Alex Wyllie bag while on a hunting expedition during the 1970 All Black tour of South Africa?

— A 300-pound (136 kilogram) hartebeest.

Q. How many scrum heels against the head did All Black hooker Bruce McLeod win when the 1970 All Blacks played South West Africa?

— Ten.

Q. Against which opposition did Colin Meads receive a broken arm during the All Blacks 1970 tour to South Africa?

— Eastern Transvaal.

Q. The crowd for the 1970 All Blacks game against Transvaal at Ellis Park, Johannesburg, was a world record for a provincial match. How many were present (to the nearest thousand)?

— 66,000.

Q. Which team did Louis Luyt, the highly influential South African fertiliser millionaire, play in against the 1960 All Blacks?

— Orange Free State.

Q. What olfactory offence was committed by one of the

All Black tourists at a formal function during the 1970 tour of South Africa?

– He let off a stink bomb.

Q. What unusual activity did Grahame Thorne get up to while the 1970 All Blacks were flying to Rhodesia?

– He donned a stewardess' hat and helped serve complimentary drinks.

Q. Andy MacDonald, who played for the 1965 Springboks against the All Blacks, encountered a maul off the field as well as on. What did the off-field mauling involve?

– He was seriously mauled by a lion, but after 480 stitches and a certain passage of time, survived the ordeal.

Q. What position did Blair Furlong, a five-eighth on the 1970 All Black tour of South Africa, play against Rhodesia, and how many goals did he kick?

– He played at fullback and kicked five goals.

Q. Members of which well-known organisation acted as ushers for spectators with grandstand seats when the 1970 All Blacks played

the Springboks in the first test at Pretoria?

– Girl Guides.

Q. The second test between the 1970 All Blacks and Springboks featured some 'uncompromising' play. How many stitches were needed to fix up players at the end of the game?

– Twenty-two.

Q. What was All Black fullback Fergie McCormick doing in the second test of the 1970 series against South Africa when Mr Ernest Grundlingh from Paarl in Western Cape Province collapsed and died?

– He was kicking the winning penalty goal.

Q. The 1970 All Blacks played a match at Outeniqua Park. In which town was that?

– George.

Q. Colin Meads was captain of the day for the 1970 All Blacks match against South Western Districts. How long was his team talk?

– Forty-five minutes.

Q. How did Alan Smith, an All Black in South Africa in 1970, break his wrist during the tour?

– He ran into a goalpost at training.

Q. Three halfbacks were considered for the fourth test of the 1970 series between the All Blacks and the Springboks. One was Chris Laidlaw, another Sid Going. Who was the third?

– Fullback Fergie McCormick, but only because Chris Laidlaw was out following an appendectomy and Sid Going was carrying an injury. In the event, Going played.

Q. How many members of parliament from South Africa and Rhodesia were among the 67,000 spectators who watched the All Blacks play the Springboks in the fourth test in 1970?

– Twenty-one, including the South African State President, Mr Fouche, South African Prime Minister B.J. Vorster, Rhodesian Prime Minister Ian Smith and sixteen South African and two Rhodesian Cabinet Ministers.

Q. Ian McCullum, a slightly built

Springbok fullback, kicked three early long-range penalty goals to set South Africa on its way to beat New Zealand in the fourth test in 1970. From what distances (in yards)?

– From 55, 45 and 60 yards.

Q. Alan Smith played two games at No. 8 during the 1970 All Black tour. What position did he normally play?

– Lock.

Q. What was the score between the 1905 All Blacks and Wellington in the national side's final preliminary game before touring Britain?

– Wellington won 3-nil.

Q. What visually challenging game was a popular pursuit on board ship while the 1905 All Blacks travelled to Britain?

– Blindfold boxing.

Q. The 1905 All Blacks beat Devon 55-4. Who scored Devon's points, and how?

– A player by the name of Lillicrap, who kicked a dropped goal.

Q. Aside from having been visited by the 1905 All Blacks, what is the main claim to fame of the Dolcoath mine in Cornwall?

— It is claimed to be the oldest mine in the world.

Q. What scrum-time ruse was employed by the halfback of several of the teams that played against the 1905 All Blacks?

— Bouncing the ball off the outside legs of their forwards at scrum time.

Q. The 1905 All Blacks won three of their tour games by the score of 41-nil. What teams did they defeat by this margin?

— Cornwall and Bristol (in successive games), and then later in the tour, Bedford.

Q. In what event did 1905 All Blacks Tyler, Newton, Hunter, and Roberts plus F. Garrity, an Aucklander in England, take part in while in London?

— A relay race at the Hornsey Swimming Club's gala.

Q. What was the somewhat apt surname of the halfback who represented Middlesex against the 1905 All Blacks?

— Stoop.

Q. Even with today's video refs, decisions about tries are still occasionally contentious. But why was the apparently legitimate try scored by 1905 All Black George Smith against Leicester denied?

— Opposing players lifted him bodily back into the field of play and the try was ruled out.

Q. What unusual event delayed the kick-off of the game between the 1905 All Blacks and Durham?

— Two of the Durham players had missed their train connection.

Q. What was unusual about the ground at which the 1905 All Blacks played Northumberland at North Shields?

— The field sloped. New Zealand had the advantage of the slope and a strong wind in the first half.

Q. Who kicked off for the All Blacks in their match against Devonport Albion in 1905?

— The Rev. Gordon Ponsonby.

Q. Dr A.N. Fell was chosen to play for Scotland against the 1905 All Blacks. Why did he withdraw from the team?

– For patriotic reasons – he was a New Zealander.

Q. What was unusual about the field on which the 1905 All Blacks played West of Scotland?

– It was a soccer field.

Q. Of which team was it said the 1905 All Blacks were 'captivated by the[ir] frank charm'?

– Ireland.

Q. What two items of clothing did the referee for the 1905 New Zealand-Wales match wear that would be regarded as highly unusual today?

– He wore ordinary walking boots – on a muddy field – and an orthodox high collar.

Q. What was the date when the 1905 All Blacks played France?

– 1 January 1906.

Q. Players in which of New Zealand's 1905 tour opposition teams 'carried superfluous flesh', indicating the need for more training?

– Players in the French team.

Q. At which two unlikely venues did the 1905 All Blacks play against British Columbia?

– Berkeley and San Francisco.

Q. The match between the 1905 New Zealand team and British Columbia was not played on the field originally assigned for the purpose. The latter, because of the rain, had become 'a perfect quagmire', and an adjacent field was used. What were the two unusual aspects of this field?

– As appeared to be the American practice, the game was played on soil that had been harrowed before the game, rather than grass. Furthermore the field was found to be about 15 yards too narrow and the sideline was extended, leaving the goalposts stranded to one side.

Q. Which team were the 1905 All Blacks playing when commentators noted there were 'a great many ladies' in the crowd to watch a one-sided game that contained 'numerous pretty bouts of passing'?

– British Columbia.

Q. How many times did Alex McDonald play for the All Blacks and what non-playing positions did he later take up?

— He made 41 appearances for the All Blacks and went on to become a selector and coach. Even at 60 plus years of age he was in the habit of throwing himself in front of practice forward rushes to show players the appropriate way to go down on the ball.

Q. After the 1905–1906 All Blacks' match against Surrey, it was suggested that instead of rushing to secure the jersey of 'the man who had scored' as a trophy, everyone should try to obtain what?

— The referee's whistle, which had been used excessively during the game.

Q. What injury kept All Black Jack Finlay out of the second test against Australia in 1946?

— He injured an eye when a window opened as he was running down the platform of Frankton Junction station — on his way for a quick cuppa at the cafeteria.

Q. How many specialist locks played in the All Black pack in the second test against Australia in 1946?

— Four — Tom Budd and Charlie Willocks (at lock), Ken Elliott (at No. 8) and Maurie McHugh (at breakaway).

Q. Charlie Willocks received seven stitches in his eyebrow and missed the last two matches of the 1947 All Black tour to Australia. How did he get injured?

— He was accidentally punched by one of his own players.

Q. The 1949 All Black tourists to South Africa were farewelled by the Governor General and blessed by an archbishop. What was the result of the series?

— They lost the test series 4–nil.

Q. How long elapsed between the time the 1949 All Blacks were selected and the time they played their first match in South Africa?

— Eight months. The team was selected on 2 October 1948 and first played on 31 May 1949.

Q. Why could the 1928 All Blacks to South Africa not call on the services of the outstanding George Nepia and Jimmy Mill?

— Because they were Maori.

Q. Mark Nicholls, the master tactician with the 1928 All Blacks in South Africa, was left out of the first three tests. What was thought to be the reason?

— It is rumoured he was the victim of a South Island clique within the team.

Q. In what year did the Springboks first fail to win a single test in a series against the All Blacks?

— 1994. They lost the first two tests and drew the third.

Q. How long each day did All Black Ron Jarden spend practising centre kicking?

— Ninety minutes each day, with a jersey placed in the middle of the field as his target.

Q. When Ron Jarden was playing, wingers threw the ball into line-outs. What unusual tactic did Jarden employ to hone this skill?

— He practised by throwing the ball into a bucket.

Q. What was possibly the biggest problem facing the All Black

forwards on the long sea voyage from New Zealand to South Africa in 1949?

— A lack of exercise. Some forwards gained 19 kg in weight because of a lack of training facilities on board. All the players could do was jog around the deck and play vigorous games of cards. When the team arrived in South Africa they found themselves booked into a place called Hermanus, the 'Riviera of South Africa', where there were no adequate training fields but plenty of socialising. Weight-gains were not really addressed.

Q. Why was Vince Bevan barred from touring with the 1949 All Blacks?

— Because of his Maori blood. Ironically, Maori folk at the time didn't think that he had enough Maori blood to allow him to play for the New Zealand Maori team.

Q. South Africa won the first test against the 1949 All Blacks 15-11. They used four goal-kickers: Jack van der Schyff, Floris Duvenage, Hannes Brewis and who?

— Okey Geffin, who kicked five penalty goals to give his team the victory.

Q. Springbok Jaap Bekker, who played against the 1956 All Blacks, had a fearsome reputation. It was said that he used to pack down against the goalposts and snap them with brute strength. What did New Zealand's Ian Clarke used to pack down against?

— Fence posts.

Q. What injury caused Brian Lochore to miss the first three weeks of the 1970 tour of South Africa, who captained the team in his absence and what happened to him on Lochore's return?

— Lochore broke his thumb playing in Perth on the way to South Africa. In this time Colin Meads captained the team. In Lochore's first game back from injury, Meads had his arm broken.

Q. Colin Meads preferred to run on to the field last. It was a matter of superstition. Where in the line-up did he run on to the field on the day his arm was broken?

— He ran on to the field

second — as vice captain — behind Lochore.

Q. What action did referee Clive Norling take with eight minutes to go in the 1981 'flour bomb' test between South Africa and New Zealand?

— He asked the captains if they wanted the game called off.

Q. Who replaced George Aitken, the All Black captain for the first two tests against the 1921 Springboks, for the third test?

— Teddy Roberts.

Q. What unusual action did Maurice Brownlie, captain of the 1928 All Blacks in South Africa, take prior to the last test?

— He ordered a week's holiday for his team. The All Blacks subsequently won the game, 13-5.

Q. What was unusual about All Black Freddy Roberts replacing Peter Harvey in the South Island side for the 1902 inter-island match?

— Roberts, from Wellington, never played for a South Island province.

Q. Name the first father and son combination to play for New Zealand.

– Harry and Teddy Roberts.

Q. What unusual feat of strength is All Black Maurice Brownlie reputed to have performed?

– He is said to have single-handedly pulled the family car out of a river after it had left the road.

Q. Who was the first All Black captain to play in all tests on a tour to Britain?

– Jack Manchester, in 1935–1936.

Q. All Black Ron King's provincial record spanned 18 seasons from 1928 to 1945. Which province did he play for?

– West Coast.

Q. Who was the first front-rower to captain New Zealand in a test?

– Kevin Skinner, against Australia in 1952.

Q. Ex-All Black test captain Ian Clarke took on what role in 1993?

– President of the NZRFU (the first ex-All Black captain to hold this role).

Q. What position did Wilson Whineray first play for the Auckland Grammar First XV?

– Halfback. He later became a No. 8, before shifting to prop.

Q. What eminent educational institution did Wilson Whineray attend in the late 1960s?

– Harvard Business School.

Q. What rank did Wilson Whineray hold with the first New Zealand SAS?

– Honorary Colonel.

Q. What was the title of Chris Laidlaw's 1999 book about New Zealand's national identity?

– *Right of Passage*.

Q. How many copies (to the nearest thousand) did Colin Meads' first biography, *Colin Meads All Black*, sell?

– It sold 57,000 copies.

Q. Who is the oldest All Black captain to have led the team in a test match?

– Tane Norton, at 35 years, 136 days, when he led New Zealand against the 1977 British Lions.

Q. Colin Meads was 35 years, 72 days when he led New Zealand against which team?

— The 1971 British Lions.

Q. What was the title of Graham Mourie's biography, released in 1982?

— Graham Mourie – Captain.

Q. What consequence did Graham Mourie suffer after the release of his biography?

— He accepted payment for it, thereby becoming a professional.

Q. Who was offered the captaincy of the 1978 'Grand Slam' All Blacks before it was given to Graham Mourie?

— Frank Oliver.

Q. What position did Sean Fitzpatrick hold with Coca-Cola after his retirement from rugby?

— Marketing consultant.

Q. What sport did Paul Koteka take up after moving to Perth?

— Triathlon.

Q. Which Italian club did All Black Brad Johnstone coach?

— The Scavaline club in A'Quila.

Q. When Scavaline were scheduled to play a game against Catania, in Sicily, why did Johnstone have difficulty drumming up a team?

— Because they had to travel to Mafia territory.

Q. What size boots did Todd Blackadder wear?

— Size 16.

Q. What insect-related challenge did Brad Johnstone have to deal with when coaching Italy?

— His fly half was traumatised when he found cockroaches in his hotel room.

Q. What was Grahame Thorne doing when ordered off for 'fighting' in a club match in South Africa?

— He was actually trying to break up a fight.

Q. What did Grahame Thorne do before playing his first game for Auckland University and before his first All Black trial in 1967?

— He vomited.

Q. What did Grahame Thorne do in 1972 to celebrate the birth of his son that made him play poorly for Northern Transvaal against

Rhodesia the next day?

— He drank a bottle of brandy.

Q. What protest action did Grahame Thorne take after missing selection following his outstanding performance in the 1972 Springbok trials?

— He grew his hair long — a desperate thing to do in South Africa in those days.

Q. What unlawful activity was Grahame Thorne a victim of when he visited South Africa as a member of the New Zealand Parliamentarians rugby side during the 1995 World Cup tournament?

— He was mugged, as were many visitors during the World Cup, a few days before the World Cup final.

Q. Why did Josh Kronfeld miss out on a place in the New Zealand Colts in 1992?

— Because a selector was nonplussed by his hair, which had been plaited with coloured rubber bands to stop it flapping around.

Q. What did Josh Kronfeld typically do during the playing of the

national anthem prior to test matches?

— He used to jiggle his head from side to side.

Q. What act of devotion did Kevin Boroevich show for Jan Cressy, his girlfriend and classmate in Standard Three at Te Kuiti Primary School?

— He wrote her a love song (titled 'Janeo').

Q. What machine did Kevin Boroevich invent while playing in France?

— The 'Borok' line-out machine.

Q. To the nearest hour, how long did hooker Warren Gatland, who played in Sean Fitzpatrick's shadow, spend warming the reserves bench during his All Black days?

— Eighteen hours.

Q. For which company was Tabai Matson working when he became an All Black?

— He was working as a rep for Coca-Cola in France. The All Blacks just happened to be touring France in 1995 while Matson was based there and, when injuries beset the tourists, he was whistled up.

Q. What was the title of 1928 All Black James Burrows' biography, published in 1974?

– Pathway Among Men.

Q. Champion wingers of their day, John Dick and Jack Steel, are related to which All Black wingers of the 1960s?

– Tony Steel, Malcolm Dick.

Q. Who was New Zealand's first double All Black?

– George Dickinson, who played cricket as a fast bowler for New Zealand against Victoria in 1924–1925.

Q. Name the two front-rowers who played for the All Blacks in the 1990s, and who shared a surname yet were not related.

– Craig William Dowd and Graham William Dowd.

Q. Such was Sean Fitzpatrick's longevity that in 1997 he played with the son of a former team-mate. Who was the son and who was his father?

– The son was Jeremy Stanley and his father was Joe Stanley, who made his All Black debut the same day as Fitzpatrick.

Q. All Black Paul Henderson suffered an unusual, debilitating infection to which part of his body while travelling by plane?

– His eye.

Q. What is the name of Paul Henderson's twin brother, who played for Southland?

– David.

Q. Which two All Blacks were known as 'the Taranaki twins'?

– 1905 tourists 'Simon' Mynott and Jimmy Hunter.

Q. How did Eric Tindill score his only points for the All Blacks?

– He kicked five dropped goals.

Q. What unusual piece of apparel was 1905 All Black William 'Billy' or 'Carbine' Wallace, wearing when he scored a try against Cornwall?

– A sun hat.

Q. What was the title of the book written by Mark Nicholls in 1928?

– With the All Blacks in Springbokland.

Q. How many times did William Michael 'Bill' Osborne, an All

Black from Wanganui, retire from test rugby?

— Three times — in 1981, 1982 and 1985.

Q. All Black Jeff Wilson once scored 66 points in one game while playing for his First XV side at Cargill High School. How were the points scored?

— Nine tries and 15 conversions.

Q. Jazz Muller claimed he would need to play more games on the All Blacks tour to South Africa in 1970. Why?

— In order to get fit for coach Ivan Vodanovich's training runs.

Q. Who scored New Zealand's last 2-point try, in 1893?

— James Lambie.

Q. As of 2005 the All Blacks had only won the Rugby World Cup once. But what other World Cup competition distinction did they hold?

— They were the only team to have been placed among the top four sides at each World Cup.

Q. How many points had the All

Blacks scored in World Cup matches at the end of 2005?

— They are the only team to have cracked the 1000-points mark, having scored 1384 points.

Q. To whom is the Dave Gallaher Cup awarded?

— To the winner of the first match between France and New Zealand in any given year.

Q. The All Blacks won three consecutive test series against South Africa. In what years were the series played?

— In 1981, 1994 and 1996.

Q. What is the record number of successive tests that the All Blacks have lost to South Africa?

— Six — the final two of the 1937 series and the four-match Springbok clean-sweep of 1949.

Q. Who kicked the All Blacks' first penalty goal against Australia in 1903?

— Billy Wallace.

Q. Who refereed all four tests of the 1928 New Zealand-South Africa series?

— South African referee
Boet Neser.

Q. What was the name of the
referee who failed to award two
penalty tries to the All Blacks
in the fourth test against the
Springboks in 1976?

— Gert Bezeidenhout.

Q. In the first test of the 1976 series
between New Zealand and
South Africa, who scored a try
after Grant Batty pulled off a
spectacular interception?

— Lyn Jaffray.

Q. In the first test of the 1977
series against the British Lions,
who scored a try after Grant
Batty pulled off a spectacular
interception?

— Grant Batty himself.

Q. What did Kel Tremain always
carry a second pair of when
playing for the All Blacks?

— Boots.

Q. Don Clarke once borrowed Kel
Tremain's 'lucky' second pair of
boots, having forgotten to pack
his own. What happened when
Clarke attempted a long-range
penalty wearing these boots?

— Tremain's boot disinte-

grated. The ball went
one way and bits of boot
flew to all points of the
compass.

Q. All Black Charlie Fletcher broke
his ankle in a warm-up match in
New Zealand and the NZRFU,
not unreasonably, omitted him
from the 1920 team to tour
Australia. How, then, did he
come to be part of the touring
party?

— His fellow All Blacks wanted
Fletcher — a popular fellow
— along for the ride. Player
solidarity resulted in a 'No
Fletcher, no tour' edict,
which saw Fletcher hobbling
on to the boat as a non-
playing member of the
team.

Q. What unusual action did Fred
Allen take before the final two
tests of the 1949 series between
New Zealand and South Africa?

— He dropped himself from
the team.

Q. Who were the three All Black
test captains in the years 1999–
2001?

— Taine Randell, Todd
Blackadder and Anton
Oliver.

Q. Before the 1989 All Blacks played Llanelli, weather conditions resulted in what ruling being made?

– The wind was so strong that a temporary grandstand was deemed unsafe to use.

Q. During the 1961 'Hurricane' test between the All Blacks and France at Athletic Park, Wellington, the team used a roving extra back to cover contingencies. Who took the role?

– Flanker John Graham.

Q. Colin Meads suffered a wound to the head in the 1967 test match against France, which required stitches after the game. How did his actions here add to his legendary hard man image?

– He didn't bother with anaesthetic as the stitches were inserted.

Q. Which French club did All Black prop Graham Purvis play for, and for how many seasons?

– He played 11 seasons for Ussel. In Purvis' first match the Ussel captain had his nose broken when an angry touch judge whacked him with his flag.

Q. Which player, at the age of 18, became New Zealand's youngest-ever first-class captain when he led Hawke's Bay? He later became an All Black.

– Richard Turner.

Q. Which All Black was the first foreign player to be signed up by Agen, one of France's leading clubs?

– Murray Mexted. Although he hadn't actually played for the All Blacks at that time, Agen officials were happy to advertise their new New Zealand player as 'Mexted the great All Black'.

Q. In what position did Doug Bruce play for New Zealand against Queensland Country in 1974?

– Fullback. He was normally a first five-eighth.

Q. In what position did Ian Kirkpatrick play at primary school?

– Prop.

Q. In the early part of his All Black playing days, how many miles a week did 'Tiny' White run to keep his edge of fitness?

– A hundred.

Q. Who used to sing and make motor car noises as he raced through gaps in the midfield, while playing for Auckland Grammar First XV?

– Grahame Thorne.

Q. When the 1972 All Blacks beat the touring Australians in the first test, the final score was 29-6. How many of the 46 line-outs did Australia win?

– Seven.

Q. When Andy Leslie made his debut for Wellington Colts, he scored a try and kicked two conversions. Who was the opposition?

– Horowhenua.

Q. Which other future All Black shared the kicking duties with Andy Leslie during his debut match for Wellington Colts?

– Gerald Kember.

Q. Johnny Smith, prior to an All Black match in Australia, made the claim that the first of his team-mates to score a try would have his name go forward as the second name for his recently born daughter, Raewyn. Early in the game Smith found a gap and was in a position where he could have easily scored himself. However, he couldn't face the prospect of a daughter named Raewyn Smith Smith. So he weaved about looking for support. The first player he spied was his brother Peter, also an All Black and also a Smith, so not a contender to receive the ball. Who did he eventually pass to?

– Winger Wally Argus, who did score the try. Johnny Smith's daughter became Raewyn Argus Smith.

Q. What number jersey did Michael Jones wear when he took the field as a reserve against South Africa in the third test of 1994?

– He wore jersey number 23. Bearing in mind that team jersey numbers range from 1 to 22, Jones' 23 was an oddity. Jones had left his number 22 jersey behind in his rush to catch the team bus, so when he got to Eden Park he was obliged to don jersey number 23 from the pile of 'extra' jerseys in the All Blacks' gear bag.

Q. How many penalty goals were kicked in the 1975 'water polo' test between New Zealand and Scotland on a sodden Eden Park, won 24-nil by the All Blacks?

– None. No penalty goal

attempts were even made because of the foul conditions.

Q. How many conversions were kicked during the 1975 'water polo' test?

– Four, all by Joe Karam, the All Black fullback.

Q. What was the title of the biography written by Johan le Roux, the Springbok prop notorious for biting Sean Fitzpatrick's ear?

– Biting Back.

Q. Who turned up for an All Black trial in 1974 wearing red striped leather shoes, pink trousers and a brightly coloured shirt?

– Kit Fawcett.

Q. What was unusual about the dressing room used by the All Blacks prior to playing British Columbia at Vancouver on their 1972–1973 tour?

– It was the ladies dressing room.

Q. Who was the only Maori included in the 1935–1936 All Black touring team to Britain?

– 'Tori' Reid.

Q. What were 'Tori' Reid's Christian names?

– Sana Torium.

Q. How many All Blacks did the 1927 Wairarapa team contain?

– Eleven.

Q. What post-match statement by All Black Peter Jones did the *New Zealand Herald* decide not to print?

– His 'absolutely buggered' comment after the deciding fourth test between New Zealand and South Africa.

Q. In 1907–1908 a group of eight New Zealand reps signed up with Bert Baskeville's league tour of Australia and Britain. Originally they were called the Professional All Blacks; what were they later called?

– The All Golds.

Q. How many league tests did George Nepia play for New Zealand?

– One – against Australia in 1937.

Q. The reinstatement of which league-playing All Black created a sensation when he was selected to play for the All Blacks in the third test of the 1921 series against South Africa?

— Karl Ifwerson, who represented New Zealand at league from 1913 to 1920.

Q. For what unusual offence was Joe Karam nearly sent off in a test match between Australia and New Zealand in 1974 by referee Dr Roger Vanderfield?

— For back-chatting.

Q. Which future New Zealand cricket captain was a team-mate of Fergie McCormick in the Canterbury Colts?

— Graham Dowling.

Q. How old (in years only) was Joe Stanley when he made his test debut?

— He was 29.

Q. How many dropped goals did halfback Chris Laidlaw kick for New Zealand?

— Five.

Q. Which former All Black great collaborated with Phil Kingsley-Jones to write several rugby yarn books?

— Stu Wilson.

Q. What are the titles of the two biographies of Sean Fitzpatrick?

— Fronting Up (published in 1994) and Turning Point (published in 1998).

Q. What is the most commonly held position for All Black test captains?

— Loose forward.

Q. Who charged down Scotsman Ian McGeechan's attempted drop kick against the 1978 All Blacks and who scored the All Black try that resulted from that action?

— The charge-down was made by Doug Bruce and the counterattack saw Bruce Robertson score at the other end.

Q. In what year was the first Grand Slam by an All Black team to Britain achieved?

— 1978.

Q. What role did Brian McKenzie have with the All Blacks when the team visited Britain in 1978?

— Physiotherapist — he was the first physio to accompany an All Black touring team.

202

Q. In 1978 the All Blacks suffered two major drubbings, losing one game 16-30 and another nil-12. Who beat them?

— Australia (30-16 at Auckland) and Munster (12-0 at Limerick).

Q. At what artistic pursuit does Doug Bruce excel?

— He is a dab hand at painting in watercolours.

Q. In what year did the All Blacks play their first test match in New Zealand, and in what city?

— In Wellington in 1904, when they beat Great Britain 9-nil.

Q. What was the All Blacks' first loss in a test match?

— The 3-nil loss to Wales in 1905.

Q. At what other sport did Ian Jones excel during his teenage years?

— He was a very good backstroke swimmer.

Q. Who kicked the first 3-point dropped goal for the All Blacks, against Eastern Transvaal in 1949?

— Jim Kearney.

Q. Who kicked the last 4-point dropped goal, against Combined Northern at Newcastle, during the All Blacks' 1947 tour?

— Thomas Webster.

Q. What unfortunate fate did Ian Kirkpatrick suffer within five minutes of making his test debut against France in 1967?

— He received a broken nose.

Q. Which All Black lock once sidestepped Bob Scott, a famous defender, in a match between the All Blacks and Auckland in 1951?

— 'Tiny' White.

Q. After a 1967 test Ian MacRae suffered from a broken tooth, a black eye and, several hours later, diarrhoea. Which team had MacRae played against?

— Wales.

Q. Which All Black played league in Whangarei for the West End Jumbos, in 1977?

— Joe Stanley.

Q. What is the highest score by the All Blacks against any New Zealand team in New Zealand?

— Fifty-nine, against Marlborough in 1972.

Q. Who kicked the winning penalty goal for the Springboks against the 1965 All Blacks in the third test, causing Gert Brynard, the Bok winger, to turn a joyful somersault?

– 'Tiny' Naude.

Q. What possible beauty treatment did Colin Meads receive from Springbok centre John Gainsford after the Springboks' late win in the third test of 1965 against New Zealand?

– Meads got a face full of mud.

Q. What injury was 'Moke' Belliss suffering from when he scored a crucial try in the first ever test between New Zealand and South Africa in 1921?

– He had a seriously strained ankle.

Q. What was the weight advantage of the Springbok pack in the first test of the 1921 series between South Africa and New Zealand?

– They were heavier by 90 kilograms.

Q. Why was All Black lock Geoff Alley's amateur status called into doubt by a Natal journalist in 1928?

– Alley had once won first prize and 10 shillings in the shot put event at a sports carnival in Southland.

Q. What were the colour of the shorts worn by the Springboks for the first test of the 1928 series between New Zealand and South Africa?

– They wore black shorts, reputedly to confuse the referee at ruck-time as to which side was lying on the ball.

Q. Who was the first New Zealander to score 100 tries in first-class rugby?

– Bert Cooke, the All Black mid-field back.

Q. During which tour did the term 'dirt-trackers', denoting mid-week All Black teams, emerge?

– During the 1928 All Black tour to South Africa, when the mid-weekers played on dusty fields.

Q. What was the nickname given to the fourth test between New Zealand and South Africa in 1928?

– It was known as the 'umbrella test', because of the wet conditions.

Q. What action by the New Zealand referee revealed his slight impartiality when All Black first five Dave Trevathan kicked a dropped goal in the first test between the 1937 All Blacks and Springboks?

— He jumped with glee.

Q. What strange behaviour did Springbok forward 'Boy' Louw exhibit after receiving a knock to the head during the second test of the 1937 series between New Zealand and South Africa?

— He giggled uncontrollably for the rest of the match — even while punching All Black prop Doug Dalton to the ground.

Q. Why was Manawatu All Black Rod McKenzie officially reprimanded by the NZRFU after the first test of the 1937 New Zealand-South Africa series?

— He hadn't handed in his shorts, which had been badly torn during the test match.

Q. From what potentially debilitating disease did Bob Scott suffer as a child?

— Poliomyelitis.

Q. What did Fred Allen do with his boots on the boat ferrying the unsuccessful 1949 All Blacks back to New Zealand?

— He place-kicked them into the ocean.

Q. What focusing technique did the Springboks use prior to the second test of the 1956 series between New Zealand and South Africa?

— They stared at a rugby ball for 15 minutes.

Q. What action by All Black winger Ron Jarden led to Springbok tries when New Zealand lost the second test of 1956?

— He missed two important tackles.

Q. When Don Clarke was first selected to play for New Zealand, what record did he establish?

— He was the largest back to play for the All Blacks.

Q. During one of the test matches of the 1956 New Zealand-South Africa series, who asked the All Blacks, during a stoppage caused by punching, if they needed a hand?

— A policeman who had been patrolling the touchline.

Q. Who missed an easy penalty attempt late in the fourth test between the 1959 All Blacks and British Lions, meaning New Zealand lost 6-9?

— Don Clarke.

Q. What was the occupation of Ray Prosser, a prop for the 1959 British Lions against the All Blacks?

— He was a bulldozer driver.

Q. What action was taken by would-be spectators outside Carisbrook, Dunedin, shortly after the start of the first test between the 1966 All Blacks and the British Lions?

— They lifted a large gate off its hinges and 200 fans poured into the ground.

Q. How many forward passes are believed to have been made in the move leading to a try by All Black Tony Steel in the fourth test against the 1966 British Lions?

— Two.

Q. How many times did All Black halfback Chris Laidlaw handle the ball in the fourth test against the 1966 British Lions?

— Thirty-nine times.

Q. What lay legal position is held by Andy Leslie?

— He is a Justice of the Peace.

Q. Which All Black once hit 106 runs in a cricket match between Bay of Islands and Rodney?

— Johnny Smith.

Q. Which All Black, after retiring from playing rugby, achieved Ranfurly Shield immortality by coaching the Marlborough team that lifted the shield from Canterbury?

— Ralph Caulton.

Q. When Robin Archer was injured in the third test against the 1956 Springboks, forward Bill Clark moved into which position?

— Centre.

Q. How did 'Brushy' Mitchell get his nickname?

— It was a consequence of the excessive amount of hair brushing he did as a boy, to discipline his highly tensile, wavy hair.

Q. What type of surgery did Don Clarke undergo in both 1952 and 1955?

— Knee surgery. He had both right knee cartilages removed by surgery in 1952. One of his left knee cartilages was removed in 1955.

Q. Which All Black test match was watched by Mr J. Shanks, an Otago Gliding Club instructor, from his glider, hovering over Carisbrook, Dunedin?

— The first test between the All Blacks and British Lions in 1971.

Q. Which British Lion nearly ran down All Black Grant Batty as the latter headed in for the deciding try in the first test against the 1977 British Lions?

— Graham Price, the Lions prop.

Q. What kept 3000 paid-up, would-be spectators away from the first test between the 1977 All Blacks and British Lions at Athletic Park, Wellington?

— A strong southerly wind on the day.

Q. Of which game did one commentator say that the standard of play was so poor that he would have preferred the New Zealand Army band, who trundled their wares prior to kick-off, to continue playing for another hour and a half?

— The second test between the 1977 All Blacks and British Lions.

Q. Who was sprayed with beer by a spectator after sliding over the deadball line in the act of preventing an All Black try in the second test against the 1977 British Lions?

— Lions winger J.J. Williams.

Q. What action did the 1977 All Blacks take in an attempt to nullify the dominance of the British Lions' scrum in the fourth test?

— They opted to pack down a three-man scrum.

Q. The All Blacks have twice beaten the British Lions in the first test by 16-12. In what years?

— In 1977 and 1983.

Q. Protesters against what clashed with rugby supporters prior to the final test between the 1983 All Blacks and British Lions?

— Apartheid.

Q. Whose try, scored in the final test between the 1983 All Blacks and British Lions, went largely unnoticed by spectators, because it was missed by TV coverage and was so quick and simple that many spectators at Eden Park also didn't see it happen?

— Jock Hobbs' try, a simple pick-up and dot-down as a scrum screwed on the Lions goal-line.

Q. Which All Black made the trials for the 1950 Empire Games, came last in the backstroke, and so decided to concentrate on other sports?

— Wilson Whineray.

Q. In South Africa in 1960 All Black Don Clarke found himself very much a marked man because of his exploits on the playing field, and on the morning of the third test his boots disappeared from his hotel room. Why did this not concern Clarke?

— He had taken to the habit of placing his practice boots near his bed, and entrusting his match and replacement boots to other members of the touring party for safe keeping.

Q. With what did All Black Tony Davies once fix the toe of his ill-repaired right boot to provide a hard edge for goal-kicking?

— He used a piece of orange peel.

Q. What strategy did 1980 All Black coach Eric Watson use at practice sessions to discourage dropped passes?

208

— The players were forced to pass bricks instead of balls, on the assumption that they would be less inclined to drop the bricks because of the threat of pain to their feet.

Q. During the 1987 World Cup semi-final between New Zealand and Wales, Welsh lock Huw Richards attacked Gary Whetton. What happened to Richards before referee Kerry Fitzgerald could send him from the field?

— He was hit by a retaliatory right cross from Buck Shelford and went down for the count.

Q. During the third test between the 1930 All Blacks and British Lions, the game became quite confused. Why?

— There were two balls on the field and in play. The All Blacks made good progress with one while, for the Lions, Parker of Wales made a long run with the other.

Q. What unusual missiles were thrown from the embankment at Eden Park during the playing of the fourth test in 1950?

— Leeks.

Q. What event brought a temporary halt to the 1991 Bledisloe Cup match between New Zealand and Australia?

— The invasion of Eden Park by two scantily clad streakers — members of the Cheeky Chicks strip troupe.

Q. In what year at the age of 31 did Bryan Williams play his final season of first-class rugby, and in what position?

— In 1982, as a fullback.

Q. How old was Wilson Whineray when he first played senior rugby for Waikaia in Southland?

— Sixteen.

Q. How many consecutive games did Andy Leslie play for Wellington?

— Ninety-nine.

Q. How old was 'Has' Catley when he played in his first All Black trial in 1935?

— Nineteen.

Q. How old was 'Has' Catley when he made his debut for the All Blacks?

— Thirty.

Q. What distinctive look did Bill Clark sport on the field?

– He wore white canvas headgear, made by a friend of the family.

Q. Why was 17 tonnes of straw needed when New Zealand played England on the 1953–1954 tour of Britain?

– It had to be spread on the playing surface to prevent the ground from freezing.

Q. Why did team manager Vinnie Meredith drop leading players Joey Sadler, George Hart and Jack Griffiths for the game against England at Twickenham on 4 January 1936?

– He caught the three of them breaking curfew on New Year's Eve. The All Blacks subsequently lost to England nil–13.

Q. What coaching triumph did Wilson Whineray achieve in 1972?

– He coached Auckland senior club Grammar to Gallaher Shield success.

Q. Against which side did Auckland All Black Frank McMullen make his rep debut in 1953?

– Wanganui, which beat Auckland 26–9.

Q. What medical condition has been suggested as the reason Andy Haden dived out of a line-out against Wales in 1978, in an attempt to secure the match-winning penalty?

– It has been said, humorously, that he was suffering from an inner ear infection, which upset his balance.

Q. Whereabouts in Auckland was the 1958 test match between New Zealand and Australia played?

– At the Epsom Showgrounds, Eden Park being closed for renovations.

Q. Andy Leslie played only two first-class games in 1965 and 1966, both for Wellington B. Which team was he playing against on both occasions?

– Golden Bay-Motueka.

Q. What move, popularised in recent years by Carlos Spencer, was also executed many years earlier by Johnny Smith?

– The 'banana' kick.

Q. When 'Has' Catley was 12 he played for South Auckland on Carlaw Park, in what sport?

— Rugby league.

Q. Why did coach Laurie Mains accuse Marc Ellis of being greedy during the 1995 World Cup?

— Because he scored six tries against Japan.

Q. How did Bill Clark, the lightweight All Black loose forward, boost his weight to 13 stone (82.5 kg) prior to weigh-ins?

— He secreted strategically placed lead about his person.

Q. Ten trial matches, involving 188 players, of whom 108 played once, 42 twice, 34 three times and four played four times. Which tour?

— The 1935–1936 All Black tour to Britain.

Q. All Blacks 'Brushy' Mitchell, Cyril Pepper and Dave Solomon had something in common that may have helped in the formation of their life-long friendship. What was it?

— None of them drank alcohol.

Q. What was especially notable about the scrumhalf and fly-half (Haydn Tanner and Willie Davies) who played for the Swansea side that beat the 1935–1936 All Blacks?

— They were both schoolboys. Swansea was only able to use their talents after making sincere exhortations to their headmaster.

Q. Joe Karam's father and three uncles all represented which province at rugby?

— King Country.

Q. Wilson Whineray came out of retirement for which game for Auckland in 1966?

— The Ranfurly Shield defence against Waikato. Waikato won 15–11.

Q. Jack Steel, the All Black winger, once scored a try by running 50 yards after catching the ball awkwardly somewhere about his shoulder blades. Rather than risk dropping the ball by attempting to transfer it to his hands, Steel just continued running at top pace with one hand steadying the ball in the region of his shoulders. Which team was he playing against?

— The 1921 Springboks.

Q. In the third test between the 1930 All Blacks and British Lions, who scored a vital try for New Zealand after scooping up a 'tactical' punt by Mark Nicholls, widely thought to be a failed dropped goal attempt?

— Winger Fred Lucas.

Q. The 1974 All Black tourists to Australia beat South Australia 117-6. How many of their points were scored in the second half of the game?

— Seventy-eight, including six converted tries from the final six kick-offs.

Q. Two individuals who would become mayors locked the All Black scrum on several occasions, most notably in all four tests against the 1956 Springboks. Who were they?

— 'Tiny' White, who was mayor of Gisborne from 1977 to 1983, and fellow lock Bob Duff, who became mayor of Lyttelton.

Q. How did Andy Leslie react the day after learning he was to be the All Blacks' new captain in 1974?

— He was violently sick.

Q. What position was Frank Bunce playing when he was initially 'discovered' while playing for the Manukau club's fifth grade team?

— Loose forward.

Q. In 1946 'Has' Catley made his All Black debut against Australia and won the scrums 23 to 6. What happened to him then?

— He was dropped.

Q. For the first test against the 1963 English tourists at Eden Park in Auckland, Ralph Caulton was called in as a late replacement for fellow Wellingtonian Rod Heeps. Why, then, a few hours before kick-off were All Black management making arrangements for an Auckland club winger to prepare to play?

— Caulton had had his flight travel plans disrupted by bad weather. He did arrive on time, however and, despite everything, scored two tries.

Q. What identity crisis is thought to have contributed to Cyril Brownlie being sent off against England?

— It is thought that the referee confused him with his brother Maurice, who

had earlier received a
warning.

Q. How many pre-match haka were
performed by the 1972–1973 All
Blacks to Britain and France?

– Just the one, when they
played the Barbarians.

Q. At Carisbrook in Dunedin
in 1997 New Zealand beat
Australia 36-24. What was so
strange about the scoring?

– All 60 points were scored
at one end of the park.

Q. Two All Blacks played in the
Waikato-Wairarapa Hawke
Cup cricket challenge match in
Masterton in the 1950s. One was
Don Clarke, who had to be flown
down in a Tiger Moth aircraft
and arrived a couple of hours
after play got under way but still
managed to take 8 wickets for
41, Waikato winning the cup.
Who was the other All Black to
play that day, and what notable
feat did he achieve?

– Ron Hemi, a very good
opening batsman, who
scored a century.

Q. What material were Joe Karam's
first rugby boots made of?

– Plastic.

Q. Which two All Black locks were
given the nickname 'Bacon
and eggs' because of their tight
combination?

– Charlie Willocks and Harry
Frazer.

Q. 1967 All Black Phil Clarke
of Marlborough was such an
unknown quantity that he wasn't
even nominated for the All Black
trials. An injury to who gave him
his big chance?

– Brian Stack of Buller.

Q. Why did the All Blacks not go
on their scheduled tour of South
Africa in 1939?

– Because of the outbreak
of the Second World War.

Q. Why did the 1967 All Blacks
not visit or play against Ireland
during their UK tour?

– Because of an outbreak of
foot and mouth disease.

Q. With three minutes to play in
the All Blacks game against
the Barbarians in 1967, New
Zealand was trailing 6-3.
What was the final score?

– The All Blacks won 11-6.
They managed two late
tries – to Ian MacRae
and Tony Steel.

Q. How many points did Fergie McCormick score on the British Isles and French legs of the 1967 All Black tour?

— Exactly 100.

Q. How many tries did Bill Birtwistle score in his first five games on the 1967 All Black tour to Britain, France and Canada?

— Six.

Q. Which famous pop star did Ian Jones meet while touring Rarotonga with a Kamo High School team?

— David Bowie, who was making a movie at the time.

Q. On which radio station does Chris Laidlaw have a regular Sunday morning programme?

— National Radio.

Q. In 1974 against a Welsh XV at Cardiff, Joe Karam nearly concocted an unlikely try for Bryan Williams, by taking a quick tap and angling a diagonal kick towards the unmarked winger. Why did the try not eventuate?

— The referee, caught un- awares, ruled off-side play.

Q. Ian Kirkpatrick scored tries on debut for Poverty Bay and the All Blacks, and also scored in his first test. Can you name the opponents and the venues in each instance?

— Against East Coast at Gisborne (1966), against Eastern Canada at Montreal (1967) and against France at Paris (1967).

Q. What was remarkable about Ian Kirkpatrick's four appearances in France — at Lyon, Toulouse, Bayonne and Paris — on the 1967 All Black tour?

— He scored tries in all four matches.

Q. What did fans from Whangarei, Tauranga, Rotorua and Taumarunui have in common before the third test between the British Lions and the All Blacks at Auckland in 1930?

— They were able to travel to the test thanks to special train services being laid on.

Q. The Mt Albert Borough Council arranged for the flying of a kite over Eden Park during the third test between the All Blacks and Lions in 1930. What four-word phrase was on the kite?

— 'Welcome to Mt Albert'.

Q. When the first test between the British Lions and the All Blacks in 1950 was broadcast, what increase in power usage (rounded to the nearest per cent) was noted between 2 and 4 p.m.?

— Ten per cent.

Q. What superstitious action was taken by sailors from the British frigate *Veryan Bay*, which was in port at Auckland when the fourth test between the Lions and the All Blacks was played in 1950?

— They attached a good luck charm to the crossbar on one of the sets of goalposts at Eden Park.

Q. When the All Blacks played the Wallabies at Athletic Park, Wellington in 1913, the foul weather caused the referee to do what?

— To split the game into four quarters, rather than two halves.

Q. Which former All Black refereed

the third test between New Zealand and Australia at Lancaster Park in 1913?

— George Nicholson.

Q. Name three former All Blacks who played for Bay of Plenty in 1962.

— Bill Gray, Mark Irwin and 'Red' Conway.

Q. In the 1967 match between New Zealand and the Barbarians, Fergie McCormick, whistled up to attempt the conversion that could win the match after Ian MacRae had scored a late try, found he had been winded. Who feigned injury to give McCormick time to recover?

— Colin Meads.

Q. What is unusual about the fact that Joe Stanley once played in a New Zealand Maori league trial?

— Both his parents are Samoan.

Q. Name two All Blacks who both share a love of cricket and who kicked crucial last-minute penalty goals enabling New Zealand to win test matches.

— Brian McKechnie and Allan Hewson. McKechnie's famous goal came in 1978 against

Wales, and Hewson's against South Africa in 1981.

Q. Despite suffering a dramatic loss of form with his goal-kicking during the course of the All Blacks 1963–1964 tour of Britain and France, how many points did Don Clarke amass during the tour?

– 149.

Q. In two successive test matches against South Africa, New Zealand failed to score any points. What years were the two games played?

– Although they were successive games, they were seven years apart, one in 1921 (0-0 at Wellington) and the next in 1928 (0-17 at Durban).

Q. How many nil-all draws have the All Blacks fought out and against which teams?

– They have been involved in three nil-all draws – against South Africa in 1921 at Wellington, New South Wales in 1929 at Sydney and Scotland in 1964 at Edinburgh.

Q. The All Blacks have twice gone down nil-17. Against which teams?

– New South Wales in 1921 and South Africa in 1928.

Q. Who is the youngest New Zealander to play in a first-class match in New Zealand?

– Joe Warbrick, a New Zealand rep in 1884, who played for Auckland Provincial Clubs against Otago in 1877 when he was a 15-year-old schoolboy at St Stephen's Native School.

Q. Which All Black scored an 80-yard solo try against Eastern Province in 1970 after initially dropping the ball behind him and back-heeling the ball before regaining possession?

– Bryan Williams.

Q. Three generations of Mehrtens have played rugby for New Zealand rep teams. Name them.

– Andrew Mehrtens, his father Terry (a Junior All Black) and his grandfather George (who played for the All Blacks in 1928).

Q. How many Otago reps were in the 1949 All Black touring team to South Africa?

— Eleven, with another four in the All Black team that played the 1949 Australians at home.

Q. Name the three first five-eighths and the one winger who played at second five-eighth during the All Blacks' 1963–1964 tour to Great Britain and France.

— The first five-eighths were Bruce Watt, Earle Kirton and Mac Herewini, and the winger was Malcolm Dick.

Q. In his first two seasons of senior club rugby Fergie McCormick played in five different positions. Name them.

— First five-eighth, second five-eighth, centre, wing and fullback.

Q. In 1982 Joe Stanley was dropped from the Auckland team. How many games had he played for them?

— One.

Q. Which great All Black fullback was Stan Meads' hero?

— Bob Scott.

Q. When the 1962 All Blacks beat Northern New South Wales by 103 to nil, who were the only two All Blacks not to score?

— Stan Meads and Neil Wolfe.

Q. Stan Meads received a painkilling injection in his broken little toe prior to playing against the 1966 British Lions. Who had caused Stan's broken toe?

— His brother Colin.

Q. Andrew Mehrtens could have been forgiven for getting confused in 1991. He played alongside two men of the same name, one in his High School Old Boys club side, the other in rep and international games. What was the name that these two players shared?

— Justin Marshall.

Q. For a number of years the Canterbury backline featured several players whose name began with 'M'. Name eight players from this extended era.

— Mark Mayerhofler, Justin Marshall, Andrew Mehrtens, Tabai Matson and later Aaron and Nathan Mauger, Joe Maddock and Leon MacDonald.

Q. When the 1976 All Blacks arrived at their hotel in Buenos

Aires, Argentina, it was raining heavily. What did the bus driver do to stop the players and their gear getting too wet?

– He drove up six steps to the hotel doors.

Q. Who scored a critical try for the 1992 All Blacks against South Africa at Ellis Park, after taking an audacious tap kick from a close-range penalty?

– Zinzan Brooke.

Q. How many games did Robin Brooke play on the 1993 All Black tour of England and Scotland?

– None. He was selected, but suffered a calf muscle injury before leaving New Zealand, yet still toured.

Q. What university qualification does backgammon fan Olo Brown hold?

– A Bachelor of Commerce.

Q. What unusual occupation did Ross Brown take for the summer of 1955 in order to improve his strength and fitness for the 1956 series against the Springboks?

– He took on a job loading railway sleepers at Manunui in the King Country.

Q. Why did Joe Karam, in his first test for New Zealand, take seven paces back from the ball, instead of his usual two, when he kicked the first of his five penalty goals against Wales in 1972?

– His knees were trembling so much he needed the extra distance to steady himself, even though the kick was only 22 metres out and right in front of the posts.

Q. What terrible fate befell English centre Danny Hearn after he tackled Ian MacRae in the 1967 game between Midland Counties and the All Blacks?

– He broke his neck and was left a paraplegic.

Q. At what food did All Black prop Graham Purvis draw the line while living and playing in France?

– Donkey sausages.

Q. What was Murray Mexted's occupation while he was playing for Agen in France?

– He drove a cheese truck.

Q. Two All Black first-fives can claim the Canterbury settlement of Southbridge as their hometown. Who?

— Doug Bruce and Dan Carter.

Q. When Don Clarke kicked the match-drawing wide-angled conversion in the third test of the 1960 series between New Zealand and South Africa, where was his brother and fellow tourist, Ian Clarke?

— He was standing at the goal posts, as he was one of the touch judges. He began waving his flag long before the ball reached the posts.

Q. Who was the first All Black to be affected by the food poisoning that afflicted the 1995 World Cup All Blacks?

— Andrew Mehrtens.

Q. Where was Stu Wilson when he first heard he had become an All Black?

— In a Dunedin urinal.

Q. Who did Murray Mexted marry in 1986 ?

— Miss Universe, Lorraine Downes.

Q. Name two companies set up by Murray Mexted in 2002.

— A global placement

specialist agency called Mexsport, and the International Rugby Academy, which was run by Mexted, Sean Fitzpatrick, Eddie Tonks and Kevin Roberts.

Q. Which position did both Colin and Stan Meads play at primary school?

— Hooker.

Q. What item of clothing did Stan Meads use to protect his appendix scar when he played in several matches in the later stage of the 1963–1964 All Black tour to Britain and France?

— A woman's 'roll-on' corset.

Q. What was Stu Wilson presented with at the end of the 1980 All Blacks' match against Llanelli, a game in which he frequently dropped the ball?

— A saucepan.

Q. What was the original first given name of Zinzan Brooke?

— Murray, but because there were several Murrays at his school at Ahuroa, the teacher asked if anyone wanted to change their name. Zinzan suggested 'Zinzan', his

second, family name and
it stuck.

Q. How did Zinzan Brooke
acquire his second given name
— Valentine?

– He changed his name to
Zinzan Valentine Brooke
in recognition of his birth
date – Valentine's Day.

Q. Which two positions did Andrew
McLean play for the All Blacks
in 1921 and 1923?

– He played as a side-row
forward against the
1921 Springboks, scoring
New Zealand's only try in
the second test of the
series. In 1923 he played
in the final game against
the touring New South
Welshmen – as a fullback
– and kicked 14 points.

Q. Which All Black once scored
all his team's 45 points — nine
tries and nine conversions
— in a junior match in the King
Country?

– Joe Karam.

Q. Referees are often the focus of
contentious discussion, but prior
to one game in New Zealand an
imposter dressed as a referee
attempted to take the field.

Which two teams was he hoping
to make a ruling on?

– The 1981 All Blacks and
Springboks. His intention,
as an anti-tour protestor
was probably to send both
teams off the field.

Q. Don Clarke played one game
for Waikato in 1958. In what
position did he play?

– Centre.

Q. During a trial match for the
Ponsonby club, which All Black
was subjected to interference at
the line-out by one of his own
players?

– Andy Haden.

Q. Who, as a youngster, used to
side-step through the crowds
leaving Eden Park after a big
match?

– Grahame Thorne.

Q. Which All Black team is said
to have lost to the Springboks
because they won too much ball?

– The 1949 All Blacks.

Q. Andy Haden had some
possessions stolen from his
car after attending a training
session at the Ponsonby club in
Auckland. What happened after

he mentioned the break-in at the clubrooms?

— The items were put back in his car after the next training session.

Q. Ian Kirkpatrick, who had broken his thumb early on during the All Blacks' 1968 tour to Australia, was named as a reserve for the first test. He had to go on during the game. Who did he replace, and why?

— He replaced Brian Lochore who, with a certain lack of originality, broke his thumb as well. Kirkpatrick promptly scored three tries.

Q. What pre-tour complication nearly saw Andy Haden withdraw from the 1972–1973 All Black tour to Britain and France?

— He reacted badly to a smallpox jab.

Q. What on-field function did hooker Ron Hemi fulfil at secondary school level and during the early part of his senior club rugby days?

— He was a goal-kicker.

Q. What aspiration did Grahame Thorne announce after he gained

selection for the All Blacks in 1967?

— He stated that he wanted to become a double international and represent New Zealand at cricket as well. In the conservatism of the times he was labelled a bit of a 'big head' for actually verbalising his goals.

Q. If, during the All Blacks' match against the Barbarians in London in 1974, the referee gave three blasts on his whistle, what would it have meant?

— That a bomb threat loomed. If this occurred the players had been instructed to sprint from the field.

Q. Why did Frank Bunce take the field for the match between Western Samoa and Wales in 1991 with his bootlaces undone?

— He was so nervous he had forgotten to tie them.

Q. Which four All Blacks played for their country before playing provincial rugby?

— Robert Wilson (1884), George Dickinson (1922), Grahame Thorne (1967-70) and Graeme Bachop (1987-1995).

Q. During his playing days Graeme Bachop sometimes had his name mis-spelled. He was even listed in match programmes as Graham Bauchop and Graeme Gachop. What was his nickname?

— 'Grim'.

Q. How many players from the Auckland representative side were in the 1983 All Black touring team to England and Scotland?

— None.

Q. Who, after boarding the team bus prior to the test match against Scotland in 1983, found he had forgotten his mouthguard, so nipped back to his hotel room to collect it, then caught a taxi to Murrayfield because the bus had departed without him?

— Robbie Deans.

Q. What caused All Black Warwick Taylor to miss the first two games of the Cavaliers tour to South Africa in 1986?

— Haemorrhoids.

Q. What unusual tour did the 1972 All Blacks undertake?

— They went on an internal tour, playing New Zealand Juniors and several provincial teams. It was the first tour of its kind in All Black history.

Q. Which All Black line-out legend was able to jump and clap his hands over the top of the crossbar?

— 'Tiny' White.

Q. Who nearly lost an ear following indiscriminate rucking by the Springboks in the third test of the 1976 New Zealand-South Africa series?

— Peter Whiting.

Q. In the early 1990s, which All Black helped coach the Zagara club in Catania, Sicily?

— Joe Stanley.

Q. Mark Irwin, Ron Hemi and Tony Davies, All Black tourists to South Africa in 1960, were involved in what sort of incident while on tour?

— A car accident between Johannesburg and Pretoria. The car was a write-off, but luckily no serious injuries were sustained.

Q. When Kel Tremain, in his first year out of school and playing club rugby in Poverty Bay, participated in the Ngatapa versus Te Araroa sub-union clash, which famous All Black was the referee?

– George Nepia.

Q. When Ian Kirkpatrick, in the second test against the 1971 British Lions, scored a famous long-range solo try, how many times did he fend off famous Lions fullback J.P.R. Williams?

– Three times.

Q. How tall — in feet and inches — was Andy Haden's great-grandfather?

– He was six foot, nine inches.

Q. Why did Kel Tremain's father, who was selected to play soccer for New Zealand, have to withdraw from the team?

– He came down with the flu.

Q. Which All Black missed out on selection for the Wellington College First XV because he could never crack the 9-stone minimum weight restriction?

– Ralph Caulton.

Q. What did both Andy Haden and Peter Whiting study at university?

– Geology.

Q. Playing cricket, which All Black once scored 150 for the Auckland Grammar School First XI?

– Grahame Thorne.

Q. After the All Blacks and Springboks had drawn the third test of the series 18-all in 1994, which team official made the comment that a draw was like kissing your sister?

– Springbok coach Ian McIntosh.

Q. In the second test between New Zealand and South Africa in 1994, who scored the deciding push-over try following the unthinkable — the South African forwards being backpeddled over their own line?

– No. 8 Zinzan Brooke.

Q. In 1956 Don Clarke faced the Springboks three times — twice for New Zealand and once for Waikato. How many points did he score on each occasion?

– Eight points each time, and each time his team won.

Q. Which All Black kicked a goal from a mark to enable Hawke's Bay to beat Wellington 6-5 in 1965?

– Kel Tremain.

Q. Who were the only three All Blacks who did not succumb to the violent stomach symptoms that affected the team prior to the 1995 World Cup final?

– Sean Fitzpatrick, and Robin and Zinzan Brooke, who had a commitment elsewhere so did not eat the fated lunch.

Q. What item of rugby clothing did South African President Nelson Mandela wear when he attended the Rugby World Cup final between New Zealand and South Africa in 1995?

– A Springbok jersey with the number 6 on the back, which was the same number as Springbok captain Francois Pienaar.

Q. Prior to the 1995 World Cup final, a jumbo jet flew low over Ellis Park with what three-word slogan painted on its undercarriage?

– 'Good luck Bokke'.

Q. Which All Black was offered $10,000 by Australian league scouts after the 1960 All Black tour to South Africa?

– Kel Tremain.

Q. In 1981 Andy Haden was ordered off in an Auckland club match, and his subsequent suspension meant he missed the first test against the touring Scottish side. Who took his place?

– Hud Rickit of Waikato, who retained it for the second test. Ironically, Graeme Higginson, the other lock, withdrew because of injury, so Haden made it back into the test team alongside Rickit.

Q. How many times did Kel Tremain, while captain of the Ranfurly Shield-holding Hawke's Bay side from 1966 to 1969, win the toss prior to the 22 shield games?

– Eighteen.

Q. Which All Black was late-tackled three times by Springbok flanker Jan Ellis during the third test of the 1970 series between New Zealand and South Africa?

– Earle Kirton.

Q. Andy Haden played for the Algida club in Italy in 1977. A couple of years later he played for them again, but in the intervening time they had changed their name to accommodate a sponsor. What was the club's new name?

— They were known as the Jaffa club.

Q. The 1976 All Blacks beat the Quaggas-Barbarians on their South African tour by scoring two tries (one converted) in what unusual circumstances?

— They were both scored in injury time.

Q. Henry Tromp, a Springbok hooker against the All Blacks in 1996, had been convicted of what crime in 1992?

— He was convicted of assault with intention to do grievous bodily harm, after he and his father thrashed a black farm labourer with a fan belt. The man later died of his wounds.

Q. Which Springbok with suspected concussion, carried from the field on a stretcher during one of the tests against the 1996 All Blacks, later denied he had been concussed, saying he was simply 'fed-up' with the All Blacks' dominance?

— Prop Os du Randt.

Q. In the weeks leading up to a test match between New Zealand and South Africa a billboard showing Sean Fitzpatrick as Jesus Christ and fellow All Blacks posing like the Apostles at the Last Supper was displayed prominently. The slogan accompanying the billboard read: 'All fifteen of them are ordering the Wildebeest Stew'. In which year and at which city?

— The 1996 test at Christchurch.

Q. Who was the replacement hooker for Ron Hemi on the All Blacks' 1960 South Africa tour, who soon succumbed to injury himself?

— Roger Boon from Taranaki.

Q. How many games for Canterbury had Graeme Bachop played at the end of his second All Black tour?

— One.

Q. Which player, selected for the All Blacks in 1987, had Buck Shelford, the captain, never heard of?

— Graeme Bachop.

Q. Why was Johnny Smith's apparently legitimate try, scored after he transferred the ball from his left arm to his right arm, disallowed?

− The referee reckoned Smith had thrown a forward pass − to himself!

Q. Kel Tremain scored 143 first class tries. For which rep team did he score his very first try?

− Southland, in a game against North Auckland, which was lost by Southland, 23-3.

Q. How many tries did the 1949 All Blacks in South Africa concede in their 24 matches?

− Eight.

Q. The 1978 Grand Slam All Blacks had an 11-match sequence in which they did not concede any tries. Name the player who finally breached their defences in the Scottish international.

- Bruce Hay.

Q. Who was the coach of the 1924–1925 All Blacks, the 'Invincibles'?

− They didn't have one.

Q. Who scored a try after picking up a charged-down drop-kick by Mac Herewini, against the 1966 British Isles?

− Malcolm Dick.

Q. Who scored a try after picking up a skewed Grant Fox drop-kick, against France in the World Cup final, 1987?

− Michael Jones.

Q. In 1959 Don Clarke scored in the second test against the Lions from a dribble pass. In 1960, Frank McMullen scored a try at the end of a movement that started with a dribble pass. Who threw both dribble passes?

− Kevin Briscoe.

Q. Who kicked New Zealand's first dropped goal in a test?

− Michael O'Leary, at Carisbrook in 1913.

Q. How many test match dropped goals did Zinzan Brooke kick?

− Three.

Q. How many test match dropped goals did Andrew Mehrtens kick?

− Ten, including two in a single test against Australia.

Q. How many goals from a mark did Billy Wallace kick in New Zealand's first test against Australia at Sydney in 1903?

− Two.

Q. Who kicked the last goal from a mark in tests for New Zealand before they became outmoded?

— Don Clarke, against England in 1963.

Q. Dennis Hugh Cameron (Mid-Canterbury) and Philip Hipkins Clarke (Marlborough) both gained selection for All Black touring teams after scoring three tries in trial matches. What happened next?

— Neither played for New Zealand again.

Q. What illness afflicted Bevan Holmes on the 1970 All Black tour to South Africa?

— Pleurisy.

Q. What illness afflicted Keith Murdoch on the 1970 All Black tour to South Africa?

— A rumbling appendix.

Q. What was odd about the attire of Kit Fawcett when he scored a try for the All Blacks against Northern Transvaal in 1976?

— He was minus his right boot.

Q. Name the two dentists, or dentists-to-be, in the 1963–1964 All Blacks in Britain and France.

— Earle Kirton and Keith Nelson.

Q. Name the three different first five-eighths who played for the 1972 All Blacks in the three-match home series against Australia.

— John Dougan, Lyn Jaffray and Bob Burgess.

Q. How many test matches did the All Blacks lose in 1949?

— Six (four against South Africa and two against Australia).

Q. How many test matches did the All Blacks lose in 1998?

— Five (three against Australia and two against South Africa).

Q. How many Poverty Bay fullbacks have played for the All Blacks?

— None.

Q. Which two Waikato players, in 1956, represented the largest fullback and the smallest halfback to play for New Zealand?

— Don Clarke and Ponty Reid.

Q. Who is the only New Zealand halfback to have kicked a dropped goal in his first test?

— Chris Laidlaw, against France in 1964.

Q. What distinction was shared between the All Black pack that played in the four tests against South Africa in 1965 and the pack that played against the 1966 British Lions?

— In both cases, the same players appeared in all test matches. In fact, the only difference was that 'Red' Conway and Wilson Whineray played in 1965 and Waka Nathan and Jack Hazlett in 1966.

Q. What did All Black Pat Vincent, when playing for Canterbury, used to practice in the dressing room prior to big games?

— Yoga.

Q. In the third test of the 1960 series between New Zealand and South Africa, who — at 5 foot 8 inches — was the shortest member of the front row, and who — at 6 foot 4 inches — was the tallest?

— The shortest was Dennis Young and the tallest was Nev MacEwan.

Q. What tragic fate awaited Peter Ogden, fullback for British Columbia against the 1913 All Blacks on tour to North America?

— He died on his way to hospital after being knocked out twice during the game.

Q. The 1949 All Blacks in South Africa beat Natal 8-nil, Orange Free State 14-9 and drew with Cape Town Clubs 11-all. What was the common feature in all of these games?

— In each case the All Blacks scored two tries, and in each case the same player dotted down twice. Fred Allen scored both tries against Natal, Ian Botting scored both tries against Orange Free State and Pat Crowley scored both tries against Cape Town Clubs.

Q. How many All Black selectors did New Zealand have in 1924?

— Seven.

Q. The highest number of spectators to watch a test match involving the All Blacks was 109,878 in 2000. At which ground, and against which team?

– At Stadium Australia, against Australia.

Q. What temporary vantage point did spectators use to take advantage back in the 1920s if they could not get in to Eden Park on test match day?

– Tram roofs.

Q. Who was the first All Black to sport really long hair?

– Bob Burgess.

Q. What sort of hairstyle did Jeff Wilson have when he played against the 1996 Springboks?

– None – he shaved his head.

Q. Who is the most recent ginger-haired All Black?

– James Ryan, in 2005.

Q. What happened to Gary Knight in his first test for New Zealand against France in 1977?

– He was eye-gouged.

Q. What unusual security precautions were taken for the All Blacks' game against Ulster in 1973?

– The team was surrounded by armed army personnel as it took the field.

Q. Which three All Blacks featured on the fuselage of the Boeing 747 used to transport the 1999 World Cup All Blacks?

– Carl Hoeft, Anton Oliver and Kees Meeuws.

Q. Which Springbok rendered All Black halfback Byron Kelleher concussed in the first Tri-Nation test match between New Zealand and South Africa in 2005?

– Victor Matfield.

Q. Which Springbok lock knocked out All Black halfback Chris Laidlaw in the first test between the two countries in 1970?

– Frik Du Preez.

Q. Which front-row forward with the 1924–1925 All Blacks in Britain, accounted for New Zealand's winning margin of 6-nil against Gloucestershire by scoring two tries?

– Quentin Donald.

Q. What feat did All Black forward Cyril Brownlie achieve against London Counties and Selection Français during the 1924–1925 tour of Britain and France?

– He scored a hat-trick of tries against both teams.

Q. What mode of scoring accounted for the 16 points scored by halfback Merv Corner on the 1932 All Blacks tour of Australia?

— Eight conversions.

Q. Who was the first player in excess of 16 stone to be selected for the All Blacks?

— Donald Max, from Nelson, who toured Australia with the 1934 All Blacks.

Q. Who was King Country's first All Black?

— Wing Bill Phillips, who played in the second test against the 1937 Springboks in New Zealand.

Q. Who was King Country's second All Black?

— Jack McLean, in 1947, who was also a wing.

Q. During their tour of South Africa in 1949, the All Blacks managed two or fewer tries in how many of their 24 matches?

— Nineteen.

Q. Who was the first forward from King Country to make the All Blacks?

— Ron Bryers, in 1949. At 17 stone and 7 pounds he was the heaviest All Black to play for New Zealand up to that time.

Q. Who was the only New Zealand player to score points in the two games that the 1953–1954 All Blacks played in France?

— Jack Kelly. He scored a try and kicked a conversion and dropped goal in the 8–11 loss at Bordeaux. The test was lost 0–3.

Q. What tragic fate awaited 'Ebbo' Bastard, a member of the 1937 Springbok team against New Zealand?

— He was later murdered, shot with an elephant gun.

Q. What was the occupation of Nick Shehadie, who played for Australia against the All Blacks?

— He ran a dry-cleaning business at Manly, Sydney. The sign outside his shop read: 'Drop your tweeds at Nick Shehadie's.'

Q. Name the five positions at which Danie Craven, who played for South Africa against New Zealand, turned out for his country.

— Halfback, first-five, centre, fullback and No. 8.

Q. Don Clarke was well known as 'The Boot', but what was the other nickname he went by?

— 'Camel'. He acquired this when someone saw him kissing his girlfriend under the light of a lamppost — he had to bend down a long way and so looked like a camel.

Q. Name the All Black prop in 1976 who never played in an All Black trial.

— Perry Harris.

Q. Name the positions and teams of the two Mark Robinsons who have played for the All Blacks in recent times.

— The North Harbour halfback and the Canterbury centre.

Q. Name the former Wellington representative, who, while playing for French Club Biarritz, was placed on standby when the All Blacks were touring France in 1977. He acted as back reserve for the final two matches of the tour but never played.

— Brian Hegarty.

Q. What athletics title did Dennis Young win before becoming serious about rugby?

— The New Zealand junior discus title.

Q. Name the two unrelated All Blacks who shared a surname and played against the 1904 Great Britain touring team.

— Duncan and Robert McGregor.

Q. Name the two props who have each scored two tries in a test for the All Blacks.

— Wilson Whineray, at Wellington in 1958 against Australia; Kees Meeuws, against Fiji at Wellington in 2002.

Q. Who was the first All Black to officially weigh at least 15 stone?

— Frederick 'Fatty' Newton, an All Black in 1905 and 1906.

Q. The 1914 All Blacks in Australia scored eight tries in their opening match against New South Wales. How many of these were converted?

— None.

Q. How many All Blacks kicked conversions when the 1920 All Blacks in Australia beat Metropolitan Union 79-5 at Sydney?

– Seven.

Q. How many of the All Blacks who toured Britain in 1924–1925 were listed as being under 10 stone in weight?

– Two – Bert Cooke and 'Gus' Hart, who each weighed 9 st 12 lb.

Q. How many of the All Blacks who toured Britain in 1924–1925 were listed as being under 11 stone in weight?

– Eight.

Q. When the All Blacks toured Australia in 1947 they had four Maori players in the backline. Who were they?

– Johnny and Peter Smith, Ben Couch and Vince Bevan. None of these players were subsequently eligible for the 1949 tour to South Africa because of apartheid issues.

Q. Name the six Wellington backs in the 1953–1954 All Blacks touring team to Britain.

– Halfback Vince Bevan, five-eighths Guy Bowers and Brian Fitzpatrick, and threequarters Ron Jarden, Jim Fitzgerald and Colin Loader.

Q. Who was the first All Black forward to be officially listed as being 6 ft 4 in in height?

– Colin Meads.

Q. When the 1957 All Blacks in Australia beat Riverina at Wagga Wagga 48-11, how many of the nine tries were scored by the surname sound-alikes Levien and Lineen?

– Six.

Q. In the 1962 test series between New Zealand and Australia in Australia, New Zealand scored six tries. How many of these were scored by Bruce Watt and how many by Russell Watt?

– Bruce scored two and Russell scored one.

Q. Name four test-match All Blacks who have received knighthoods, or the equivalent thereof.

– Harcourt Caughey, Brian Lochore, Colin Meads and Wilson Whineray.

Q. What was unusual about the combination of halfback Des Connor and first five-eighth Neil Wolfe for the All Blacks against France in 1961?

— They were the tallest halfback and shortest first five-eighth combination to play for New Zealand.

Q. Name the 1961 All Black front-row against France.

— Ian Clarke, Dennis Young and Wilson Whineray. This was one of the smallest front rows of the post-war era.

Q. Peter Brown, a Scottish No. 8 who played against the All Blacks, was also a goal-kicker with a bizarre mannerism. What did he used to do?

— He used to turn his back on the ball prior to commencing his run up.

Q. Who was the first All Black to score a try and kick a dropped goal in his first test match?

— Mac Herewini, against the 1962 Australians.

Q. In the first test against England at Eden Park in 1963, the All Blacks fielded one of the smallest mid-field combinations in All Black history. Who was at second five-eighth and who was at centre?

— Neil Wolfe and Ian Uttley, respectively.

Q. Name the three positions at which both Colin and Stan Meads played test rugby.

— Lock, flanker and No. 8.

Q. In which test match did 'Red' Conway score his only test match try?

— In his last test — against South Africa in the fourth test of the 1965 series.

Q. List the ways in which Don Clarke scored his 15 points in the first test against England at Eden Park in 1963.

— He scored in four ways — a try, three conversions, one penalty and a dropped goal.

Q. Name the two first five-eighths selected for the All Blacks' 1963–1964 tour to Britain and France.

— Bob Burgess and Ian Stevens.

Q. Who were the only three members of the 30-man All Black touring team to South Africa in 1970 not to play in a test match?

– Bevan Holmes, Bruce Hunter and Jake Burns.

Q. What unusual incident involving All Black Howard Joseph occurred during a test match against the 1971 British Lions?

– He tripped over a dog.

Q. Who scored the All Blacks' only points in the third test against the 1971 British Lions at Wellington when he dotted down for a try?

– Laurie Mains. The score was remarkable for the fact that Mains was not regarded as a try-scoring fullback, and because he missed the straightforward conversion of the try, having been included in the team to shore up the goal-kicking.

Q. In the first test against the 1971 British Lions, whose clearing kick was charged down, leading to the only try in the game, and a 9-3 victory to the Lions?

– Alan Sutherland. Before he had a chance to atone he broke his leg while playing in a match before the second test and took no further part in the series.

Q. The All Blacks scored 16 tries in the test series against the 1908 Anglo-Welsh tourists. How many of these were converted?

– Five.

Q. Who was the first All Black to be officially measured as 6 foot 6 inches in height?

– Peter Whiting.

Q. A brief but nasty brawl between the 1976 All Blacks and Uruguay was notable for what event?

– A spectator came on to the field and entered the fray.

Q. The two captains in the 1913 third test between Australia and New Zealand played at which position?

– Fullback. Michael O'Leary was the New Zealand captain and Larry Dwyer led Australia.

Q. Who was hit on the head by a flour bomb during the third test of 1981 against South Africa?

– Gary Knight.

Q. In which game did Gary Knight score his only test match try?

— The third test against the 1981 Springboks.

Q. How many Canterbury representatives participated in the 2002 test match between New Zealand and Ireland at Eden Park, a game the All Blacks won 40-8?

— Fifteen (six backs, all eight forwards and one sub).

Q. In the 1973 All Blacks-Barbarians game, robust Welsh flanker Tom David was in a side-line skirmish with which diminutive All Black?

— Grant Batty.

Q. The 1996 All Blacks were welcomed home with a ticker-tape parade down Queen Street, in recognition of what achievement?

— They had beaten the Springboks in a series in South Africa for the first time.

Q. Why was New Zealand referee Pat Murphy replaced by touch judge Alan Taylor during the third test between New Zealand and South Africa in 1965?

— He pulled a hamstring.

Q. What do Carl Hayman, Billy Bush, Andy Haden and Gary Knight all have in common?

— They have all sported beards during their All Black careers.

Q. What colour jerseys did the 1930 All Blacks wear to avoid clashing with the dark blue of the British Isles?

— White.

Q. What weather conditions dramatically affected the game when the 1972–1973 All Blacks played East Glamorgan?

— Heavy fog covered the ground.

Q. What scoring manoeuvre led to the All Blacks beating Australia in the final seconds of the second test in Brisbane in 1968?

— A penalty try was awarded to Grahame Thorne.

Q. The All Blacks were awarded penalty tries against South Africa in successive Tri-Nations campaigns in which years?

— In 2001 (at Auckland) and 2002 (at Durban).

Q. What signal did the All Blacks of the 1960s use to indicate to team-mates that they were being assailed by 'heavies' or boring supporters?

– They rubbed their right ears.

Q. Who coached the New Zealand Juniors team that in 1973 beat the All Blacks at Carisbrook?

– Eric Watson.

Q. Who was the surprise selection as hooker for the 1970 All Blacks to South Africa?

– Ron Urlich, who ended up scoring six tries and playing in two tests.

Q. What nationality were the parents of Brian 'Jazz' Muller?

– Swiss.

Q. Did Jules Le Lievre play for France or the All Blacks?

– He was an All Black prop with red hair and freckles.

Q. Which All Black and corporal in the New Zealand army was feted by 13 full generals of the South African army during the 1970 tour of South Africa?

– Henare 'Buff' Milner.

Q. Who missed out on a try in the first test of the 1976 series between New Zealand and South Africa, when the rolling ball took a turn for the worse and came to rest behind a goal-post, with the fast-following player over-running it?

— Andy Leslie.

Q. Name the three All Black second five-eighths produced by the Poverty Bay union.

— Brian Fitzpatrick, John Collins and Mike Parkinson.

Q. Which ex-All Black coached Tonga to victory over New Zealand Maori not once but twice in 1969?

— Dennis Young.

Q. When New Zealand played at Wellington in 1901, the gate takings of £420 represented a record for the colony. The attendance figure of 8000 was also a record. Who was the opposition?

— New South Wales.

Q. Which three All Blacks played in all 11 matches on the All Blacks 1903 tour to Australia?

— Billy Wallace, 'Opai' Asher and George Tyler.

Q. Name the four All Black forwards on the 1972–1973 tour to Britain who weighed over 17 stone.

— Alan Sutherland, Andy Haden, Keith Murdoch and Graham Whiting.

Q. How many players named James Ryan have played for the All Blacks?

— Two: the utility back in 1910 and 1914, and the Otago lock in 2005.

Q. To what dietary cause did Colin Meads attribute the lack of red-bloodedness in recent All Black forwards?

— He suggested they might be eating too much pasta and not enough red meat.

Q. How many players with the surname of Wilson have played for New Zealand?

— Fifteen: Alexander, Alfred Leonard, Bevan William, Douglas Dawson, Frank Reginald, Hector William, Hedley Brett, Henry Clarke, Jeffrey William, Nathaniel Arthur, Norman Leslie, Richard George, Robert J., Stuart Sinclair and Vivian Whitta.

Q. How many players with the surname of Clark/Clarke have played for New Zealand?

— Ten: Donald William, Francis Leslie, Lindsay Alan, William Henry, Adrian Hipkins, Donald Barry, Eroni, Ian James, Philip Hipkins and Ray Lancelot.

Q. Name the 12 cities or towns in which the All Black trials for the 1949 South African tour were played.

— Whangarei, Auckland, Hamilton, Gisborne, Wanganui, Palmerston North, Napier, Wellington, Motueka, Christchurch, Timaru and Invercargill.

Q. How did Charlie Willocks, one of the 1949 All Blacks in South Africa, injure his shoulder?

— He was involved in a train crash, as was the rest of the team.

Q. What do George Aitken, Colin Gilray, David Kirk and Chris Laidlaw have in common?

— They were All Blacks who became Rhodes Scholars.

Q. What mythical act of strength is attributed to All Black prop Brian 'Jazz' Muller?

— It is said he used to trim his mother's hedge with a lawnmower.

Q. What mythical act of strength is attributed to All Black Colin Meads?

— It is said he used to carry a sheep under each arm.

Q. What mythical act of strength is attributed to All Black 'Has' Catley?

— It is said he was capable of heaving bags of superphosphate.

Q. How did Colin Meads score in his first game for King Country?

— He kicked a dropped goal and scored a try.

Q. When playing for New Zealand Universities against the 1965 Springboks, what did Chris Laidlaw once do after returning to the field following treatment for a head injury?

— He kicked a dropped goal but doesn't remember it.

Q. Of what standard French cuisine did the 1977 All Blacks in France develop a loathing?

— Raw steak and salad.

Q. Which All Black, playing for Canterbury against West Coast, thought he had dived across the goal-line for a try, but found to his embarrassment that he had dived across the 25-yard line?

– Dennis Young.

Q. When the 1907 All Blacks in Australia beat Queensland 17-11, who scored all of their five tries?

– Winger Frank Fryer.

Q. How many penalty goals did Don Clarke kick in his final two tests against the Wallabies at Lancaster Park and Athletic Park in 1964?

– None.

Q. What was especially notable about Don Clarke's farewell test appearance, against Australia at Athletic Park in 1964?

– The All Blacks took a 20-5 walloping.

Q. What was the occupation of Poverty Bay All Black Laurie Knight?

– Doctor. An official All Black doctor had not yet been appointed to accompany the team, so Knight's medical knowledge and prowess were put to good use. This was particularly so during the All Blacks' 1976 tour to South Africa.

Q. What was the occupation of Canterbury All Black Hugh Burry?

– He was a doctor.

Q. Which modern-day All Black saved the Ranfurly Shield for Canterbury by scoring a late try against Wellington to tie the game up, and then kicked a side-line conversion to sneak the win?

– Ben Blair.

Q. What was Jerry Collins' occupation before he became a professional rugby player?

– He was a rubbish collector for Wellington City Council.

Q. For which district did Ben Blair's father and grandfather play?

– Buller.

Q. How is Jerry Collins related to Tana Umaga?

– They are cousins.

Q. Who was the goal-kicking fullback for the 1979 All Blacks against the touring French team?

– Bevan Wilson.

Q. Who was the goal-kicking fullback for the 1979 All Blacks against the touring Argentinians?

– Richard Wilson.

Q. When the All Blacks toured England and Scotland at the end of 1979, an All-Counties front row was included. Name the players involved.

– John Spiers, Andy Dalton and Rod Ketels.

Q. Why did Taranaki's Ross Fraser, named in the New Zealand team to play Argentina at Dunedin in in 1979, never become an All Black?

– He had the misfortune to break his leg on the very day he was named in the squad.

Q. What height was the shortest player in the forward pack when the 1979 All Blacks played Queensland B?

– Six foot (1.83 metres).

Q. Allan Hewson played in all three tests against the 1981 Springboks. How many penalties did he kick?

– Seven, including the match-winner in the third test.

Q. What role did Samuel Sleigh, the manager of the 1884 New Zealand side, fulfil when his team played New South Wales?

– He acted as the referee.

Q. Name the two Hawke's Bay reps who appeared against the 1982 Wallabies.

– Mark Taylor and Graeme Higginson. They had first played for New Zealand while representing other provinces, Taylor for Bay of Plenty and Higginson for Canterbury.

Q. The All Blacks could manage only one try in each of the first three tests against the 1983 British Lions. How many did they score in the fourth test?

– Six.

Q. Who was Wanganui's first All Black halfback ?

– Andy Donald.

Q. Why did Joe Warbrick, a member of the 1884 New Zealand team that toured New South Wales, travel to Australia separately from the rest of his team members?

– He missed the boat linking the Auckland players with

the rest of the team in Wellington and had to take a steamer directly to Sydney.

Q. Which All Black became the Highlanders' unofficial bus driver in 2000?

– Joe McDonnell.

Q. The annual Peter Johnstone Memorial Bowls Tournament at Mt Maunganui, geared for bowlers who've etched a career in rugby, is named after the All Black captain from which two years?

– 1950 and 1951.

Q. Which two All Blacks both coached the Italian rugby team?

– Brad Johnstone and John Kirwan.

Q. What is the occupation of 1961 All Black Don McKay?

– He runs a pharmacy on Auckland's North Shore. At the time of first touching the ball in test rugby (and promptly scoring a very early try against the 1961 Frenchmen), he said that he felt as if he had a block of ice in his stomach.

Q. Laurie Mains coached the Super 12 Cats in 2000 and 2001 and each time they reached the semi-finals. Where did they finish in 1999 and 2002?

– They finished last.

Q. What amazing golfing feat did Bob Scott once achieve on a Petone golf course?

– He landed a hole-in-one.

Q. Which ex-All Black became President of the Auckland Rugby Union in 2003?

– Waka Nathan.

Q. In what years did Eric Rush represent New Zealand at sevens rugby?

– Every year from 1988 to 2004.

Q. Which ex-All Black became President of Bowls New Zealand?

– Johnny Simpson.

Q. Which three ex-All Blacks were all MPs at the same time?

– Tony Steel, Grahame Thorne and Chris Laidlaw. Laidlaw made it by way of a by-election.

Q. Of which company is the late Mick Williment the founder?

– Williment Travel, the NZRFU's official travel agent.

Q. Name two All Black Wilsons who hold a trotting trainer's licence.

– Jeff and Bevan.

Q. Where did Luke McAlister spend his primary school years?

– In Lancashire, England.

Q. With which union did Carl Hoeft play his rugby before representing Otago and New Zealand?

– Thames Valley.

Q. What is Joe McDonnell's occupation?

– He works with disadvantaged children in Dunedin.

Q. How many McLeans have played for New Zealand?

– Five: Andrew Leslie McLean, Charles McLean, Hubert Foster McLean, John Kenneth McLean and Robert John McLean.

Q. What is Robin Brooke's occupation?

– He is the manager of the New World Supermarket at Milford, Auckland.

Q. Which secondary school did Chris Jack attend?

– Shirley Boy's High School.

Q. Which sport other than rugby does Campbell Johnstone have a desire to play?

– American football – he has hankerings to be a quarterback for the Dallas Cowboys.

Q. How did Josh Kronfeld demonstrate his opposition to French nuclear testing in the Pacific during the All Blacks 1995 tour to France?

– He wore an anti-nuclear logo on his headgear.

Q. What is the first name of Sione Lauaki's league-playing brother?

– Hame.

Q. Name the two Thorn(e)s who played in the Canterbury forward pack in recent years.

– Reuben Thorne and Brad Thorn.

Q. Three players with the surname Clarke played in the third test against the 1958 Australians. What were their first names?

– Brothers Don and Ian Clarke and Auckland five-eighth Adrian Clarke.

Q. At one stage Clark(e) was such a popular All Black name that there were two Don Clark(e)s playing in the same test series — against Australia in 1964. In what positions?

– They were Don Clarke the fullback and Don Clark the Otago loose forward.

Q. What is Joe McDonnell's nickname?

– 'Pudding'.

Q. Which All Black set a record for test match tries by a prop in a calendar year when he scored five tries in 2002?

– Kees Meeuws.

Q. How are Kees Meeuws and the late All Black Ron Rangi related?

– They are second cousins.

Q. What colour jerseys were worn by the Australians when they played the 1907 All Blacks?

– Maroon with blue hoops.

Q. Prior to touring Australia in 1925, the All Blacks played a match against Wellington. What was the result?

– The All Blacks lost 6-10. They scored two tries, but couldn't convert either.

Q. What injury did Fred Allen suffer during the Second World War?

– He got a piece of shrapnel in the neck.

Q. Why did John Ashworth's weight soar to 18 stone (114 kg) during the 1977 All Black tour to France?

– It was a result of all the bread he had eaten on tour.

Q. What was the first provincial match that Fred Allen played?

– Canterbury against West Coast. The result was a 6-all draw.

Q. Which representative team did Keith Murdoch's father John play for?

– Otago.

Q. When Waka Nathan played in a club trial for Otahuhu in 1958, what was unusual about his attire?

— He was wearing boots but no socks.

Q. How old was Fred Allen when he was made captain of Canterbury?

— 20 — and he weighed little more than 10 stone (63.5 kg).

Q. What viral infection did 1978 All Black John Ashworth have the misfortune to contract from the player he was packing down against in the match with Cambridge University.

— Facial herpes. Ashworth passed the condition on to cohorts Gary Knight and Andy Haden at training.

Q. Three candidates for which competition greeted the 1947 All Blacks when they played Combined Northern at Newcastle?

— The Miss Australia beauty pageant.

Q. Why was Des Connor not available for the first test between Australia and New Zealand in 1964?

— Because he was attending a friend's wedding.

Q. What caused John Spencer, a member of the 1903 All Blacks' tour to Australia, to miss the first four games of the tour?

— He fell and injured a leg, the victim of a rough sea crossing on the Moeraki.

Q. What caused a 30-minute delay to the kick-off between the All Blacks and Wellington Province at Wellington in 1905?

— They needed the time to look for a suitable ball.

Q. When Grant Fox played in the Auckland Grammar School's First XV, who was his coach?

— Graham Henry.

Q. Bad weather caused the 1905 New Zealand-Australia test match to be transferred from the Caledonian ground in Dunedin to where?

— Tahuna Park.

Q. How many of the players in the All Black backline that played against Australia at Dunedin in 1905 (while the Originals were in the UK) went on to play for New Zealand again?

— None.

Q. What caused John Dick to withdraw from the 1938 All Black tour to Australia?

— German measles.

Q. The first test after the Second World War was played between the All Blacks and Australia, the latter losing 8-31. Where was it played and in what year?

— At Dunedin in 1946.

Q. Which All Black trialist missed selection for the Canterbury Country team at loose-head prop for their annual clash against Town in 1977?

— John Ashworth.

Q. Which All Black loose forward was obliged to play fullback for the 1926 All Blacks in their 'home-coming' match against Auckland?

— Ron Stewart. The actual fullback, Donald Stevenson, was ill and several other more appropriate substitutes were injured. The All Blacks won 11-6.

Q. The All Blacks on tour in

Australia in which year were entertained at a barbecue by the St George Rugby Club at Garie Beach?

— 1947. Refreshments and sustenance included 300 dozen oysters, 150 pounds of steak and 54 gallons of beer.

Q. Which future All Black played for Auckland Colts in the curtain-raiser to the infamous 'flour-bomb' test of 1981 between New Zealand and South Africa?

— Grant Fox.

Q. With which act of valour is Keith Murdoch credited?

— He is said to have saved the life of a young boy who fell into a swimming pool in 1979.

Q. Which future All Black scored a late dropped goal in the Otahuhu College v. Seddon Memorial Technical College game, played as the curtain-raiser to the fourth test between New Zealand and South Africa in 1956, to give his team the victory by one point?

— Mac Herewini.

Q. In which year did the New Zealand touring team to New South Wales and Queensland play matches against a New South Wales Junior XVIII and a Queensland Second XVIII?

– 1893.

Q. In what year was the inaugural inter-island match staged?

– It was in 1897 and possibly because there were no Southland reps named in that year's New Zealand team to tour Australia, the Southland union barred their players from playing in the match.

Q. In the early days, matches between New Zealand and which side were known as inter-colonial encounters?

– New South Wales.

Q. What do Bill Hardcastle, Evan Jessep, Keith Gudsell and Owen Stephens have in common?

– They were All Blacks who later played for Australia. By contrast, Des Connor was a Wallaby who went on to play for New Zealand.

Q. Which future All Black once kicked a goal from halfway in bare feet while touring Fiji with a school team?

– Grant Fox.

Q. John Gallagher once beat Zinzan Brooke in what sort of contest in Brisbane?

– A hamburger-eating contest.

Q. Name the first set of brothers to play for the All Blacks.

– The Purdue brothers, Charles and 'Pat'.

Q. During the 1938 New Zealand tour to Australia, what incident caused All Black Jack Taylor to suffer head injuries that precluded him playing in the next match?

– He and Charlie Saxton were involved in a motor accident when the car in which they were travelling left the road, snapped off a eucalyptus tree and flipped over. Saxton suffered only minor bruising.

Q. What was the occupation of Fred Allen's father?

– He was a railway guard.

Q. What elementary error did lock Geoff Alley make while attempting to touch down for a try closer to the posts during the All Blacks' 1926 game against a New South Wales XV?

– He ran over the dead-ball line.

Q. Grant Fox once represented Bay of Plenty in what capacity in a Hawke Cup cricket match against Nelson?

– He played as a batsman, coming in at number three.

Q. How many players named Stewart have played for New Zealand?

– Seven – Allan James Stewart, David Stewart, Edward Barrie Stewart, James Douglas Stewart, Kenneth William Stewart, Ronald Terowie Stewart and Vance Edmond Stewart.

Q. What was different about the haka performed by the All Blacks when they played Australian Capital Territory at Canberra in 1947?

– They performed a haka to both sides of the field prior to kick-off.

Q. For how many consecutive years starting in 1957 did King Country enjoy All Black representation?

– For 17 years, from 1957 through to 1973. Colin Meads carried the mantle from 1957 to 1971, assisted by his brother Stan, who was an All Black from 1961 to 1966. Prop forward Graham Whiting then represented New Zealand from 1972 to 1973.

Q. Which ex-All Black coach went on to coach Argentina, getting them through to the quarter-finals of the 1999 World Cup?

– Alex Wyllie.

Q. What was the measurement of Keith Murdoch's chest?

– 50 inches (about 1.27 metres).

Q. What was the first name of Waka Nathan's brother who represented New Zealand schoolboys at league?

– Cowley.

Q. Against which team did Grant Fox play his first test?

– Argentina.

Q. Who was the All Black goal-kicker in Grant Fox's first test?

— Fullback Kieran Crowley.

Q. Who was the first All Black produced by the Oriental-Rongotai club?

— John Gallagher.

Q. In what year did the All Blacks and New South Wales in Sydney meet for a celebratory dinner at the A.B.C. Café after the first match of the tour?

— 1907.

Q. Which All Black played Hawke Cup cricket for Wairarapa as a wicketkeeper and was once twice dismissed by New Zealand fast bowler Ewen Chatfield in a match against Hutt Valley?

— Stu Wilson.

Q. The 1972–1973 All Black tourists to Britain and France scored seven test match tries. How many of these were scored by Sid Going and the loose forwards?

— Five.

Q. Keith Murdoch had what emergency sleeping arrangements?

— He used to carry a mattress in the back of his old Holden, in which he used to bunk down from time to time.

Q. What permanent medical condition does Jason O'Halloran suffer from?

— He is an insulin-dependent diabetic.

Q. Centre Mark Robinson achieved honours degrees in political studies and philosophy from which university?

— Cambridge University.

Q. Which All Black front-rower spent a year in South Africa on a Rotary Scholarship as a schoolboy and represented Border Secondary Schools?

— Greg Somerville.

Q. Gary Whetton attended which well-known confidence and team-building course?

— Outward Bound.

Q. Prior to the 1987 World Cup match against Scotland the All Black forwards were subjected to a training session that included the packing down of how many scrums?

— Eighty.

Q. What was unusual about the second-half attire of some players in the Cumberland County when they played the 1884 New Zealand team?

– They did not wear any boots.

Q. Who made Grant Batty's first rugby jersey?

– It was knitted by his grandmother.

Q. How much did Sid Going weigh when he played his first game of organised rugby?

– Three stone and three pounds.

Q. How many times did the three Brooke brothers — Robin, Zinzan and Marty — start together in the same game for Auckland?

– Only once, in 1987 against East Coast. Robin played No. 8, Zinzan flanker and Marty lock.

Q. Which position did Robbie Deans play for Canterbury in 1979 before being summarily dropped, leading to his decision to concentrate on the fullback position?

– First-five.

Q. What was unusual about the 1884 New Zealand team's match against Combined Suburbs XVII in Sydney?

– There was no referee.

Q. What did a disappointed Alan Whetton do in 1986 after the second test against Australia, in the knowledge he was about to be dropped?

– He drank too much port.

Q. What was one effect of the multiple concussions that Sid Going received during his career?

– He couldn't remember the number of times he had been concussed.

Q. In his early flatting days in Christchurch, what did All Black Wayne Smith and his flatmates used to do to keep warm?

– They stole strainer posts from a nearby farm and burnt them.

Q. Which All Black, in 1993, played for the Castres club in the French final and scored his side's only try in a 14-11 victory?

– Gary Whetton. After the game Whetton got to shake the hand of French President François

Mitterand, before doing a one-man haka live on French TV.

Q. As their careers matured, Sid Going played halfback and his brother Ken played fullback. What positions did they play before settling down into these roles?

– Sid was a fullback and Ken was often the halfback.

Q. How many club games had Grant Batty played before he got selected for an All Black trial?

– Five.

Q. How long were the two halves in the 1884 game between New Zealand and New South Wales?

– Fifty minutes each.

Q. How many dropped goals did the 1884 New Zealand team in New South Wales score in their nine matches (including the preliminary match against a Wellington XV)?

– Nine. All but one of the dropped goals were notched by the threequarters, Helmore, Ryan and Warbrick.

Q. Which All Black spent 1963–1964 in Canada, where he was based as a Mormon missionary?

– Sid Going. In his first club match at fullback after returning he was so out of condition that on one occasion when he was supposed to come into the backline, he was unable to make it.

Q. How many All Blacks have lived to be 100?

– None. The oldest have been Phillippe 'Sid' Cabot, who reached 98, Jock Richardson, who made 95, Charlie Sonntag, who died at 94, and Billy Wallace and Frank Mitchison, who both celebrated their 93rd birthdays.

Q. Which All Black coach played cricket for Canterbury and Otago in the 1960s as a wicketkeeper and right-hand batsman?

– Graham Henry.

Q. Which All Black was awarded the Pierre de Coubertin Trophy for Fair Play for stopping to attend to Welsh captain Colin Charvis, who was in danger of swallowing his tongue during a test match in Hamilton in 2003?

— Tana Umaga. Recipients of the award in other sports include Arthur Ashe, Bobby Charlton, Martina Navratilova and Sergei Bubka.

Q. Which All Black became the first player in the world to kick 50 penalty goals against one opponent, in this case, South Africa?

— Andrew Mehrtens.

Q. Which 2004–2005 All Black has a brother, father, uncle and grandfather who have all represented Taranaki?

— Conrad Smith.

Q. Which Gore establishment did Justin Marshall once list as his favourite restaurant?

— The Gore pie cart, where, he claimed, 'you were always satisfied'.

Q. What item was produced to commemorate the victory by Welsh club Llanelli over the 1972–1973 All Blacks?

— An official commemorative tie.

Q. Which All Black scored two tries against the All Blacks for the New Zealand President's XV in 1973?

— Sid Going.

Q. What did Wayne Smith win for being named the *Sunday News*' Player of the Match when the 1980 All Blacks drew 13-all with Sydney?

— A toaster.

Q. Why did the All Blacks of 1953–1954 have to swear that they were not 'Communist, Fascist, Nazi or Falangist' in their travels to Britain?

— They were travelling via the USA and in the era of McCarthyism, this was part of the entry requirements.

Q. What was run up the masthead of their ship as the 1884 New Zealand tourists to New South Wales entered Sydney Harbour?

— A rugby ball.

Q. When the 1893 New Zealand team played a Combined XV at Petone, what strip did the Combined team wear?

— They played in jerseys of many different colours.

Q. In what game was the first try

scored against a New Zealand team?

– In the 1884 game that New Zealand played against a Combined Suburbs XVII at Sydney.

Q. What did both Grant Batty and Sid Going promise to do if the 1974 All Black tourists to Ireland, Wales and England emerged undefeated?

– They swore to shave off their beards. Both players arrived back in New Zealand clean-shaven.

Q. What non-rugby sporting competition did the 1884 New Zealand tourists to New South Wales conduct while traveling across the Tasman on the *Hauroto*?

– A North v. South tug-of-war bout. The North Island won by two pulls to one.

Q. How many tries did Christian Cullen score in his first two tests?

– Seven – three against Western Samoa and four against Scotland.

Q. Who were the first two All Blacks to sign a contract with the New Zealand Rugby Union, as opposed to the World Rugby Corporation, when rugby turned professional in 1995?

– Josh Kronfeld and Jeff Wilson.

Q. Pat Lam played one game for the All Blacks. In what year and against which team?

– Against Sydney in 1992. Lam had been summoned as a tour replacement and was himself replaced during the match, which New Zealand lost 40-17.

Q. Why did Cecil Badeley, originally named as captain of the 1924–1925 All Blacks to Britain and France, lose the captaincy to Cliff Porter before the team left New Zealand?

– He suffered a persistent knee injury.

Q. Aside from being brothers and All Blacks, what else did Adrian and Philip Clarke share in the way of nomenclature?

– They both had the same second name – Hipkins.

Q. The All Blacks have played at Wellington in which three different countries?

– Australia, where the 1932

© DARY CRIMP

tourists took on New South Wales Western Districts; South Africa, where the 1949 and 1960 All Blacks engaged Boland, and, of course, New Zealand.

Q. All Blacks Glenn Taylor and Ian Kirkpatrick once met in a game at the Northland township of Tangiteroria. What sport were they playing?

– Polo. Glenn's father John and Ian's brothers David and Colin all represented New Zealand at polo.

Q. Which 1930s All Black who won the Military Cross played soccer for the Army against Auckland during the war years?

– Merv Corner.

Q. How many players with the surname starting with 'B' have represented the All Blacks?

– Ninety-nine.

Bibliography

Anon, *Thirty five years of Rugby News*, 2005, Rugby Press International, Auckland.

Chester, R.H. and McMillan, N.A.C., *Centenary — 100 Years of All Black Rugby*, 1984, Moa Publications, Auckland.

————, *The Encyclopedia of New Zealand Rugby*, 1981, Moa Publications, Auckland.

Chester, R.H., McMillan, N. and Palenski, Ron, *The Encyclopedia of New Zealand Rugby* (3rd edn), 1998, Hodder Moa Beckett, Auckland.

Dixon, George H., *The Triumphant Tour of the New Zealand Footballers, 1905*, 1999, David Ling Publishing Ltd, Auckland.

Howitt, Bob, *Rugby Greats* (rev. edn), 2004, Hodder Moa Beckett, Auckland.

Howitt, Bob and Haworth, Dianne, *1905 Originals*, 2005, HarperCollins, Auckland.

————, *All Black Magic*, 2003, HarperCollins, Auckland.

————, *Rugby Nomads*, 2002, HarperCollins, Auckland.

Hutchins, Graham, *Rugby Shorts*, 2001, Celebrity Books, Auckland.

Matheson, John, *Rushie*, 2002, Hodder Moa Beckett, Auckland.

McCarthy, Winston, *Haka! The All Blacks Story*, 1968, Pelham Books, London.

McLean, T.P., *The All Blacks*, 1991, Sidgwick and Jackson, London.

————, *New Zealand Rugby Legends*, 1987, Moa Publications, Auckland.

————, *Winter of Discontent*, 1977, A.H. and A.W. Reed, Wellington.

————, *Goodbye to Glory*, 1976, A.H. and A.W. Reed, Wellington.

————, *Battling the Boks*, 1970, A.H. and A.W. Reed, Wellington.

————, *Red Dragon of Rugby*, 1969, A.H. and A.W. Reed, Wellington.

————, *Willie Away*, 1964, A.H. and A.W. Reed, Wellington.

Miller, Geoff, *Bateman's Rugby Facts of New Zealand*, 2004, David Bateman Ltd, Auckland.

New Zealand Herald, *Rivals — 75 Years of the Lions v the All Blacks*, 2005, Random House, Auckland.

Palenski, Ron, *All Blacks and Lions*, 2005, Hodder Moa Beckett, Auckland.

————, *Century in Black*, 2003, Hodder Moa Beckett, Auckland.

————, *The Jersey*, 2001, Hodder Moa Beckett, Auckland.

Quinn, Keith, *Outrageous Rugby Moments*, 2002, Hodder Moa Beckett, Auckland.

————, *Legends of the All Blacks*, 1999, Hodder Moa Beckett, Auckland.

Scott, R.W.H. and McLean, T.P., *The Bob Scott Story*, 1956, A.H. and A.W. Reed, Wellington.

Zavos, Spiro, *Winters of Revenge*, 1997, Penguin Books, Auckland.

Zavos, Spiros and Bray, Gordon, *Two Mighty Tribes — the Story of the All Blacks vs the Wallabies*, 2003, Penguin Books, Auckland.